Jimmy Du's Essential Chinese

Jimmy Du's Essential Chinese:

Jimmy Du's Natural Language Works
Second Edition

By

Zhengming Du

Cambridge
Scholars
Publishing

Jimmy Du's Essential Chinese:
Jimmy Du's Natural Language Works
Second Edition

By Zhengming Du

The first edition of this book was published in 2013, the present paperback binding is a new edition with enriched contents, published 2016

Cambridge Scholars Publishing

Lady Stephenson Library, Newcastle upon Tyne, NE6 2PA, UK

British Library Cataloguing in Publication Data
A catalogue record for this book is available from the British Library

Audio voice by Xuan Yang and Ryan Martin

ISBN (10): 1-4438-8812-5
ISBN (13): 978-1-4438-8812-7

CONTENTS

INTRODUCTION

Welcome to Jimmy Du's Essential Chinese of Jimmy Du Natural Language Works.

This is a specially designed self-teaching course to help you master Mandarin Chinese in the shortest time possible. We promise you will just "pick it up" if you spend only a little time following this course while relaxing at home, taking a walk, commuting to work or traveling. You don't have to sit in a classroom, consult the dictionary, study grammar, or do any written exercises. This least-effort principle is based on the understanding that we human beings all have an innate aptitude for acquiring any human language, native or foreign. All you need to do is keep learning what you can immediately understand, imitate, and put to use. The least effort means the highest efficiency. For this reason, we've provided easy-to-understand explanations and translations of everything in the text. The text contents are arranged in a natural order, beginning with the essential words, phrases and short sentences, all carefully selected so that they will not only serve as a basis for you to expand your vocabulary, but also help you learn the nature of the Chinese language and how it works. On this solid foundation, you will find no difficulty in developing your comprehension of more complicated structures and, ultimately, your fluency.

OK! Let's begin!

PREPARATION

CHINESE PINYIN SPELLING AND PRONUNCIATION

Standard Mandarin Chinese is also called Putonghua, which means "common speech". As you come to learn it, you actually may not encounter as much difficulty as you expected because the letters used in Chinese Pinyin for spelling words are the same as those used in English, with only one exception: the letter "ü". This "ü" is written as the letter "u" but with two dots on the top as in German. In computer input with Pinyin software, the key used for it is "v", a letter which by coincidence is not used in Chinese Pinyin spelling.

Chinese Pinyin letters have two categories, the initials and finals. The initials are the same as the English consonant letters, and the finals use the English vowel letters. The two are usually combined to spell a word. This means that Chinese is basically an open-syllable language in which words will end with a vowel sound, as in Italian or Japanese.

There are only three exceptions to this general rule. They are the nasal sound letters "n" and "ng" and the retroflex sound "r". Since many Pinyin letters are pronounced very much like those in English, we only have to make a few notes on those exceptions that are essentially different.

Let's first go through the six basic Pinyin finals. They will be read twice after their corresponding English letters.

Letter a: a

Letter o: o

Letter e: e

Letter i: i

Letter u: u

Letter u with two dots on the top: ü

Now we can try some examples of the above Pinyin letters by combining each of them with an initial letter. Let's pick out the letter "o" and the letter "e" for example.

b: b(o)
p: p(o)
m: m(o)
f: f(o)
d: d(e)
t: t(e)
n: n(e)
l: l(e)
g: g(e)
k: k(e)
h: h(e)

We can see that these initial letters have very similar pronunciations as the English consonant letters. However, since Chinese is an open-syllable language, they will end with the additional vowel sound "o" or "e" if they stand alone as Pinyin letter names.

OK! Now let's come to some initials that are somewhat different from their English counterpart letters.

Letter z: z(i)

It is pronounced as "ds" as in the English "beds" or "words".

Letter c: c(i)

It is pronounced as "ts" as in "its" or "let's".

The English letter "s" belongs to the same group as "z" and "c" in the Pinyin system, but it is not changed so much, except that it ends with a weak schwa. When followed by a final sound, it is similar to its counterpart in English, just as in "speak" or "say".

Letter s: s(i)

Let's now listen and repeat. And pay attention to the ending of these letters as open syllables.

z: z(i)
c: c(i)
s: s(i)

Letter j: j(i)

It is pronounced somewhat like the English "g" in "Jesus" or "jeep"

Letter q: q(i)

It is pronounced somewhat like the English beginning consonant in "cheese" or "cheap".

Letter x: x(i)

It is similar in pronunciation to the beginning consonant in the English "sheep", but with the tongue tip touching the root of the upper teeth.

In fact, what is special in the pronunciation of these three letters—"j, q, x"—is that they are all articulated between the tongue tip and the gums of the upper teeth. Let's listen again.

Letters j, q, x: j(i), q(i), x(i)

Now let's learn to pronounce the letter "r" in Pinyin. It has two different pronunciations. As a Pinyin initial it is pronounced in the same way as the second consonant in "pleasure" or "measure"; but when placed at the end of a vowel sound, it is the same as in the American English "worker" or "marker". This is an exception to the rule that consonants will generally be the initial position in Chinese. Now listen and repeat.

Letter r in the initial position: r(i)

Letter r in the end position: r—(e)r

OK. Let's go on.

Letter w: w(u)

It is pronounced somewhat as in English "woo" in "the boy wooed the girl", but with some friction between the lips.

Letter y: y(i)

It is pronounced similar to that in the English "yeast" in fermentation.

Now we see that these two Pinyin initial letters are pronounced exactly like two other final letters, that is, the English letters "u" and "i". As a rule in spelling a word in Pinyin that has either "w" or "u", or either "y" or "i", both letters will be written.

OK. Now we have learned the basic single letters, let's have a review to make sure we remember them. Listen to repeat.

a: a

o: o

e: e

i: y(i)

u: (w)u

u with two dots on the top: (y)ü

z: z(i)

c: c(i)

s: s(i)

j: j(i)

q: q(i)

x: x(i)

b: b(o)

p: p(o)

m: m(o)

f: f(o)
d: d(e)
t: t(e)
n: n(e)
l: l(e)
g: g(e)
k: k(e)
h: h(e)
r in the initial position: r(i)
r in the end position: (e)r
y and i: y(i)
w and u: w(u)

Apart from these single letters that may be a little difficult in Pinyin pronunciation, there are also a few combinations that deserve our attention. Let's listen and repeat three such combinations in the initial position.

combination of c and h: ch(i)
combination of s and h: sh(i)
combination of z and h: zh(i)

Among these three combinations, the first two are comparable to their English counterparts, although in Pinyin they are pronounced with the tongue tip curled up.

ch: ch(i)
sh: sh(i)

The Pinyin combination of "z" and "h" doesn't exist in English. It is somewhat like the consonant sound in the English names "George" and "Joe" but pronounced in Chinese with the tip of the tongue drawn back and curled up. Now, let's listen again and repeat.

z and h: zh(i)
c and h: ch(i)
s and h: sh(i)

To some people, these three combinations may be confusing with the three single-letter initials that are counterparts of "j", "q" and "x" in English. Let's compare them.

j and z-h combination: j(i); zh(i)
q and c-h combination: q(i); ch(i)
x and s-h combination: x(i); sh(i)

Have you noticed the differences? Yes. When you pronounce the single-letter initials "j", "q" and "x", your tongue tip is kept close to the ridge of the gums of the upper teeth; but when you pronounce the combinations "zh", "ch" and "sh", you have your tongue curled up. Let's listen to the three pairs together and repeat.

Single Pinyin finals j, q, and x;

Initial Pinyin combinations zh, ch and sh: zh(i), ch(i) and sh(i)

There is one special rule to note about using the single initial letters "j", "q", and "x" in spelling. That is, when they are spelt with another final sound, there will always be the extra letter "i" attached at the end even though the pronunciation is not changed. Here are a few examples.

j plus a: j-i-a, jia

q plus a: q-i-a, qia

x plus a: x-i-a, xia

We should note that when the final letter "e" (counterpart of the English letter "e") follows these three initials, its pronunciation is changed and will become somewhat like the English "e" as in "yes".

j plus e: j-i-e, jie

q plus e: q-i-e, qie

x plus e: x-i-e, xie

Please remember: in pronouncing these three Pinyin sounds, you should start with the tip of the tongue closer to the ridge of the gums of the upper teeth, which makes the sounds different from the English consonants as in "just", "chair" and "sheet". Listen once more.

jie, qie, xie

All right! So far, we have learned almost all the Pinyin sounds that can pose a challenge to foreign learners. Although there are more final letter combinations, they are nevertheless much easier to imitate, because they are similar to the English diphthongs and triphthongs.

If you can remember all that we have learned, you can now immediately put them to use as you go on to Lesson 1. If you don't, you'd better go through it once more.

Lesson 1 第一课

The Musical Chinese Tones (Part 1)

你好（NI^3HAO^3）AND 再见（ZAI^4JIAN^4）

As we know, Chinese is by nature a tonal language, in which the meaning of a word is not only determined by its pronunciation but also by its tone. In fact, there are many homophones in Chinese—words with the same pronunciations. Misuse of the tones may cause misunderstanding. Therefore, it is necessary to follow the exact tones in spoken Chinese as you learn the pronunciation, just as if you were learning to sing.

Let's now listen to the most common Chinese greetings. As you listen, pay attention to the ups and downs in the tones and try to repeat.

Hello! Or, how do you do? (informal speech)!

你好！ ni^3hao^3!

Hello! Or, how do you do? (formal speech)!

您好！ nin^2hao^3!

When you leave a friend, you say—

Goodbye!

再见！ zai^4jian^4!

The musical pattern of 你好 and 您好 is rising up, dipping down, and then rising a little again. And the pattern of the tones in 再见 is a repetition of a falling tone.

In Mandarin Chinese, there are four pitched tones plus one that is not pitched. We simply call them the first, second, third, fourth and the light tone. The four pitched tones are marked in writing with their corresponding numbers in superscript. The light tone, also called the neutral tone, is just like any unstressed syllable in English. It is either left unmarked or marked by a "zero" in superscript.

Of the four pitched tones, we have now learned three, the second tone in 您, the third tone in 你 and 好, and the fourth tone in each syllable of 再见. Now let's take two words of the remaining first tone.

The first word in this tone is "ta", which actually has three distinct written characters, respectively for the masculine and feminine third person pronouns and for the impersonal pronoun "it".

他/她/它 ta^1

The second word in the first tone is a marker of a question used at the end of a sentence.

吗—ma^1

The function of 吗 is to change an indicative sentence into a general question without changing the order.

To speakers of English and other languages that are not tonal, probably the third tone is the most difficult. Let's listen to it in the first person pronoun.

I or me, 我 wo^3

Since the Chinese word for any form of the English linking verb "to be" is 是 (shi^4), we simply say the following:

I am...

我是…… wo^3 shi^4...

You are...

你是…… ni^3 shi^4...

He is or she is...

他/她是…… ta^1 shi^4...

In Chinese, sentence subjects are not always necessary. So we can reverse the word order of the above and say the following as complete sentences:

It's me.

是我。shi^4 wo^3.

It's you.

是你。shi^4 ni^3.

It's he, or it's she.

是他/她。shi^4 ta^1.

To make a negation, we simply say—

Not or no 不 bu^4

I'm not.

我不是。wo^3 bu^4 shi^4.

You are not.

你不是。ni^3 bu^4 shi^4.

He is not or she is not.

他/她不是。ta^1 bu^4 shi^4.

Here we should note that the negative 不 in 不是 is primarily a fourth tone word, although what you hear is in the second tone. This is because the tone is naturally changed in the tonal context for easy and smooth flow of speech. ***In this course book, we will mark the original tones of words in the sentences, but you should follow the recording to find out occasional changes****. So let's listen again—*

No. It's not me.

不，不是我。bu^{4}, bu^{4} shi^{4} wo^{3}—bu^{4} shi^{4} wo^{3}.

No. It's not you.

不，不是你。bu^{4}, bu^{4} shi^{4} ni^{3}—bu^{4}, shi^{4} ni^{3}.

No. It's not him or it's not her.

不，不是他/她。bu^{4}, bu^{4} shi^{4} ta^{1}—bu^{4}, bu^{4} shi^{4} ta^{1}.

We should know that the function of the Chinese 是 is not exactly the same with the English linking verb "to be", because it has a strong affirmative function and can actually mean YES, OK or RIGHT. Let's listen to the following:

Is it or is it right?

是吗？shi^{4} ma^{1}?

Yes.

是。shi^{4}.

Isn't it or isn't it right?

不是吗？bu^{4} shi^{4} ma^{1}?

No. It isn't.

不, 不是。bu^{4}, bu^{4} shi^{4}.

Are you Mr. Wang?

你是王先生吗？ni^{3} shi^{4} wang^{2} xian^{1}sheng ma^{1}?

No. I'm not him.

不，我不是他。bu^{4}, wo^{3} bu^{4} shi^{4} ta^{1}.

I'm not Mr. Wang.

我不是王先生。wo^{3} bu^{4} shi^{4} wang^{2} xian^{1}sheng.

I am; he is not.

我是，他不是。wo^{3} shi^{4}。ta^{1} bu^{4} shi^{4}.

He is; I'm not.

他是，我不是。ta^{1} shi^{4}, wo^{3} bu^{4} shi^{4}.

It is me, not him.

是我，不是他。shi^{4} wo^{3}, bu^{4} shi^{4} ta^{1}.

It is he, not I.

是他，不是我。shi^{4} ta^{1}, bu^{4} shi^{4} wo^{3}.

In fact, the affirmative function of 是 in Chinese is much more important than its function as a linking verb, simply because a Chinese sentence can directly take an adjective word without using a verb. For example:

Literally, "you good", but in effect, "How do you do!"

你好！ ni^{3}hao^{3}!

The weather is fine.

天气好！ tian^{1}qi^{4} hao^{3}!

I'm hard-working, or I'm diligent.

我努力。wo^{3} nu^{3}li^{4}.

He is intelligent.

他聪明。ta^{1} cong^{1}ming.

We are all fine.

我们都好。wo^{3}men dou^{1} hao^{3}.

OK!

We know that the Chinese tones are generally fixed, one tone for each syllable— that is to say, for each single character. However, there are occasional changes because tones may influence one another in the natural flow of speech. For instance, in a word or phrase of two third tones, the first will be changed to the second tone if you speak naturally fast. Now, listen to the simple Chinese greeting again and see this for yourself. It is read twice, first separately and then as connected speech.

How do you do! 你 (ni^{3}), 好 (hao^{3})：你好 ni^{3} hao^{3}!

Therefore, although the two words of the 2nd person pronouns 你 and 您 differ in tones, the difference no longer exists when they are followed by the 3rd tone word 好. Let's listen.

Formal greeting: How do you do! 您好！ nin^{2} hao^{3}!

Casual greeting: How do you do! 你好 ni^{3} hao^{3}!

Let's listen to some two-character combinations that repeat the third tone. They are read twice, first separately and then in combination.

Very good, very well 很 hen^{3}, 好 hao^{3}— 很好 hen^{3} hao^{3}.

I think 我 wo^{3}, 想 xiang^{3}— 我想 wo^{3} xiang^{3}

You and me 你 ni^{3}, 我 wo^{3}— 你我 ni^{3} wo^{3}

You think 你 ni^{3}, 想, xiang^{3}— 你想 ni^{3} xiang^{3}

In Chinese, there are many two-character words in which both characters are in the third tone, but in actual use, the first one is changed to the second. Let's listen and repeat.

Where or which place 哪 na^{3}, 里 li^{3}— 哪里 na^{3} li^{3}

May or can 可 ke^{3}, 以 yi^{3}— 可以 ke^{3}yi^{3}

OK! Then what if more than two third tones follow one another? The answer is: it is usually the first character of the more closely related two that is changed. Let's just listen to some examples.

I'm very well, or I'm very good.

我很好。wo^{3} hen^{3} hao^{3}.

I very much want or miss... Or I really want or miss...
我很想……wo^3 hen^3 xiang^3...
I want to write.
我想写。wo^3 xiang^3 xie^3.
I miss you.
我想你。wo^3 xiang^3 ni^3.
I miss you very much.
我很想你。wo^3 hen^3 xiang^3 ni^3.

For practice, let's now go through all the basic tones as we learn more Chinese words. Please try to repeat without changing the tones.

The first tone
Hear or listen 听 ting^1— 听 ting^1
Speak or say 说 shuo^1— 说 shuo^1
Hear people say, or it is heard 听说 ting^1 shuo^1
He or she 他/她 ta^1— 他/她 ta^1
He or she hears them say; he or she hears that 他/她听说 ta^1 ting^1 shuo^1
Listen to him or her say. Or, hear him or her say. 听他/她说 ting^1 ta^1 shuo^1.

The second tone
You (the polite form) 您 nin^2— 您 nin^2
Come 来 lai^2— 来 lai^2
Read 读 du^2— 读 du^2
Learn 学 xue^2— 学 xue^2
You come to read, or you please read.
您来读。nin^2 lai^2 du^2.
You come to learn, or you please learn.
您来学。nin^2 lai^2 xue^2.

The third tone
You 你 ni^3— 你 ni^3
I or me 我 wo^3— 我 wo^3
Good, or well 好 hao^3— 好 hao^3
Write 写 xie^3— 写 xie^3

Here again, we should know that the tone change of the first syllable in a word of two third-tone syllables is natural for easy flow of speech. You don't have to bother about this, because it would be hard for you to keep the original tones when you speak naturally fast with the least effort.

How do you do!
你好。ni^3 hao^3— 你好 ni^3 hao^3.
You and me 你我 ni^3 wo^3— 你我 ni^3 wo^3

You write 你写 ni³ xie³— 你写 ni³ xie³
The fourth tone
Again, or once more 再 zai⁴— 再 zai⁴
See or meet 见 jian⁴— 见 jian⁴
Goodbye!
再见！ zai⁴jian⁴!
Look 看 kan⁴— 看 kan⁴
Look again.
再看 zai⁴kan⁴
See, or look and see 看见 kan⁴jian⁴

Here the single-character words 看 and 见 respectively mean "look" and "see". When they are used together as a two-character word, the meaning is "see".

All right! Now we have learned the four basic tones, all we need to do is practice them as we go on to the next lesson.

LESSON 2 第二课

THE MUSICAL CHINESE TONES (PART 2)

LISTENING AND SPEAKING

听听说说 TING^{1}TING^{1}SHUO^{1}SHUO^1

In this lesson, we will continue to consolidate our foundation in using all possible musical patterns of Chinese; we'll learn two other things that make the Chinese language even more musical, that is, the use of word repetition and the light tone.

When the same word is repeated, there is usually some additional nuance of meaning, depending on the function of the word. For example, if a verb is repeated, the additional meaning is to keep doing it for a while or give it a try. Let's listen and repeat.

1st tone repetition

Listen for a while or give it a try

听听 ting^1 ting^1

Speak for a while or give it a try

说说 shuo^1 shuo^1

Listen and speak for a while

听听说说 ting^1 ting shuo^1 shuo^1

2nd tone repetition

Read for a while or give it a try

读读 du^2 du^2

Learn for a while

学学 xue^{2}xue^2

Read and learn for a while

读读学学 du^{2}du^2, xue^{2}xue^2

3rd tone repetition, with the first syllable naturally changed to the 2nd tone.

Think for a while

想想 xiang^3 xiang^3
Write for a while
写写 xie^3 xie^3
Think and write for a while
想想写写 xiang^3 xiang^3 xie^3 xie^3
4th tone repetition
Take a look
看看 kan^{4}kan^4
Go and have a look
去看看 qu^4 kan^4 kan^4
Go and have a look again
再去看看 zai^4 qu^4 kan^4 kan^4

In the above repetitions, the Chinese word 一 (yi^1) for "one" could be put in the middle without changing the meaning. And the thing to note is that its tone is sometimes changed because of the influence of the preceding or succeeding tones. Let's listen to the following.

Listen for a while or just for a try.
听一听 ting^1 yi^1 ting^1
Read for a while or just for a try.
读一读 du^2 yi^1 du^2
Think for a while or just for a try.
想一想 xiang^3 yi^1 xiang^3
Take a look 看一看 kan^4 yi^1 kan^4
All right. Let's do more practice.
You (polite form) come and learn for a short while or give it a try.
您来学学。nin^2 lai^2 xue^2 xue^2.
You (polite form) read 您读 nin^2 du^2
You (polite form) come and read for a try.
您来读读。nin^2 lai^2 du^2 du^2.
Goodbye, literally again see
再见 zai^4 jian^4
Look and see. Or simply see
看见 kan^4 jian^4
Look again, literally again look
再看 zai^4 kan^4

Since tones may influence one another in connected speech or occasionally change for special emphasis, the first-tone word 一 (yi^1) inserted in the verb repetitions is sometimes changed according to the tone of the repeated word. But you don't have to worry about this, because you will tend to get the right tone if you just make the least effort when *speaking. So let's listen again. And as you listen and repeat, pay attention to the tone changes of the word 一(yi^1).*

Listen for a while or just for a try
听一听 ting^1 yi^1 ting^1
Read for a while or just for a try
读一读 du^2 yi^1 du^2
Think for a while or just for a try
想一想 xiang^3 yi^1 xiang^3
Take a look
看一看 kan^4 yi^2 kan^4

Please note that the third-tone 好 may be repeated too, and then it means "seriously" or "well". It actually has two different tone patterns, determined by whether it is used in formal speech or informal speech. In informal speech, there is usually the "er" syllable added to the end. So, let's listen and repeat.

Listen seriously and well (formal speech)
好好听 hao^2 hao^3 ting^1
Listen seriously and well (informal)
好好儿听 hao^3 hao'r^2 ting^1
Speak seriously and well (formal)
好好说 hao^2 hao^3 shuo^1
Speak seriously and well (informal)
好好儿说 hao^3 hao'r^2 shuo^1
Read seriously and well (formal)
好好读 hao^2 hao^3 du^2
Read seriously and well (informal)
好好儿读 hao^3 hao'r^2 du^2

OK! Now, after learning so much of repetitions of single-character or single-syllable words, we should know that the two-character words can also be repeated. Here are a few examples.

Learn or study 学习 xue^{2}xi^2
Learn or study for a while
学习学习 xue^{2}xi^2 xue^{2}xi^2
Consider or think 考虑 kao^{3}lv^4
Take time to consider or think for a while
考虑考虑 kao^{3}lv^4 kao^{3}lv^4
Take a rest 休息 xiu^{1}xi
Take some rest or rest for a while
休息休息 xiu^{1}xi xiu^{1}xi
Take a real good rest

好好休息休息 hao^{3}hao^3 xiu^{1}xi xiu^{1}xi

In the two-syllable word 休息, the second syllable is actually a synonym to the first and is only complementary; it is uttered in the light tone. For the same reason, we repeat 休息 as one word. However, if the relation between the two is coordinating or contrasting, then each character is repeated separately, and the original tones are kept unchanged. For example—

Listen and read 听读 ting^1 du^2

Listen and read for a while

听听读读 ting^1 ting^1 du^{2}du^2

Read and write 读写 du^{2}xie^3

Read and write for a while

读读写写 du^{2}du^2 xie^{3}xie^3

Eat and drink 吃喝 chi^1 he^1

Keep eating and drinking, indulge in food and comfort

吃吃喝喝 chi^1 chi^1 he^1 he^1

Talk and laugh, be happy 说笑 shuo^1 xiao^4

Enjoy talking with friends and be happy

说说笑笑 shuo^1 shuo^1 xiao^4 xiao^4

Play and be merry 玩乐 wan^2 le^4

Enjoy pleasures

玩玩乐乐 wan^2 wan^2 le^4 le^4

Pretty, nice, or beautiful 漂亮 piao^4 liang^4

Very pretty, nice or beautiful

漂漂亮亮 piao^4 piao^4 liang^4 liang^4

Serious or seriously 认真 ren^4 zhen^1

Very serious or seriously

认认真真 ren^4 ren^4 zhen^1 zhen^1

All right! From the above, we see how repetitions contribute to the musicality of the Chinese language. In fact, not only verbs can be repeated, but also nouns, adjectives, and adverbs. However, when words of different parts of speech are repeated, the change of meaning will be different.

Let's first learn repetitions of some nouns that are related to time.

Day (informal) 天 tian^1

Day by day, every day (informal)

天天 tian^{1}tian^1

Day (formal) 日 ri^4

Day by day, every day (formal speech)

日日 ri^{4}ri^4

Night 夜 ye^4

Night by night, every night
夜夜 ye^{4} ye^{4}
All days and nights, all time
日日夜夜 ri^{4}ri^{4} ye^{4}ye^{4}
Time, hour 时 shi^{4}
Time and again, now and then
时时 shi^{2}shi^{2}
A quarter of an hour 刻 ke^{4}
Every quarter of an hour
刻刻 ke^{4} ke^{4}
Every now and then, often
时时刻刻 shi^{2} shi^{2} ke^{4}ke^{4}
Month 月 yue^{4}
Every month
月月 yue^{4}yue^{4}
Year 年 nian^{2}
Every year
年年 nian^{2}nian^{2}
Each year and each month, all time
年年月月 nian^{2}nian^{2} yue^{4}yue^{4}

OK! These are repetitions of time words. The following examples are some words related to people.

Person, man 人 ren^{2}
Each person, everybody
人人 ren^{2}ren^{2}
Family, home or house 家 jia^{1}
Every family, all families
家家 jia^{1}jia^{1}
Male and female 男女 nan^{2}nv^{3}
All males and females, all the people
男男女女 nan^{2}nan^{2} nv^{3}nv^{3}
Mountain and water, the landscape 山水 shan^{1} shui^{3}
All mountains and waters
山山水水 shan^{1}shan^{1} shui^{3}shui^{3}
Street and alley 街巷 jie^{1}xiang^{4} All streets and alleys, the whole town
街街巷巷 jie^{1}jie^{1} xiang^{4}xiang^{4}

Next, let's see some repetitions of words that can be used as adjectives and adverbs.

Big, large 大 da^{4}
Quite big, considerably large

大大的 da^{4}da^{4} de
Small 小 xiao^{4}
Quite small
小小的 xiao^{2} xiao^{3} de
Of big and small, of various sizes
大大小小的 da^{4}da^{4} xiao^{4}xiao^{4} de
Long 长 chang^{2}
Quite long
长长的 chang^{2}chang^{2} de
Short 短 duan^{3}
Quite short
短短的 duan^{3} duan^{3} de
Long and short, of various lengths
长长短短的 chang^{2}chang^{2} duan^{3}duan^{3} de
Tall, high 高 gao^{1}
Low, short 低 di^{1}
Of various heights
高高低低 gao^{1}gao^{1} di^{1}di^{1}
Red 红 hong^{2}
Quite red, fairly red
红红的 hong^{2}hong^{2} de
Green 绿 lv^{4}
Quite green, fairly green
绿绿的 lv^{4}lv^{4} de
Of various colors, colorful
红红绿绿的 hong^{2}hong^{2} lv^{4}lv^{4} de
Blue 蓝 lan^{2}
Quite blue, fairly blue
蓝蓝的 lan^{2}lan^{2} de
Yellow or brown 黄 huang^{2}
Quite yellow or brown
黄黄的 huang^{2}huang^{2} de
Often 常 chang^{2}
Quite often, very frequently
常常 chang^{2}chang^{2}
Fast, quick 快 kuai^{4}
Quite fast, fairly quick
快快 kuai^{4}kuai^{4}
Slow 慢 man^{4}
Quite slow, taking one's time (in doing something)

慢慢 man^{4}man^4
Now quick, now slow; at different speeds
快快慢慢 kuai^{4}kuai^4 man^{4}man^4
Clear, easy to see or understand 清楚 qing^1 chu^3
Very clear and easy to see or understand
清清楚楚 qing^{1}qing^1 chu^{3}chu^3
Clean 干净 gan^1 jing^4
Very clean
干干净净 gan^{1}gan^1 jing^{4}jing^4
Orderly, in good order 整齐 zheng^3 qi^2
In very good order
整整齐齐 zheng^{2}zheng^3 qi^{2}qi^2

Very good! We have now learned many words and their repetitions. You can practice a few times to get used to the interesting play of Chinese tones in actual use. However, we should know that not every word in Chinese can be repeated, and so it is still necessary to learn from native speakers what words actually can be.

LESSON 3 第三课

PERSONAL PRONOUNS AND THE LIGHT TONE 我们 WO^{3}MEN，你们 NI^{3}MEN，他们 TA^{1}MEN

In this lesson, we will learn more about the musicality of Mandarin Chinese through the use of the light tone and word repetition. The light tone is also called as the neutral tone. It is easier to learn than the pitched tones simply because it is just like any unstressed syllable in English. Characters using the light tone are usually those that serve the function of word suffixes or particles that only have a complementary meaning. Let's first take the plural suffix of personal pronouns for example.

The plural suffix of personal pronouns 们 men^{2}

As we hear, this character is pronounced in the second tone— that is, the rising tone. However, it is often changed to the unstressed light tone in natural speech if the plurality is not emphasized. Let's listen.

I or me 我 wo^{3}

We or us 我们 wo^{3}men^{2}— 我们 wo^{3}men

You (singular) 你 ni^{3}

You (plural) 你们 ni^{3}men^{2}— 你们 ni^{3}men

He or she 他/她 ta^{1}

They or them 他们 ta^{1}men^{2}— 他们 ta^{1}men

When the plural meaning is especially emphasized in contrast to the singular, the original second tone of 们 (men^{2}) is kept unchanged. For example:

It's me, not us.

是我, 不是我们。shi^{4} wo^{3}, bu^{4} shi^{4} wo^{3}men^{2}.

It's you in the singular, not you in the plural.

是你, 不是你们。shi^{4} ni^{3}, bu^{4} shi^{4} ni^{3}men^{2}.

In Chinese, this suffix can be added to a noun referring to people. Please listen and repeat.

Person or man 人 ren^{2}

People 人们 ren^{2}men
Male, man 男人 nan^{2}ren
Men 男人们 nan^{2}renmen
Female, woman 女人 nv^{3}ren^2
Women 女人们 nv^{3}ren^{2}men
Friend 朋友 peng^{2}you
Friends 朋友们 peng^{2}youmen
Child 孩子 hai^{2}zi
Children 孩子们 hai^{2}zimen

As we hear, the light tone is actually used not only in the plural suffix 们, but also in the second syllable of the two-syllable words. This often happens when the second syllable is only complementary in meaning, or when it is affected by the preceding tone for the sake of natural and effortless flow of speech.

So let's listen again.

People 人们 ren^{2}men
Male, man 男人 nan^{2}ren
Men 男人们 nan^{2}renmen
Female, woman 女人 nv^{3}ren^2
Women 女人们 nv^{3}ren^{2}men
Friend 朋友 peng^{2}you^3
Friends 朋友们 peng^{2}you^{3}men
Child 孩子 hai^{2}zi
Children 孩子们 hai^{2}zimen

The single character word 子 (zi) which is originally pronounced in the third tone also changes to the light tone, since it's used as a suffix. For example:

Son 儿子 er^{2}zi
Grandson 孙子 sun^{1}zi
Wife 妻子 qi^{1}zi

Now let's change them into the plural form by adding the suffix 们 men

Sons 儿子们 er^{2}zimen
Grandsons 孙子们 sun^{1}zimen
Wives 妻子们 qi^{1}zimen
Children 孩子们 hai^{2}zimen

Apart from the suffixes, the repetition of the same noun words often changes to the light tone, especially when it adds no meaning except suggesting an informal way of talking. Let's listen and repeat.

Dad 爸爸 ba^{4}ba
Mom 妈妈 ma^{1}ma

Elder sister 姐姐 jie^{3}jie
Younger sister 妹妹 mei^{4}mei
Elder brother 哥哥 ge^{1}ge
Younger brother 弟弟 di^{4}di
Grandpa 爷爷 ye^{2}ye
Granny 奶奶 nai^{3}nai
Uncle on the mother's side 舅舅 jiu^{4}jiu
Younger uncle on the father's side 叔叔 shu^{1}shu
Elder uncle on the father's side 伯伯 bo^{2}bo
Aunt on the father's side 姑姑 gu^{1}gu

OK. Now let's learn another frequently used light-tone word, the possessive marker and nominalizer.

My or mine 我的 wo^{3} de
My father 我的爸爸 wo^{3} de ba^{4}ba
My wife 我的妻子 wo^{3} de qi^{1}zi
Your or yours (singular) 你的 ni^{3} de
Your mother 你的妈妈 ni^{3} de ma^{1}ma
Yours or your (plural) 你们的 ni^{3}men^{2} de
Yours or your (plural) grandpa 你们的爷爷 ni^{3}men^{2} de ye^{2}ye
His or her or hers 他/她的 ta^{1} de-
His or her elder sister 他/她的姐姐 ta^{1} de jie^{3}jie
His or her elder brother 他/她的哥哥 ta^{1} de ge^{1}ge
Their children 他们的孩子 ta^{1}men de hai^{2}zi
Our or ours 我们的 wo^{3}men de
Our friends 我们的朋友 wo^{3}men de peng^{2}you
The children's 孩子们的 hai^{2}zimen de
The children's uncle on the mother's side 孩子们的舅舅 hai^{2}zimen de jiu^{4}jiu

Now let's practice the musical Chinese tones with more easy phrases using 的(de)

His father's 他的爸爸的 ta^{1} de ba^{4}ba de
His mother's 他的妈妈的 ta^{1} de ma^{1}ma de
My grandpa's or of my grandpa's 我的爷爷的 wo^{3} de ye^{2}ye de
My elder sister's or of my elder sister 我的姐姐的 wo^{3} de jie^{3}jie de
My elder brother's 我的哥哥的 wo^{3} de ge^{1}ge de
My younger brother's 我的弟弟的 wo^{3} de di^{4}di de
Your elder sister's 你的姐姐的 ni^{3} de jie^{3}jie de
Your younger sister's 你的妹妹的 ni^{3} de mei^{4}mei de
Your sister's 你的姐妹的 ni^{3} de jie^{3}mei^{4} de
Her boyfriend's 她的男朋友的 ta^{1} de nan^{2}peng^{2}you^{3} de

His girlfriend's 他的女朋友的 ta^{1} de nv^{3}peng^{2}you^{3} de
Our company's 我们的公司的 wo^{3}men^{2} de gong^{1}si^{1} de
Your factory's 你们的工厂的 ni^{3}men^{2} de gong^{1}chang^{3} de

Please note that the possessive marker 的 (de) is not always necessary. For instance, in all the phrases above, the first 的 can be omitted. So let's have a review of them and leave out the first 的.

His father's 他爸爸的 ta^{1}ba^{4}ba de
His mother's 他妈妈的 ta^{1} ma^{1}ma de
My grandpa's or of my grandpa's 我爷爷的 wo^{3} ye^{2}ye de
My elder sister's or of my elder sister 我姐姐的 wo^{3} jie^{3}jie de
My elder brother's 我哥哥的 wo^{3} ge^{1}ge de
My younger brother's 我弟弟的 wo^{3} di^{4}di de
Your elder sister's 你姐姐的 ni^{3} jie^{3}jie de
Your younger sister's 你妹妹的 ni^{3} mei^{4}mei de
Your sister's 你姐妹的 ni^{3} jie^{3}mei^{4} de
Her boyfriend's 她男朋友的 ta^{1} nan^{2}peng^{2}you^{3} de
His girlfriend's 他女朋友的 ta^{1} nv^{3}peng^{2}you^{3} de
Our company's 我们公司的 wo^{3}men^{2} gong^{1}si^{1} de
Your factory's 你们工厂的 ni^{3}men^{2} gong^{1}chang^{3} de

The next thing to learn about the word 的 (de) is its function as a nominalizer. This is to say, it is used after a verb to make a noun phrase.

What is heard or listened to 听的 ting^{1} de
What is said or spoken 说的 shuo^{1} de
What is being thought about 想的 xiang^{3} de
What is read 读的 du^{2} de
What is learned 学的 xue^{2} de
What comes or who comes 来的 lai^{2} de
What is written 写的 xie^{3} de
What is looked at 看的 kan^{4} de
What is seen or what is met with 见的 jian^{4} de
What is seen 看见的 kan^{4}jian^{4} de
What is done or made 做的 zuo^{4} de

Let's do more practice of the tones, using a subject word we have learned. Listen and repeat.

What mother says or said 妈妈说的 ma^{1}ma shuo^{1} de
What grandma listens to or hears 奶奶听的 nai^{3}nai ting^{1} de
What grandpa thinks or has thought. 爷爷想的 ye^{2}ye xiang^{3} de
What father's younger brother writes or wrote 叔叔写的 shu^{1}shu xie^{3} de
What the younger brother learns or learned 弟弟学的 di^{4}di xue^{2} de

What the younger sister reads or has read 妹妹读的 mei^{4}mei du^2 de
What the elder brother looks at or looked at 哥哥看的 ge^{1}ge kan^4 de
What the elder sister sees or has seen 姐姐见的 jie^{3}jie jian^4 de
Or
What the elder sister sees or has seen 姐姐看见的 jie^{3}jie kan^{4}jian^4 de
What we make or do, or what we have made or done 我们做的 wo^{3}men zuo^4 de

Another important use of the light tone is with the past or perfect tense marker 了 (le). Let's listen and repeat.

Said or have said 说了 shuo^1 le
Heard or have heard 听了 ting^1 le
Read or have read 读了 du^2 le
Learned or have learned 学了 xue^2 le
Came or have come 来了 lai^2 le
Became good or have become good; or, it's OK now 好了 hao^3 le
Wrote or have written 写了 xie^3 le
Looked or have looked 看了 kan^4 le
Saw or have seen; met or have met 见了 jian^4 le
Saw or have seen 看见了 kan^{4}jian^4 le
Did, made or have done or have made 做了 zuo^4 le

EXTRA EXERCISE

Now, after learning possible tone changes in repetitions, we will listen to some short sentences using all the tones. Please try to keep the ups and downs of the tones in each sentence as you repeat.

He has listened, or he listened.
他听了。ta^1 ting^1 le.
They heard, or have heard.
他们听了。ta^{1}men ting^1 le.
He said, or he has said.
他说了。ta^1 shuo^1 le.
They said, or they have said.
他们说了. ta^{1}men shuo^1 le.
He has come, or he came. 他来了。ta^1 lai^{2}le.
They came, or they have come. 他们来了。ta^{1}men lai^2 le.
We read, or we have read. 我们读了。wo^{3}men du^2 le.
We learned, or we have learned. 我们学了。wo^{3}men xue^2 le.
You (polite form) have listened, or you listened. 您听了。nin^2 ting^1 le.

You (polite form) have said, or you said 您说了。nin^{2} shuo^{1} le.
You (polite form) have come. 您来了。nin^{2} lai^{2} le.
You (polite form) read, or have read. 您读了。nin^{2} du^{2} le.
You (polite form) learned, or have learned. 您学了。nin^{2} xue^{2} le.
I heard, listened, or have heard or listened. 我听了。wo^{3} ting^{1} le.
I said, or have said. 我说了。wo^{3} shuo^{1} le.
I read, or have read. 我读了。wo^{3} du^{2} le.
I have learned. 我学了。wo^{3} xue^{2} le.
I thought, or I have thought. 我想了。wo^{3} xiang^{3} le.
You wrote, or you have written. 我写了。wo^{3} xie^{3} le.
I looked, or have looked. 我看了。wo^{3} kan^{4} le.
He looked, or has taken a look. 他看了。ta^{1} kan^{4} le.
I saw, or have seen. 我见了。wo^{3} jian^{4} le.
They saw, or have seen, or have met. 他们见了。ta^{1}men jian^{4} le.
I looked and saw, or I have looked and seen. 我看见了。wo^{3} kan^{4}jian^{4} le.
Goodbye! 再见了。zai^{4}jian^{4} le.

As for the use of 了 in the last expression of the above, "再见了", we would say its function is simply a sentence final instead of a tense marker. Another case in which it is used as a sentence final is when we want to mean that something is done.

It's okay now, or it's done. 好了。hao^{3} le.

Yes. After learning all this, let's say 好了, and do more exercises on the musical tones. We will first use only one verb and the negative 不 to make short questions with the subject omitted. Listen and repeat.

Listen or not 听不听 ting^{1} bu^{4} ting^{1}
Speak or not 说不说 shuo^{1} bu^{4} shuo^{1}
Eat or not 吃不吃 chi^{1} bu^{4} chi^{1}
Come or not 来不来 lai^{2} bu^{4} lai^{2}
Learn or not 学不学 xue^{2} bu^{4} xue^{2}
Read or not 读不读 du^{2} bu^{4} du^{2}
Understand or not 懂不懂 dong^{3} bu^{4} dong^{3}
Write or not 写不写 xie^{3} bu^{4} xie^{3}
Want or not, desire or not; literally, think or not 想不想 xiang^{3} bu^{4} xiang^{3}
Okay or not 好不好 hao^{3} bu^{4} hao^{3}
Look or not, or watch or not 看不看 kan^{4} bu^{4} kan^{4}
Yes or no 是不是 shi^{4} bu^{4} shi^{4}
Correct or not 对不对 dui^{4} bu^{4} dui^{4}
Know how or don't 会不会 hui^{4} bu^{4} hui^{4}

OK! Now let's replace the negative 不 with another negative— 没, which is usually used in the perfect tense. Again, let's omit the sentence subject because it is not necessary in Chinese if we know it from the context.

Have listened or haven't 听没听 ting^{1} mei^{2} ting^{1}
Have spoken or haven't 说没说 shuo^{1} mei^{2} shuo^{1}
Have eaten or haven't 吃没吃 chi^{1} mei^{2} chi^{1}
Have come or haven't 来没来 lai^{2} mei^{2} lai^{2}
Have learned or haven't 学没学 xue^{2} mei^{2} xue^{2}
Have read or haven't 读没读 du^{2} mei^{2} du^{2}
Have written or haven't 写没写 xie^{3} mei^{2} xie^{3}
Have understood or haven't 懂没懂 dong^{3} mei^{2} dong^{3}
Have thought or haven't 想没想 xiang^{3} mei^{2} xiang^{3}
Has it been done well or haven't 好没好 hao^{3} mei^{2} hao^{3}
Have or haven't 有没有 you^{3} mei^{2} you^{3}
Have learned how or haven't 会没会 hui^{4} mei^{2} hui^{4}
Have looked or not 看没看 kan^{4} mei^{2} kan^{4}
Has it been correct or not, or has it been right or wrong 对没对 dui^{4} mei^{2} dui^{4}

All right! In the above, we have learned some important Chinese sentence structures as we practiced the tones. Please remember that all these can be directly put to use as questions as well as phrases, because the sentence subject can be dropped if the meaning is clear in context. Let's now go on consolidating our command of the tones in some more examples. Listen and repeat.

He has heard what I said, or has taken my advice.
他听了我说的。ta^{1} ting^{1} le wo^{3} shuo^{1} de.
As for what I said, he has heard or taken as advice.
我说的他听了。wo^{3} shuo^{1} de ta^{1} ting^{1} le.
They have heard what we said or taken our advice.
他们听了我们说的。ta^{1}men ting^{1} le wo^{3}men shuo^{1} de.
As for what we said, they have heard or taken as advice.
我们说的他们听了。wo^{3}men shuo^{1} de ta^{1}men ting^{1} le.
I have written down, or written about what he thinks.
我写了他想的。wo^{3} xie^{3} le ta^{1} xiang^{3} de.
As for what he thinks, I have written.
他想的我写了。ta^{1} xiang^{3} de wo^{3} xie^{3} le.
We have written about, or written down what they think.
我们写了他们想的。wo^{3}men xie^{3} le ta^{1}men xiang^{3} de.
As for what they think, we have written about, or written down.

他们想的我们写了。ta^{1}men xiang^{3} de wo^{3}men xie^{3} le.
I have seen what he has looked at, or looked through.
我见了他看的。wo^{3} jian^{4} le ta^{1} kan^{4} de.
As for what he looked at, or looked through, I have seen.
他看的我见了。ta^{1} kan^{4} de wo^{3} jian^{4} le.
We have seen what they looked at, or looked through.
我们见了他们看的。wo^{3}men jian^{4} le ta^{1}men kan^{4} de.
As for what they looked at, or looked through, we have seen.
他们看的我们见了。ta^{1}men kan^{4} de wo^{3}men jian^{4} le.
You have said what I think.
你说了我想的。ni^{3} shuo^{1} le wo^{3} xiang^{3} de.
As for what I think, you have said it.
我想的你说了。wo^{3} xiang^{3} de ni^{3} shuo^{1} le.
You have said what we think.
你们说了我们想的。ni^{3}men shuo^{1} le wo^{3}men xiang^{3} de.
As for what we think, you have spoken it out.
我们想的你们说了。wo^{3}men xiang^{3} de ni^{3}men shuo^{1} le.
He has read what I have written.
他读了我写的。ta^{1} du^{2} le wo^{3} xie^{3} de.
As for what I have written, he has read.
我写的他读了。wo^{3} xie^{3} de ta^{1} du^{2} le.
They have read what we wrote.
他们读了我们写的。ta^{1}men du^{2} le wo^{3}men xie^{3} de.
As for what we have written, they have read.
我们写的他们读了。wo^{3}men xie^{3} de ta^{1}men du^{2} le.
He has written out, or written about what I think.
他写了我想的。ta^{1} xie^{3} le wo^{3} xiang^{3} de.
As for what I think, he has written it out, or written about.
我想的他写了。wo^{3} xiang^{3} de ta^{1} xie^{3} le.
We have read what they have written.
我们看了他们写的。wo^{3}men kan^{4} le ta^{1}men xie^{3} de.
As for what they have written, we have read.
他们写的我们看了。ta^{1}men xie^{3} de wo^{3}men kan^{4} le.
What you say is what I have heard.
你说的我听过。ni^{3} shuo^{1} de wo^{3} ting^{1} guo^{4}.
I have heard what you say.
我听过你说的。wo^{3} ting^{1} guo^{4} ni^{3} shuo^{1} de.
What you hear is what I have seen.
你听的我见过。ni^{3} ting^{1} de wo^{3} jian^{4} guo^{4}.
I have seen what you talk about.

我见过你说的。wo^3 jian^1 guo^4 ni^3 shuo^1 de.
What you think about is what I have thought about.
你想的我想过。ni^3 xiang^3 de wo^3 xiang^1 guo^4.
I have thought about what you are thinking about.
我想过你想的。wo^3 xiang^3 guo^4 ni^3 xiang^3 de.
What you read is what I have read before.
你读的我读过。ni^3 du^2 de wo^3 du^2 guo^4.
I have read what you are reading.
我读过你读的。wo^3 du^2 guo^4 ni^3 du^2 de.
What you are learning is what I learned in the past.
你学的我学过。ni^3 xue^2 de wo^3 xue^2 guo^4.
I have learned what you are learning.
我学过你学的。wo^3 xue^2 guo^4 ni^3 xue^2 de.

LESSON 4 第四课

ASKING GENERAL QUESTIONS WITH "是不是" (SHI^{4}BU^{2}SHI^{4})

Having learned the affirmative word 是 (shi^{4}) and negative word 不 (bu^{4}) in lesson 1, we can now go on to their uses in asking general questions. Let's listen and repeat.

Is it or isn't it? Or, simply, is it?
是不是？ shi^{4} bu^{4} shi^{4}?
Yes or no? Or, is it true?
是不是？ shi^{4} bu^{4} shi^{4}?
Is it this one?
是不是这个？ shi^{4} bu^{4} shi^{4} zhe^{4} (/zhei^{4}) ge^{4}?
Is it that one?
是不是那个？ shi^{4} bu^{4} shi^{4} na^{4} ge^{4}?
Is this…?
这个是不是…？ zhe^{4} ge^{4} shi^{4} bu^{4} shi^{4}...?
Is this yours?
这个是不是你的？ zhe^{4} ge^{4} shi^{4} bu^{4} shi^{4} ni^{3} de?
Is that…?
那个是不是…？ na^{4} ge^{4} shi^{4} bu^{4} shi^{4}...?
Is that his?
那个是不是他的？ na^{4} ge^{4} shi^{4} bu^{4} shi^{4} ta^{1} de?
Are you a student?
你是不是学生？ ni^{3} shi^{4} bu^{4} shi^{4} xue^{2} sheng^{1}?
Are they students?
他们是不是学生？ ta^{1}men shi^{4} bu^{4} shi^{4} xue^{2}sheng^{1}?
Is he a teacher?
他是不是老师？ ta^{1} shi^{4} bu^{4} shi^{4} lao^{3}shi^{1}?
Is he your boyfriend?
他是不是你的男朋友？ ta^{1} shi^{4} bu^{4} shi^{4} ni^{3} de nan^{2}peng^{2}you^{3}?
Is she your girlfriend?
她是不是你的女朋友？ ta^{1} shi^{4} bu^{4} shi^{4} ni^{3} de nv^{3}peng^{2}you^{3}?

Is that one your son?
那个是不是你的儿子？na^{4} (/nei^{4}) ge^{4} shi^{4} bu^{4} shi^{4} ni^{3} de er^{2}zi?
Is your son that one?
你的儿子是不是那个？ni^{3} de er^{2}zi^{3} shi^{4} bu^{4} shi^{4} na^{4}(/nei^{4}) ge^{4}?
Is his daughter a student?
他的女儿是不是学生？ta^{1} de nv^{3}er^{2} shi^{4} bu^{4} shi^{4} xue^{2}sheng^{1}?
Is that student your daughter?
那个学生是不是你女儿？na^{4} ge^{4} xue^{2}sheng^{1} shi^{4} bu^{4} shi^{4} ni^{3} nv^{3}er^{2}?
Is his girlfriend a nurse?
他的女朋友是不是护士？ta^{1} de nv^{3}peng^{2}you^{3} shi^{4} bu^{4} shi^{4} hu^{4}shi^{4}?
Is the doctor this one?
医生是不是这个？yi^{1}sheng^{1} shi^{4} bu^{4} shi^{4} zhe^{4} ge^{4}?
Is this one the doctor?
这个是不是医生？zhe^{4} ge^{4} shi^{4} bu^{4} shi^{4} yi^{1}sheng^{1}?
Is the nurse this one?
护士是不是那个？hu^{4}shi^{4} shi^{4} bu^{4} shi^{4} na^{4} ge^{4}?
Is that one a nurse?
那个是不是护士？na^{4} ge^{4} shi^{4} bu^{4} shi^{4} hu^{4}shi^{4}?
Is the husband of the nurse a doctor?
护士的丈夫是不是医生？hu^{4}shi^{4} de zhang^{4}fu shi^{4} bu^{4} shi^{4} yi^{1}sheng^{1}?
Is the doctor's wife a nurse?
医生的妻子是不是护士？yi^{1}sheng^{1} de qi^{1}zi shi^{4} bu^{4} shi^{4} hu^{4}shi^{4}?
Is that one the boss?
那个是不是老板？na^{4} ge^{4} shi^{4} bu^{4} shi^{4} lao^{2}ban^{3}?
Is this one the boss's secretary?
这是不是老板的秘书？zhe^{4} shi^{4} bu^{4} shi^{4} lao^{2}ban^{3} de mi^{4}shu?

OK! Now we need to know that there is another word in Chinese for referring to people. This is 位 (wei^{4}), which means a position or seat, and is considered as a measure word. It is used as an alternative to 个 when we want to show respect to the person referred to.

这位是不是你的老师？zhe^{4} wei^{4} shi^{4} bu^{4} shi^{4} ni^{3} de lao^{3}shi^{1}?
这位是不是您的妻子？zhe^{4} wei^{4} shi^{4} bu^{4} shi^{4} nin^{2} de qi^{1}zi?
那位是不是他们的经理？na^{4} wei^{4} shi^{4} bu^{4} shi^{4} ta^{1}men de jing^{1}li^{3}?
那位是不是你们的老板？na^{4} wei^{4} shi^{4} bu^{4}shi^{4} ni^{3}men de lao^{3}ban^{3}?

OK! Let's remember that a question can also be made simply by adding the first-tone question word 吗 at the end of the indicative sentence. So let's listen to some sentences using two forms of questions.

Are they students?
他们是不是学生？ta^{1}men shi^{4} bu^{4} shi^{4} xue^{2}sheng^{1}?
他们是学生吗？ta^{1}men shi^{4} xue^{2}sheng^{1} ma^{1}?

Is he a teacher?
他是不是老师？ta^1 shi^4 bu^4 shi^4 lao^{3}shi^1?
他是老师吗？ta^1 shi^4 lao^{3}shi^1 ma^1?
Is he your boyfriend?
他是不是你的男朋友？ta^1 shi^4 bu^4 shi^4 ni^3 de nan^{2}peng^{2}you^3?
他是你的男朋友吗？ta^1 shi^4 ni^3 de nan^{2}peng^{2}you^3 ma^1?
Is she your girlfriend?
她是不是你的女朋友？ta^1 shi^4 bu^4 shi^4 ni^3 de nv^{3}peng^{2}you^3?
她是你的女朋友吗？ta^1 shi^4 ni^3 de nv^{3}peng^{2}you^3 ma^1?
Is the doctor this one?
医生是不是这位？yi^{1}sheng^1 shi^4 bu^4 shi^4 zhe^4 wei^4?
医生是这位吗？yi^{1}sheng^1 shi^4 zhe^4 wei^4 ma^1?
Is that one the nurse or a nurse?
那个是不是护士？na^4 ge^4 shi^4 bu^4 shi^4 hu^{4}shi^4?
那个是护士吗？na^4 ge^4 shi^4 hu^{4}shi^4 ma^1?
Is this one your wife?
这位是不是您的妻子？zhe^4 wei^4 shi^4 bu^4 shi^4 nin^2 de qi^{1}zi?
这位是您的妻子吗？zhe^4 wei^4 shi^4 nin^2 de qi^{1}zi ma^1?
Is the nurse that one?
护士是不是那个？hu^{4}shi^4 shi^4 bu^4 shi^4 na^4 ge^4?
护士是那个吗？hu^{4}shi^4 shi^4 na^4 ge^4 ma^1?
Is that one their manager?
那位是不是他们的经理？na^4 wei^4 shi^4 bu^4 shi^4 ta^{1}men de jing^{1}li^3?
那位是他们的经理吗？na^4 wei^4 shi^4 ta^{1}men de jing^{1}li^3 ma^1?
Is that one your boss?
那位是不是你们的老板？na^4 wei^4 shi^4 bu^4 shi^4 ni^{3}men de lao^{3}ban^3?
那位是你们的老板吗？na^4 wei^4 shi^4 ni^{3}men de lao^{3}ban^3 ma^1?
Is this one the boss's secretary?
这个是不是老板的秘书？zhe^4 ge^4 shi^4 bu^4 shi^4 lao^{3}ban^3 de mi^{4}shu?
这个是老板的秘书吗？zhe^4 ge^4 shi^4 lao^{3}ban^3 de mi^{4}shu ma^1?

In answering such general questions, we simply repeat the verb 是 or negate it with the negative word 不.

Is this one your wife?
这位是不是你妻子？zhe^4 wei^4 shi^4 bu^4 shi^4 ni^3 qi^{1}zi?
Yes. 是。shi^4.
No. 不是。bu^{4}shi^4.
Is that one his son?
那个是不是他儿子？na^4 ge^4 shi^4 bu^4 shi^4 ta^1 er^{2}zi?
不是。是他女儿。bu^4 shi^4. shi^4 ta^1 nv^{3}er^2.
Is that one the doctor?

那位是不是医生？ na4wei4 shi4 bu4 shi4 yi1sheng1?
No. She is the nurse.
不是。她是护士。bu4 shi4. ta1 shi4 hu4shi4.
Is this one your elder sister?
这个是不是你姐姐？ zhe4 ge4 shi4 bu4 shi4 ni3 jie3jie?
No. She is my younger sister.
不是。她是我妹妹。bu4 shi4. ta1 shi4 wo3 mei4mei.
Are you a student?
你是不是学生？ ni3 shi4 bu4 shi4 xue2sheng1?
No. I'm a teacher.
不是，我是老师。bu4 shi4. wo3 shi4 lao3shi1?

Now, we should learn that the negation word 不 can be inserted in the repetition of any verbal expression to change it into a general question. Listen and repeat the following:

At, in, or exist in a place 在 zai4
Are you in? Or, are you here? Are you there?
你在不在？ ni3 zai4 bu4 zai4?
At home 在家 zai4 jia1
Are you at home?
你在不在家？ ni3 zai4 bu4 zai4 jia1?
Be here 在这里 zai4 zhe4li3
Is he here?
他在不在这里？ ta1 zai4 bu4 zai4 zhe4li3?
Be there 在那里 zai4 na4li3
Is his son there?
他的儿子在不在那里？ ta1 de er2zi zai4 bu4 zai4 na4li3?
To know 知道 zhi1 dao4
Do you know?
你知道不知道？ ni3 zhi1dao4 bu4 zhi1dao4?

However, when referring to a person we know, we would use another word instead of 知道.

Literally, to recognize. Or simply, to know
认识 ren4shi
Do you know Mr. Zhang?
你认识不认识张先生？ ni3 ren4shi2 bu4 ren4shi zhang1xian1sheng?
Understand 理解 li3jie3
Does he understand?
他理解不理解？ ta1 li3jie3 bu4 li3jie3

There is a single-character synonym of 理解. That is—

懂 dong3

Do you understand?

你懂不懂？ni^{3} dong^{3} bu^{4} dong^{3}?

Do you understand what he says?

你懂不懂他说的？ni^{3} dong^{3} bu^{4} dong^{3} ta^{1}shuo^{1} de?

Apart from 理解 and 懂, there is still another synonym for "understand" or "comprehend", 明白, which originally means "clear"

Be clear 明白 ming^{2}bai

Do you understand?

你明白不明白？ni^{3} ming^{2}bai bu^{4} ming^{2}bai?

All right! Now, we need to know a special verb that doesn't use the word 不 for negation. This is 有, which means "have" or "exist". Instead of using 不 for negation, it uses the negative word 没 (mei^{3}).

Have or exist; there are; there is 有 you^{3}

Literally not have; not exist 没有 mei^{2} you^{3}

Do you have brothers?

你有没有兄弟？ni^{3} you^{3} mei^{2} you^{3} xiong^{1}di^{4}?

Do you have sisters?

你有没有姐妹？ni^{3} you^{3} mei^{2} you^{3} jie^{3}mei^{4}?

Do you have brothers and sisters?

你有没有兄弟姐妹？ni^{3} you^{3} mei^{2} you^{3} xiong^{1}di^{4} jie^{3}mei^{4}?

Does he have a computer?

他有没有电脑？ta^{1} you^{3} mei^{2} you^{3} dian^{4}nao^{3}?

Is there any email for me?

有没有我的邮件？you^{3} mei^{2} you^{3} wo^{3} de you^{2}jian^{4}?

Is there a telephone call for me?

有没有我的电话？you^{3} mei^{2} you^{2} wo^{3} de dian^{4}hua^{4}?

Is there anybody here?

这里有没有人？zhe^{4} li^{2} you^{3} mei^{2} you^{3} ren^{2}?

Is there a hotel there?

那里有没有宾馆？na^{4}li^{3} you^{3} mei^{2} you^{3} bin^{1}guan^{3}?

Of course, we can also use the interrogative word 吗 to ask the general questions.

Is this fruit expensive?

这水果贵不贵？zhe^{4} shui^{3}guo^{3} gui^{4} bu^{4} gui^{4}?

这水果贵吗？zhe^{4} shui^{3}guo^{3} gui^{4} ma^{1}

Is that dress cheap? Or, is that piece of clothing cheap?

那衣服便宜不便宜？na^{4} yi^{1}fu pian^{2}yi^{4} bu^{4} pian^{2}yi^{4}?

那衣服便宜吗？na^{4} yi^{1}fu pian^{4} yi^{4} ma^{1}?

Is this OK?

这行不行？zhe^{4} xing^{2} bu^{4} xing^{2}?

这行吗？zhe^4 xing^2 ma^1?
Do you have brothers?
你有没有兄弟？ni^3 you^3 mei^2 you^3 xiong^{1}di^4?
你有兄弟吗？ni^3 you^3 xiong^{1}di^4 ma^1?
Do you have sisters?
你有没有姐妹？ni^3 you^3 mei^2 you^3 jie^{3}mei^4?
你有姐妹吗？ni^3 you^3 jie^3 mei^4 ma^1?
Do you have brothers and sisters?
你有没有兄弟姐妹？ni^3 you^3 mei^2 you^3 xiong^{1}di^4 jie^{3}mei^4?
你有兄弟姐妹吗？ni^3 you^3 xiong^{1}di^4 jie^{3}mei^4 ma^1?
Does he have a computer?
他有没有电脑？ta^1 you^3 mei^2 you^3 dian^{4}nao^3?
他有电脑吗？ta^1 you^3 dian^{4}nao^3 ma^1?
Is there any email for me?
有没有我的邮件？you^3 mei^2 you^3 wo^3 de you^{2}jian^4?
有我的邮件吗？you^3 wo^3 de you^{3}jian^4 ma^1?
Is there any new email?
有没有新邮件？you^3 mei^2 you^3 xin^1 you^{2}jian^4?
有新邮件吗？you^3 xin^1 you^{2}jian^4 ma^1?
Is there a telephone call for me?
有没有我的电话？you^3 mei^2 you^2 wo^3 de dian^{4}hua^4?
有我的电话吗？you^3 wo^3 de dian^{4}hua^4 ma^1?
Is there anybody here?
这里有没有人？zhe^{4}li^3 you^3 mei^2 you^3 ren^2?
这里有人吗？zhe^{4}li^3 you^3 ren^2 ma^1?
Is there a hotel there?
那里有没有宾馆？na^{4}li^3 you^3 mei^2 you^3 bin^{1}guan^3?
那里有宾馆吗？na^{4}li^3 you^3 bin^{1}guan^3 ma^1?

When 有没有 is used before a verb, it marks the perfect tense, as does its English counterpart "have done or haven't done".

Has the teacher come?
老师有没有来？lao^{3}shi^1 you^3 mei^2 you^3 lai^2?
Has the student or have the students gone there?
学生有没有去？xue^{2}sheng^1 you^3 mei^2 you^3 qu^4?
Has your brother said or told?
你弟弟有没有说？ni^3 di^{4}di you^3 mei^2 you^3 shuo^1?
Has he heard or listened?
他有没有听？ta^1 you^3 mei^2 you^3 ting^1?
Have you done it?
你们有没有做？ni^{3}men you^3 mei^2 you^3 zuo^4?

Has his girlfriend gone there?
他的女朋友有没有去？ta^{1} de nv^{3}peng^{2}you^{3} you^{3} mei^{3} you^{3} qu^{4}?
Has the manager read this email?
经理有没有读这个邮件？ jing^{1}li^{3} you^{3} mei^{2} you^{3} du^{2} zhe^{4} ge^{4} you^{2}jian^{4}?
Have you written that email?
你有没有写那个邮件？ni^{3} you^{3} mei^{2} you^{3} xie^{3} na^{4} ge^{4} you^{2}jian^{4}?
Have you taken your meal?
你有没有吃饭？ni^{3} you^{3} mei^{2} you^{3} chi^{1} fan^{4}?
Have you looked? Or, have you seen?
你有没有看？ni^{3} you^{3} mei^{2} you^{3} kan^{4}?
Have you seen?
你有没有看见？ni^{3} you^{3} mei^{2} you^{3} kan^{4} jian^{4}?
Has his sister seen the movie or a movie?
他妹妹有没有看电影？ta^{1} mei^{4}mei you^{3} mei^{2} you^{3} kan^{4} dian^{4}ying^{3}?
Have you met? Or, have you met each other?
你们有没有见面？ni^{3}men you^{3} mei^{2} you^{3} jian^{4}mian^{4}?

However, in standard Mandarin Chinese, the word 有 itself is not used as a perfect tense marker. What actually marks the tense is the negative word 没. So as an alternative to 有没有 plus a verb, we can ask the same question with this word 没 inserted in the repetition of the verb. Let's turn what we have just learned into this shorter form.

Has the teacher come?
老师有没有来？lao^{3}shi^{1} you^{3} mei^{2} you^{3} lai^{2}?
老师来没来？lao^{3}shi^{1} lai^{2} mei^{2} lai^{2}?
Has the student or have the students gone there?
学生有没有去？xue^{2}sheng^{1} you^{3} mei^{2} you^{3} qu^{4}?
学生去没去？xue^{2}sheng^{1} qu^{4} mei^{2} qu^{4}?
Has your brother said or told?
你弟弟有没有说？ni^{3} di^{4}di you^{3} mei^{2} you^{3} shuo^{1}?
你弟弟说没说？ni^{3} di^{4}di shuo^{1} mei^{2} shuo^{1}?
Has he heard or listened?
他有没有听？ta^{1} you^{3} mei^{2} you^{3} ting^{1}?
他听没听？ta^{1} ting^{1} mei^{2} ting^{1}?
Have you done it?
你们有没有做？ni^{3}men you^{3} mei^{2} you^{3} zuo^{4}?
你们做没做？ni^{3}men zuo^{4} mei^{2} zuo^{4}?
Has his girlfriend gone there?
他的女朋友有没有去？ta^{1} de nv^{3}peng^{2}you^{3}you^{3} mei^{2} you^{3} qu^{4}?
他的女朋友去没去？ta^{1} de nv^{3}peng^{2}you^{3} qu^{4} mei^{2} qu^{4}?

Has the manager read this email?

经理有没有读这个邮件？jing^{1}li^{3} you^{3} mei^{2} you^{3} du^{2} zhe^{4} ge^{4} you^{2}jian^{4}?

经理读没读这个邮件？jing^{1}li^{3} du^{2} mei^{2} du^{2} zhe^{4} ge^{4} you^{2}jian^{4}?

Have you written that email?

你有没有写那个邮件？ni^{3} you^{3} mei^{2} you^{3} xie^{3} na^{4} ge^{4} you^{2}jian^{4}?

你写没写那个邮件？ni^{3} xie^{3} mei^{2} xie^{3} na^{4} ge^{4} you^{2}jian^{4}?

Have you taken your meal?

你有没有吃饭？ni^{3} you^{3} mei^{2} you^{3} chi^{1} fan^{4}?

你吃没吃饭？ni^{3} chi^{1} mei^{2} chi^{1} fan^{4}?

你吃饭没吃饭？ni^{3} chi^{1} fan^{4} mei^{2} chi^{1} fan^{4}?

Have you looked?

你有没有看？ni^{3} you^{3} mei^{2} you^{3} kan^{4}?

你看没看？ni^{3} kan^{4} mei^{2} kan^{4}?

Have you seen?

你有没有看见？ni^{3} you^{3} mei^{2} you^{3} kan^{4}jian^{4}?

你看见没看见？ni^{3} kan^{4}jian^{4} mei^{2} kan^{4}jian^{4}?

Has his sister seen the movie or a movie?

他妹妹有没有看电影？ta^{1} mei^{4}mei you^{3} mei^{2} you^{3} kan^{4} dian^{4}ying^{3}?

他妹妹看没看电影？ta^{1} mei^{4}mei kan^{4} mei^{2} kan^{4} dian^{4}ying^{3}?

Have you met each other?

你们有没有见面？ni^{3}men you^{3} mei^{2} you^{3} jian^{4}mian^{4}?

你们见面没见面？ni^{3}men jian^{4}mian^{4} mei^{2} jian^{4}mian^{4}?

你们见没见面？ni^{3}men jian^{4} mei^{2} jian^{4}mian^{4}?

One thing to note about using the verb repetition with the insertion of 没 is that they are not used along with the question word 吗. When making the question with 吗, the perfect marker 了 is used.

Has the teacher come?

老师来了吗？lao^{3}shi^{1} lai^{2} le ma^{1}?

Have the students or has the student gone?

学生去了吗？xue^{2} sheng^{1} qu^{4} le ma^{1}?

Has your younger brother said it?

你弟弟说了吗？ni^{3} di^{4} di shuo^{1} le ma^{1}?

Has he heard or listened?

他听了吗？ta^{1} ting^{1} le ma^{1}?

Have you done?

你们做了吗？ni^{3}men zuo^{4} le ma^{1}?

Has his girlfriend gone there?

他的女朋友去了吗？ta^{1} de nv^{3} peng^{3}you^{3} qu^{4} le ma^{1}?

Has the manager read this email?

经理读这个邮件了吗？jing^{1}li^{3} du^{2} zhe^{4} ge^{4} you^{2}jian^{4} le ma^{1}?
Have you written that email?
你写那个邮件了吗？ni^{3} xie^{3} na^{4} ge^{2} you^{2}jian^{4} le ma^{1}?
Have you taken your meal?
你吃饭了吗？ni^{3} chi^{1} fan^{4} le ma^{1}?
Or
你吃了吗？ni^{3} chi^{1} le ma^{1}?
Have you looked?
你看了吗？ni^{3} kan^{4} le ma^{1}?
Have you seen?
你看见了吗？ni^{3} kan^{4}jian^{4} le ma^{1}?
Has he seen the movie?
他看电影了吗？ta^{1} kan^{4} dian^{4}ying^{3} le ma^{1}?
Have you met?
你们见面了吗？ni^{3}men jian^{4}mian^{4} le ma^{1}?

If the answer to the question is yes, you can either repeat 是 or directly repeat the verb. You can, but don't have to repeat the subject because it can be omitted in Chinese.

...came or have come.
……来了。lai^{2} le.
Or
是，来了。shi^{4}, lai^{2} le.
... went or have gone there.
……去了。qu^{4} le.
Or
是，去了。shi^{4}, qu^{4} le.
... listened or have listened.
……听了。ting^{1} le.
Or
是，听了。shi^{4}, ting^{1} le.
... made, did, or have made or have done.
……做了。zuo^{4} le.
Or
是，做了。shi^{4}, zuo^{4} le.
... ate or have eaten.
……吃了。chi^{1} le.
Or
是，吃了。shi^{4}, chi^{1} le.
...met or have met.
……见面了。jian^{4}mian^{4} le;

Or

是，见面了。shi^4, jian^{4}mian^4 le;

Or

……见了。jian^4 le.

If the answer is no, you have several choices. You can say 没有 or *没, with or without repeating the verb. So the following answers are all correct, with the subject omitted in Chinese.*

Haven't or hasn't read

没有；没；没有读；没读 mei^2 you^3, mei^2, mei^2 you^3 du^2, mei^2 du^2

Haven't or hasn't written

没有；没；没有写；没写 mei^2 you^3, mei^2, mei^2 you^3 xie^3, mei^2 xie^3

Haven't or hasn't looked

没有；没；没有看；没看 mei^2 you^3, mei^2, mei^2 you^3 kan^4, mei^2 kan^4

Haven't or hasn't seen

没有；没；没有见；没见 mei^2 you^3, mei^2, mei^2 you^3 jian^4, mei^2 jian^4

We should know this pattern not only applies to verb repetition but also to adjective repetition.

OK? Or, is it good?

好不好？hao^3 bu^4 hao^3?

Is it correct? Or, am I right?

对不对？dui^4 bu^4 dui^4?

Is it big?

大不大？da^4 bu^4 da^4?

Is it small?

小不小？xiao^3 bu^4 xiao^3?

Is it tall?

高不高？gao^1 bu^4 gao^1?

Is it low?

低不低？di^1 bu^4 di^1?

Is it long?

长不长？chang^2 bu^4 chang^2?

Is it short?

短不短 duan^3 bu^4 duan^3?

Is it expensive?

贵不贵？gui^4 bu^4 gui^4?

Is it cheap?

便宜不便宜？pian^{2}yi^4 bu^4 pian^{2}yi^4?

Is it pretty? Or, is it beautiful?

漂亮不漂亮？piao^{4}liang^4 bu^4 piao^{4}liang^4?

Is it clear? Or, are you clear?

清楚不清楚？ qing^{1}chu^3 bu^4 qing^{1}chu^3?
Are you happy? Or, are you glad?
高兴不高兴？ gao^{1}xing^4 bu^4 gao^{1}xing^4?
Is it new?
新不新？ xin^1 bu^4 xin^1?
Is it old? (when referring to objects)
旧不旧？ jiu^4 bu^4 jiu^4?
Is it old? (when referring to age)
老不老？ lao^3 bu^4 lao^3?
Is this computer a new one?
这电脑新不新？ zhe^4 dian^{4}nao^3 xin^1 bu^4 xin^1?
Is this fruit dear or expensive?
这水果贵不贵？ zhe^4 shui^{3}guo^3 gui^4 bu^4 gui^4?
Is that piece of clothes cheap?
那衣服便宜不便宜？ na^4 yi^{1}fu pian^{2}yi^4 bu^4 pian^{2}yi^4?

LESSON 5 第五课

TALKING ABOUT LANGUAGE
你说什么语言？NI3 SHUO2 SHEN2ME YU3YAN2?

To talk about learning and speaking a language, we need to know words and expressions about language use. So, let's learn the following first.

Language 语言 yu3yan2
What language?
什么语言？shen2me yu3yan2?
What language do you speak?
你说什么语言？ni3 shuo1 shen2me yu3yan2?
I speak English.
我说英语。wo3 shuo1 ying1yu3.
The mother tongue 母语 mu3yu3
Is English your mother tongue?
英语是不是你的母语？ying1yu3 shi4 bu4 shi4 ni3 de mu3yu3?
No. My mother tongue is Chinese.
不是，我的母语是汉语。bu4 shi4, wo3 de mu3yu3 shi4 han4yu3.
Foreign language 外语 wai4yu3
English is my foreign language.
英语是我的外语。ying1yu3 shi4 wo3 de wai4yu3.
The first language 第一语言 di4yi1 yu3yan2
The second language 第二语言 di4er4 yu3yan2
Chinese is my first language.
汉语是我的第一语言。han4yu3 shi4 wo3 de di4yi1 yu3yan2.
English is my second language.
英语是我的第二语言。ying1yu3 shi4 wo3 de di4er4 yu3yan2.
What language does he speak?
他说什么语言？ta1 shuo1 shen2me yu3yan2?
He also speaks English.
他也说英语。ta1 ye3 shuo2 ying1yu3.
Does his wife speak English too?

他妻子也说英语吗？ta1 qi1zi ye3 shuo2 ying1yu3 ma1?

Yes. She speaks English too.

是，她也说英语。shi4, ta1 ye3 shuo1 ying1yu3.

What other languages can you speak?

你还会说什么语言？ni3 hai2 hui4 shuo1 shen2me yu3yan2?

I can also speak French and Spanish.

我还会说法语和西班牙语。wo3 hai2 hui4 shuo1 fa3yu3 he2 xi1ban1ya2yu3.

Can you speak Chinese too?

你也能说汉语吗？ni3 ye3 neng2 shuo1 han4yu3 ma1?

No. I'm learning it.

不会。我在学汉语。bu4 hui4. wo3 zai4 xue2 han4yu3.

Here in the above, the word 会 is used as a synonym of 能. So we can use them interchangeably.

Can you speak Chinese too?

你能说汉语吗？ni3 neng2 shuo1 han4yu3 ma1?

你会说汉语吗？ni3 hui4 shuo1 han4yu3 ma1?

For the word 说, Mandarin Chinese also has a synonym, 讲 (jiang3). If 说 (shuo1)is more like the English "say", then 讲 (jiang3)is more like "talk". However, there is a local difference between them: in the southern part of China, 讲 (jiang3) is often used to cover both the meanings of "say" and "talk".

What language do your parents speak?

你爸爸和妈妈讲什么语言？ni3 ba4ba he2 ma1ma jiang3 shen2me yu3yan2?

My father speaks German, and my mother Italian.

爸爸讲德语，妈妈讲意大利语。ba4ba jiang3 de2yu3, ma1ma jiang3 yi4da4li4yu3.

I hear he speaks Portuguese, does he?

听说他讲葡萄牙语，是吗？ting1 shuo1 ta1 jiang3 pu2tao2ya2yu3, shi4 ma1?

Yes. He speaks Portuguese, and also Spanish.

是的，他说葡萄牙语，也说西班牙语。shi1 de, ta1 shuo1 pu2tao2ya2yu3, ye3 shuo1 xi1ban1ya2yu3.

Can your boss speak Chinese?

你的老板能不能说汉语？ni3 de lao3ban3 neng2 bu4 neng2 shuo1 han4yu3?

No. He doesn't speak Chinese.

他不会说汉语。ta1 bu4 hui4 shuo1 han4yu3.

What he speaks is Korean.

他说的是韩语。ta^1 shuo^1 de shi^4 han^{2}yu^3.
What other language does he speak?
他还讲什么语言？ta^1 hai^2 jiang^3 shen^{2}me yu^{3}yan^2?
He also speaks Japanese.
他也讲日语。ta^1 ye^3 jiang^3 ri^{4}yu^3.
Is Japanese his mother tongue?
日语是他的母语吗？ri^{4}yu^3 shi^4 ta^1 de mu^{3}yu^3 ma^1?
No. His mother tongue is Korean.
不是，他的母语是韩语。bu^4 shi^4, ta^1 de mu^{3}yu^3 shi^4 han^{2}yu^3.
Is it Korean or Chinese?
是韩语还是汉语？shi^4 han^{2}yu^3 hai^{2}shi^4 han^{4}yu^3?
It's not Korean. It's Chinese.
不是韩语，是汉语。bu^4 shi^4 han^{2}yu^3, shi^4 han^{4}yu^3.

As we see, the word 还是 is used as the English "or" when another possibility is mentioned.

Do you speak Chinese or Korean?
你说汉语还是韩语？ni^3 shuo^1 han^{4}yu^3 hai^{2}shi^4 han^{2}yu^3?
Is his mother tongue French or German?
他的母语是法语还是德语？ta^1 de mu^{3}yu^3 shi^4 fa^{3}yu^3 hai^{2}shi^4 de^{2}yu^3?

The single-character word 还 itself means "still" or "still more".

What else?
还有什么呢？hai^2 you^3 shen^{2}me ne?
He also speaks German and Russian.
他还会说德语和俄语。ta^1 hai^2 hui^4 shuo^1 de^{2}yu^3 he^2 e^{2}yu^3.
What about your brother?
你兄弟呢？ni^3 xiong^{1}di^4 ne?
He speaks Italian and Spanish.
他说意大利语和西班牙语。ta^1 shuo^1 yi^{4}da^{4}li^{4}yu^3 he^2 xi^{1}ban^{1}ya^{2}yu^3.
How about Portuguese?
葡萄牙语呢？pu^{2}tao^{2}ya^{2}yu^3 ne^2?
Can he speak it?
他能讲吗？ta^1 neng^2 jiang^3 ma^1?
No. But he can read it.
不。但是，他能读葡萄牙语。bu^4. dan^{4}shi^4, ta^1 neng^2 du^2 pu^{2}tao^{2}ya^{2}yu^3.

As we see now, the function word 呢 is used at the end of the sentence for a further question after the previous one.

What else?
还有什么呢？hai^2 you^3 shen^{2}me ne?

Or simply—

What else? Or, anything more?
还有呢？hai2 you3 ne?
How about you?
你呢？ni3 ne?
How about your brother?
你兄弟呢？ni3 xiong1di4 ne?
How about Russian?
俄语呢？e2yu3 ne?
How about Portuguese?
葡萄牙语呢？pu2tao2ya2yu3 ne?

The Chinese equivalent of the English "but" is 但是 (dan4shi4). And there is another word that also means "but" or "however". This is:

不过 bu4guo4
I can read, but I can't speak.
我能读，不过不能说。wo3 neng2 du2, bu4guo4 bu4 neng2 shuo1.
I can read English, but I can't speak it.
我能读英语，但是不能说。wo3 neng2 du2 ying1yu3, dan4shi4 bu4 neng2 shuo1.
Only 只 zhi3
Only a little 只有一点 zhi3you3 yi1 dian3
Or
只有一点点 zhi3you3 yi1 dian3 dian3
I can speak only a little.
我只能说一点。wo3 zhi3 neng2 shuo1 yi1 dian3.
I have learned only a little.
我只学了一点点。wo3 zhi3 xue2 le yi1 dian3 dian3.
I have read only a little.
我只读了一点点。wo3 zhi3 du2 le yi1 dian3 dian3.
Not much 不多 bu4 duo1
Very little 很少 hen3 shao3.
I do not read English very much.
我读英语不多。wo3 du2 ying1yu3 bu4 duo1.
I have learned very little.
我学得很少。wo3 xue2 de hen3 shao3.
How much? Or how many?
多少？duo1shao3?
Very little
很少。hen3 shao3.
Not much
不多 bu4 duo1.

I have not learned much.
我学得不多。wo^{3} xue^{2} de bu^{4} duo^{1}.

Please note that the word 得 in 学得 sounds exactly like the possessive marker or nominalizer 的 but has a different written character as well as a different grammatical function: it is used to add a complement to the verb that describes the action or tells its result.

Well done!
干得好！ gan^{4} de hao^{3}!
Well said!
说得好！ shuo^{1} de hao^{3}
It's better to do it well than to say it well.
说得好不如干得好。shuo^{1} de hao^{3} bu^{4}ru^{2} gan^{4} de hao^{3}.
What you said is very good.
你说的话很好。ni^{3} shuo^{1} de hua^{4} hen^{3} hao^{3}.
You speak very well. Or, you speak very nicely.
你说得很好。ni^{3} shuo^{1} de hen^{3} hao^{3}.
The English I learn is very good.
我学的英语很好。wo^{3} xue^{2} de ying^{1}yu^{3} hen^{3} hao^{3}.
I have learned English very well.
英语我学得很好。ying^{1}yu^{3} wo^{3} xue^{2} de hen^{3} hao^{3}.
The book I read is very good.
我读的书很好。wo^{3} du^{2} de shu^{1} hen^{3} hao^{3}.
I read this book very well.
这本书我读得很好。zhe^{4} ben^{3} shu^{1} wo^{3} du^{2} de hen^{3} hao^{3}.
Or
我读这本书读得很好。wo^{3} du^{2} zhe^{4} ben^{3} shu^{1} du^{2} de hen^{3} hao^{3}.

Let's now take a sentence that uses both the function words and see the difference.

The car I have bought sells fast.
我买的汽车卖得快。wo^{3} mai^{3} de qiche^{1} mai^{4} de hen^{3} kuai^{4}

OK! Now we need to know the third important word that is pronounced as "de" but differs in writing and in grammatical function from both the possessive or nominal marker 的 and the verbal complement 得. This third one serves as an adverbial modifier, placed before the verb but after an adjective instead of a verb. For example:

I learn Chinese happily.
我高兴地学汉语。wo^{3} gao^{1}xing^{4} de xue^{2} han^{4}yu^{3}.
Or, to use two synonyms of 高兴—
我愉快地学汉语。wo^{3} yu^{2} kuai^{4} de xue^{2} han^{4}yu^{3}.
我快乐地学汉语。wo^{3} kuai^{4}le^{4} de xue^{2} han^{4}yu^{3}.

Here, we need to note that this third function word has the same written character as the common noun that means "land" or "ground", or "field". However, this noun is pronounced as "di^{4}" (地). For example:

On land; on the ground.

在地上 zai^{4} di^{4} shang^{4}

Sea and land

大海与陆地 da^{4}hai^{3} yu^{3} lu^{4}di^{4}

The farming field

田地 tian^{2}di^{4}

Now, to come back to the two different grammatical function words with the same pronunciation, we need to remember that one follows a verb to indicate the result of the action, and the other follows an adjective to mark condition in the process of the action. Let's now compare them in the following:

I learn Chinese happily.

我高兴地学汉语。wo^{3} gao^{1}xing^{4} de xue^{2} han^{4}yu^{3}.

I learn Chinese, and it makes me happy.

However, sometimes the two patterns may have the same meaning except that they simply emphasize different words. For example:

We all work hard.

我们都很努力地工作。wo^{3}men^{2} dou^{1} hen^{3} nu^{3}li^{4} de gong^{1}zuo^{4}.

我们都工作得很努力。wo^{3}men^{2} dou^{1} gong^{1}zuo^{4} de hen^{3} nu^{3}li^{4}.

All right. Now let's take an example that uses all the three Chinese function words, the possessive marker 的, the verbal modifier 地, and the verbal complement 得.

When he seriously speaks Chinese, he speaks very well.

他认真地说汉语的时候说得很好。ta^{1} ren^{4}zhen^{1} de shuo^{1} han^{4}yu^{3} de shi^{2}hou^{4} shuo^{1} de hen^{3} hao^{3}.

Seriously 认真地 ren^{4}zhen^{1} de

Seriously speak 认真地说 ren^{4}zhen^{1} de shuo^{1}

When he seriously speaks

他认真地说的时候 ta^{1}ren^{4}zhen^{1} de shuo^{1} de shi^{2}hou^{4} shuo^{1}

When he seriously speaks Chinese, he speaks very well.

他认真地说汉语的时候说得很好。ta^{1} ren^{4}zhen^{1} de shuo^{1} han^{4}yu^{3} de shi^{2}hou^{4} shuo^{1} de hen^{3} hao^{3}.

Now it's time for us to learn to talk about nationalities. Listen and repeat.

Which country?

哪国？na^{3} guo^{2}?

Which 哪 na^{3}

Which one?
哪个？na^{3} ge^{4}?
Which country?
哪国？na^{3} guo^{2}?
Or
Which country?
哪个国家？na^{3} ge^{4} guo^{2}jia^{1}?
To be short—
哪国 na^{3} guo^{2}
Person, man, or people 人 ren^{2}
Which country are you from? Or, what is your nationality?
你是哪国人？ni^{3} shi^{4} na^{3} guo^{2} ren^{2}?
Which country are you from?
你是哪个国家的？ni^{3} shi^{4} na^{3} ge^{4} guo^{2}jia^{1} de?
There are two ways to answer such a question.
The first way is to use 是 shi^{4}
I'm English.
我是英国人。wo^{3} shi^{4} ying^{1}guo^{2} ren^{2}.
I speak English.
我说英语。wo^{3} shuo^{1} ying^{1}yu^{3}.
I'm Chinese.
我是中国人。wo^{3} shi^{4} zhong^{1}guo^{2} ren^{2}.
I speak Chinese.
我说汉语。wo^{3} shuo^{1} han^{4}yu^{3}.
I'm Spanish.
我是西班牙人。wo^{3} shi^{4} xi^{1}ban^{1}ya^{2} ren^{2}.
I speak Spanish.
我说西班牙语。wo^{3} shuo^{1} xi^{1}ban^{1}ya^{2}yu^{3}.
I'm French.
我是法国人。wo^{3} shi^{4} fa^{3}guo^{2} ren^{2}.
I speak French.
我说法语。wo^{3} shuo^{1} fa^{3}yu^{3}.
I'm Portuguese.
我是葡萄牙人。wo^{3} shi^{4} pu^{2}tao^{2}ya^{2} ren^{2}.
I speak Portuguese.
我说葡萄牙语。wo^{3} shuo^{1} pu^{2}tao^{2}ya^{2}yu^{3}.
I'm Italian.
我是意大利人。wo^{3} shi^{4} yi^{4}da^{4}li^{4} ren^{2}.
I speak Italian.
我说意大利语。wo^{3} shuo^{1} yi^{4}da^{4}li^{4}yu^{3}.

He is German.
他是德国人。ta^{1} shi^{4} de^{2}guo^{2} ren^{2}.
He speaks German.
他说德语。ta^{1} shuo^{1} de^{2}yu^{3}.
They are Russian.
他们是俄国人。ta^{1}men shi^{4} e^{2}guo^{2} ren^{2}.
They speak Russian.
他们说俄语。ta^{1}men shuo^{1} e^{2}yu^{3}.
She is Egyptian.
她是埃及人。ta^{1} shi^{4} ai^{1}ji^{2} ren^{2}.
She speaks Arabic.
她说阿拉伯语。ta^{1} shuo^{1} a^{1}la^{1}bo^{2}yu^{3}.
You are Indian.
你是印度人。ni^{3} shi^{4} yin^{4}du^{4} ren^{2}.
You speak Hindi.
你说印度语。ni^{3} shuo^{1} yin^{4}du^{4}yu^{3}.
You (plural) are Japanese.
你们是日本人。ni^{3}men shi^{4} ri^{4}ben^{3} ren^{2}.
You (plural) speak Japanese.
你们说日语。ni^{3}men shuo^{1} ri^{4}yu^{3}.
I'm Korean.
我是韩国人。wo^{3} shi^{4} han^{2}guo^{2} ren^{2}.
I speak Korean.
我说韩语。wo^{3} shuo^{1} han^{2}yu^{3}.
I learn Chinese.
我学汉语。wo^{3} xue^{2} han^{4}yu^{3}.
The second way is to use "come from" 来自 (lai^{2}zi)^{4}.
I come from...我来自…… wo^{3} lai^{2}zi^{4}...
I come from Britain.
我来自英国。wo^{3} lai^{2}zi^{4} ying^{1}guo^{2}.
I come from the United States.
我来自美国。wo^{3} lai^{2}zi^{4} mei^{3}guo^{2}.
I come from France.
我来自法国。wo^{3} lai^{2}zi^{4} fa^{3}guo^{2}

The above are all formal expressions in Chinese. To answer the question informally, we have yet another way to say the same.

我是美国来的。wo^{3} shi^{4} mei^{3}guo^{2} lai^{2} de.
我是法国来的。wo^{3} shi^{4} fa^{3}guo^{2} lai^{2} de.
我是意大利来的。wo^{3} shi^{4} yi^{4}da^{4}li^{4} lai^{2} de.
我是澳大利亚来的。wo^{3} shi^{4} ao^{4}da^{4}li^{4}ya^{4} lai^{2} de.

Now listen to the following and try to repeat.

And 和 he^2

I speak English and French.

我说英语和法语。wo^3 shuo^1 ying^{1}yu^3 he^2 fa^{3}yu^3.

He speaks Chinese and Korean.

他说汉语和韩语。ta^1 shuo^1 han^{4}yu^3 he^2 han^{2}yu^3.

You speak Spanish and Portuguese.

你说西班牙语和葡萄牙语。ni^3 shuo^1 xi^{1}ban^{1}ya^{2}yu^3 he^2 pu^{2}tao^{2}ya^{2}yu^3.

They speak German, Italian, and Arabic.

他们说德语，意大利语和阿拉伯语。ta^{1}men shuo^1 de^{2}yu^3, yi^{4}da^{4}li^{4}yu^3 he^2 a^{1}la^{1}bo^{2}yu^3.

All right! Now, let's learn two important adverbs. One is—

Also, too 也 ye^3

And the other is—

Still more; in addition or also 还 hai^2

These two function words, 也 and 还, are similar in meaning, and so they are often interchangeable. The only difference is that 还 may also mean "what's more", or "still more".

He can speak Chinese, and English as well.

他能讲汉语，也能说英语。ta^1 neng^2 jiang^3 han^{4}yu^3, ye^3 neng^2 shuo^1 ying^{1}yu^3.

I speak French, and also German.

我说法语，还懂德语。wo^3 shuo^1 fa^{3}yu^3, hai^2 dong^3 de^{2}yu^3.

They speak Japanese and Chinese too.

他们说日语，也说汉语。ta^{1}men shuo^1 ri^{4}yu^3, ye^3 shuo^1 han^{4}yu^3.

What else?

还有什么？hai^2 you^3 shen^{2}me?

Nothing else.

没有了。mei^{2}you^3 le.

What other language do you speak?

你还说什么语言？ni^3 hai^2 shuo^1 shen^{2}me yu^{3}yan^2?

I speak Hindi too.

我还说印度语。wo^3 hai^2 shuo^1 yin^{4}du^{4}yu^3.

When 还 is used with the negative word 不 or 没, the meaning is "not yet".

Can you speak Chinese now?

现在你能说汉语吗？xian^{4}zai^4 ni^3 neng^2 shuo^1 han^{4}yu^3 ma^1?

I cannot yet.

还不能。hai^2 bu^4 neng^2.

还不行。hai^2 bu^4 xing^2.

I'm still learning.
我还在学。wo3 hai2 zai4 xue2.
OK! Now let's learn more words about languages.
Some 有些，有的 you3xie1, you3 de
What language do they speak?
他们说什么语言？ta1men shuo1 shen2me yu3yan2?
Some people speak English.
有些人说英语。you3xie1 ren2 shuo1 ying1yu3.
Some people speak Indian.
有些人说印度语。you3xie1 ren2 shuo1 yin4du4yu3
Some people speak Arabic.
有些人说阿拉伯语。you3xie1 ren2 shuo1 a1la1bo2yu3.
As with English, we can drop the word 人 for "people" and say—
Some speak English.
有些说英语。you3xie1 shuo1 ying1yu3.
Some speak Hindi.
有些说印度语。you3xie1 shuo1 yin4du4yu3.
Some speak Arabic.
有些说阿拉伯语。you3xie1 shuo1 a1la1bo2yu3.
Or we can also simply say—
有人说法语。you3 ren2 shuo1 fa3yu3.
有人说德语。you3 ren2 shuo1 de2yu3.
有人说俄语。you3 ren2 shuo1 e2yu3.
Another synonym of 有些 and 有的 is 一些
Some people speak Spanish.
一些人讲西班牙语。yi1xie1 ren2 jiang3 xi1ban1ya2yu3.
Some people speak French.
一些人讲意大利语。yi1xie1 ren2 jiang3 yi4da4li4yu3.
Still some people speak Portuguese.
还有一些人讲葡萄牙语。hai2 you3 yi1xie2 ren2 jiang3 pu2tao2ya2yu3.
I know some French and Japanese.
我懂一些法语和日语。wo3 dong3 yi1xie1 fa3yu3 he2 ri4yu3.
Now let's go on with more useful words. Listen and repeat.
All, totally 都
Totally understand, understand all 都懂 dou1 dong3
Totally understand, understand all 都理解 dou1 li3jie3
I understand everything you say.
你说的我都懂。ni3 shuo1 de wo3 dou1 dong3.
I don't understand all they say.
他们说的我不是都懂。ta1men shuo1 de wo3 bu4 shi4 dou1 dong3.

Words and sentences, or speech 话 hua^{4}
I understand all that you say.
你的话我都理解。ni^{3} de hua^{4} wo^{3} dou^{1} li^{3}jie^{3}.
Do you understand everything?
你都懂吗？ni^{3} dou^{1} dong^{3} ma^{1}?
I understand some of it, but not all.
我懂一些，不是都懂。wo^{3} dong^{3} yi^{1}xie^{1}, bu^{4} shi^{4} dou^{1} dong^{3}.
We all speak English.
我们都说英语。wo^{3}men dou^{1} shuo^{1} ying^{1}yu^{3}.
We all learn Chinese.
我们都学汉语。wo^{3}men dou^{1} xue^{2} han^{4}yu^{3}.
He and his wife are both American.
他和他妻子都是美国人。ta^{1} he^{2} ta^{1} qi^{1}zi dou^{1} shi^{4} mei^{3}guo^{2} ren^{2}.
His grandpa and grandma are both Chinese.
他爷爷和奶奶都是中国人。ta^{1} ye^{2}ye he^{2} nai^{3}nai dou^{1} shi^{4} zhong^{1}guo^{2} ren^{2}.

All right! Now we have already learned quite a few words and expressions about learning and speaking a language. If you are not sure you can remember everything and put them to use, just listen and repeat once more.

LESSON 6 第六课

LEARNING AND SPEAKING A LANGUAGE 学说语言 XUE^2 SHUO^1 YU^{1}YAN^2

As we try to communicate in the new language we are learning, probably the most useful words and expressions are as follows.

I don’t understand.
我不懂。wo^3 bu^4 dong^3.
I don’t understand as I listen.
我听不懂。wo^3 ting^1 bu^4 dong^3.
I don’t understand what you say.
我听不懂你的话。wo^3 ting^1 bu^4 dong^3 ni^3 de hua^4.
What meaning?
什么意思？shen^{2}me yi^{4}si?
What’s the meaning?
是什么意思？shi^4 shen^{2}me yi^{4}si?
What’s the meaning of that?
那是什么意思？na^4 shi^4 shen^{2}me yi^{4}si?
What’s the meaning of this?
这是什么意思？zhe^4 shi^4 shen^{2}me yi^{4}si?
What do you mean?
你说的是什么意思？ni^3 shuo^1 de shi^4 shen^{2}me yi^{4}si?
I don’t understand what you mean.
我不懂你的意思。wo^3 bu^4 dong^3 ni^3 de yi^{4}si.

As we see, there is a difference between the Chinese and English sentences. That is, in Chinese, the sentence subject can be omitted if it is known from the context.

I don’t understand.
我不懂。wo^{3}bu^4 dong^3
Or, simply
不懂。bu^4 dong^3
What’s the meaning?
什么意思？shen^{2}me yi^{4}si?

Or

是什么意思？shi^4 shen^{2}me yi^{4}si?

Of course, you may say sorry and ask for a repetition.

Sorry! Or, pardon!

对不起！dui^4 bu^4 qi^3!

Can you say it once more?

能不能再说一遍？neng^2 bu^4 neng^2 zai^4 shuo^1 yi^1 bian^4?

Or you may simply use the Chinese word for "repeat"

Sorry. Can you repeat it?

对不起，能不能重复一下？dui^4 bu^4 qi^3, neng^2 bu^4 neng^2 chong^{2}fu^4 yi^1 xia^4?

The Chinese "一遍" and "一下" both mean "once". And there is another word that also means the same—

Once, one time 一次 yi^1 ci^4

Say it once again. 再说一次。zai^4 shuo^1 yi^1 ci^4.

Then, you may need to ask about a word or phrase.

What does this word mean?

这个词是什么意思？zhe^4 ge^4 ci^2 shi^4 shen^{2}me yi^{4}si?

What does this character mean?

这个字是什么意思？zhe^4 ge^4 zi^4 shi^4 shen^{2}me yi^{4}si?

Please note that the word 词 for "word" is in the second tone while the word 次 for "time" or "times" is in the fourth tone.

Once, one time 一次 yi^1 ci^4

One word 一个词 yi^1 ge^4 ci^2

A word at a time 一次一个词 yi^1 ci^4 yi^1 ge^4 ci^2

How... 怎么...zen^{3}me...

How do you say...?

......怎么说？zen^{3}me shuo^1...

How do you say this?

这怎么说？zhe^2 zen^{3}me shuo^1?

In Chinese 在汉语里 zai^4 han^{4}yu^3 li^3

Use Chinese 用汉语 yong^4 han^{4}yu^3

In Chinese, how do you say it?

在汉语里怎么说？zai^4 han^{4}yu^3 li^3 zen^{3}me shuo^1?

In, inside, or within 在......里 zai^4...li^3

In Chinese 在汉语里 zai^4 han^{4}yu^3 li^3

How do you say this in Chinese?

这个在汉语里怎么说？zhe^4 ge^4 zai^4 han^{4}yu^3 li^3 zen^{3}me shuo^1?

How do you say that in English?

这个在英语里怎么说？zhe^4 ge^4 zai^4 ying^{1}yu^3 li^3 zen^{3}me shuo^1?

To use Chinese, how do you say it?
用汉语怎么说？yong^{4} han^{4}yu^{3} zen^{3}me shuo^{1}?
To make it short and compact, we can simply say—
How do you say it in Chinese?
汉语怎么说？han^{4}yu^{3} zen^{3}me shuo^{1}?
How do you say it in English?
英语怎么说？ying^{1}yu^{3} zen^{3}me shuo^{1}
How do you say "repeat" in Chinese?
英语"重复"怎么说？ying^{1}yu^{3} chong^{2}fu^{4} zen^{3}me shuo^{1}?
重复 chong^{2}fu^{4}
Repeat once.
重复一遍 chong^{2}fu^{4} yi^{1} bian^{4}
Please repeat once.
请再重复一遍。qing^{3} zai^{4} chong^{2}fu^{4} yi^{1} bian^{4}.
Or
请重复一次。qing^{3} chong^{2}fu^{4} yi^{1} ci^{4}.

So, we know that we may often omit something in Chinese to make the sentence simple. This is to say, the same meaning can be expressed in sentences of different lengths.

How do you say it in Chinese?
汉语怎么说？han^{4}yu^{3} zen^{3}me shuo^{1}?
汉语里怎么说？han^{4}yu^{3} li^{3} zen^{3}me shuo^{1}?
在汉语里怎么说？zai^{4} han^{4}yu^{3} li^{3} zen^{3}me shuo^{1}?
How do you say "repeat" in Chinese?
在汉语里 "repeat" 怎么说？zai^{4} han^{4}yu^{3} li^{3} "repeat" zen^{3}me shuo^{1}?
重复 chong^{2}fu^{4}
How do you say "again" in Chinese?
汉语里 "again" 怎么说？han^{4}yu^{3} li^{3} "again" zen^{3}me shuo^{1}?
再 zai^{4}
How do you say "once" in Chinese?
汉语 "once" 怎么说？han^{4}yu^{3} "once" zen^{3}me shuo^{1}?
There are three ways to say this.
一遍 yi^{1} bian^{4}
一次 yi^{1} ci^{4}
一下 yi^{1} xia^{4}
OK! Let's go on to more words and expressions.
Tell me.
告诉我。gao^{4}su^{4} wo^{3}
Can you tell me?
能不能告诉我？neng^{2} bu^{4} neng^{2} gao^{4}su^{4} wo^{3}?

Can you tell me the meaning?

能告诉我意思吗？neng^{2} gao^{4}su^{4} wo^{3} yi^{4}si ma^{1}?

What does it mean? Or literally, what meaning?

什么意思？shen^{2}me yi^{4}si?

In the above, the question 什么意思 has something omitted. The full expression should be—

这是什么意思？zhe^{4} shi^{4} shen^{2}me yi^{4}si?

Or

那是什么意思？na^{4} shi^{4} shen^{2}me yi^{4}si?

Or

你说的是什么意思？ni^{3} shuo^{1} de shi^{4} shen^{2}me yi^{4}si?

We can see that although in Chinese there is a translation equivalent of the English pronoun "it", this word is nevertheless not so frequently used as in English, because its pronunciation is exactly the same with the pronouns for "he" and "she". In many cases, it is omitted or replaced by 这 or 那, meaning respectively "this" or "that".

What does this mean?

这是什么意思？zhe^{4} shi^{4} shen^{2}me yi^{4}si?

What does this character mean?

这个字是什么意思？zhe^{4} ge^{4} zi^{4} shi^{4} shen^{2}me yi^{4}si?

What does that mean?

那是什么意思？na^{4} shi^{4} shen^{2}me yi^{4}si?

What does that word mean?

那个词是什么意思？na^{4} ge^{4} ci^{2} shi^{4} shen^{2}me yi^{4}si?

What do you mean?

你说的是什么意思？ni^{3} shuo^{1} de shi^{4} shen^{2}me yi^{4}si?

What does he or does she mean?

他/她是什么意思？

Can you tell me?

能告诉我吗？neng^{2} gao^{4}su^{4} wo^{3} ma^{1}?

Can you tell me what it means?

能告诉我是什么意思吗？neng^{2} gao^{4}su^{4} wo^{3} shi^{4} shen^{2}me yi^{4}si ma^{1}?

How do you translate it?

怎么翻译？zen^{3}me fan^{1}yi^{4}?

Can you tell me how to translate?

能告诉我怎么翻译吗？neng^{2} gao^{4}su^{4} wo^{3} zen^{3}me fan^{1}yi^{4} ma^{1}?

How do you translate it into English?

怎么翻译成英语？zen^{2}me fan^{1}yi^{4} cheng^{2} ying^{1}yu^{3}?

Or

英语怎么翻译？ying^{1}yu^{3} zen^{3}me fan^{1}yi^{4}?

Or

What's the English translation?

英语翻译是什么？ying1yu3 fan1yi4 shi4 shen2me?

How do you translate it into Chinese?

怎么翻译成汉语？zen3me fan1yi4 cheng2 han4yu3?

Or

How is the Chinese translated? Or, what is the Chinese translation?

汉语怎么翻译？han4yu3 zen3me fan1yi4?

Of course we can also say the following:

How do you say it in Chinese?

用汉语怎么说？yong4 han4yu3 zen3me shuo1?

用汉语怎么讲？yong4 han4yu3 zen3me jiang3?

汉语怎么讲？han4yu3 zen3me jiang3?

汉语怎么说？han4yu3 zen3me shuo1?

Please note that the word 怎么 in these examples is interchangeable with another word. This is:

怎样 zen3yang4

How to say it in Chinese?

用汉语怎样讲？yong4 han4yu3 zen3yang4 jiang3?

汉语怎样说？han4yu3 zen3yang4 shuo1?

To answer this question, you can say the following, with the beginning word 用 omitted if you like to.

汉语这么说…… han4yu3 zhe4me shuo1...

汉语这样讲…… han4yu3 zhe4yang4 shuo1...

All right! Now we need to know the opposite words of 这么 and 这样. They are—

那么 na4me

那样 na4yang4

Let's learn their meaning in sentences.

You can't speak or talk that way.

你不能那么讲。ni3 bu4neng2 na4me jiang3

With the sentence subject omitted—

不能那么讲。bu4neng2 na4me jiang3

Or

不能那么说。bu4neng2 na4me shuo1

Still, you can use 那样 to replace 那么.

You or we can't speak or talk that way.

不能那样讲。bu4neng2 na4yang4 jiang3.

不能那样说。bu4neng2 na4yang4 shuo1.

You can't do it that way.

不能那样做。bu4neng2 na4yang4 zuo4.

Or, we can use a less formal word for 做.

It can't be done that way.

不能那样干。bu4neng2 na4yang4 gan4.

This character cannot be written that way.

这个字不能那样写。zhe4 ge4 zi4 bu4neng2 na4yang4 xie3.

Still, you have to know that 那么 is somewhat special in that it can be used as an independent adverb, as the English "then", or "and then". For example:

Then, how to say it? Or, how should I say it?

那么，怎么说？na4me, zen3me shuo1

Then, how to explain?

那么，怎么解释？na4me, zen3me jie3shi4?

那么，怎么翻译？na4me, zen3me fan1yi4?

Then, how should it be done?

那么，怎么做？na4me, zen3me zuo4?

Or

那么，怎么办？na4me, zen3me ban4?

The verb 办 means "to deal with" or "to manage", but the 怎么办 is usually understood as "what to do".

Then, what can I do?

那么，我怎么办？na4me, wo3 zen3me ban4?

And 那么 can be short as 那.

Then, what can be done? Or, what can we do?

那怎么办？na4 zen3me ban4?

Now, we also need to know the word 怎么 as an interrogative word can be followed by the sentence final 了, which is often changed into a similar sentence final—

啦 la1

What's the matter? What happened?

怎么了？zen3me le1?

怎么啦？zen3me la1?

When you want to ask about or make an exclamation about the degree of something, you can use another word with the suffix. This is—

多么 duo1me

How difficult is Chinese?

Or, as an exclamation—

How difficult Chinese is!

汉语多么难？(！) han4 yu3 duo1me nan2? (!)

In this case, we can drop the suffix 么, and add the exclamatory word 啊 to emphasize the emotion. Then the sentence is usually an exclamation, and not a question.

汉语多难啊！ han4 yu3 duo1 nan2 a4!

Here we should note that although the exclamation word 啊 is usually considered as a light-tone word, it actually takes the fourth tone for emphasis of the emotion. For easy articulation in connected speech, you can change this 啊 (a4) to the similar exclamatory 哪 (na4)

汉语多难哪！ han4 yu3 duo1 nan2 na4!

Actually, all the three words, 这么, 那么, and 多 can be used for making exclamations, with or without the exclamatory final 啊.

So nice!

这么好！ zhe4me hao3!

So nice!

那么好！ na4me hao3!

How nice this paradise is!

这天堂多好啊! zhe4 tian1tang2 duo1 hao3 a4!

So beautiful!

多美啊！ duo1 mei3 a4!

Or, so pretty!

多漂亮啊！ duo1 piao4liang4 a4!

Of course, an exclamation may take the superficial form of a question.

How could it be so good!

怎么这么好啊！ zen3me hao3 zhe4me hao3 a4!

How could it be like this! Or, how could it be!

怎么会这样！ zen3me hui4 zhe4yang4!

How could it be like that!

怎么会那样！ zen3me hui4 na4yang4!

Or simply—

How could it be?

怎么会？ zen3me hui4!

How can it be so difficult!

怎么会这么难！ zen3me hui4 zhe4me nan2!

How can it be so expensive!

怎么会这么贵啊？ zen3me hui4 zhe4me gui4 a4?

Let's listen to more sentences using the words with the suffix 么.

It's so difficult!

这么难！ zhe4me nan2!

It's as difficult as that!

那么难！ na4me nan2!

It's so expensive!
这么贵！ zhe^{4}me gui^4!
How cheap it is!
多便宜啊！ duo^1 pian^{2}yi^4 a^4!
How can it be as cheap as that!
怎么那么便宜！ zen^{3}me na^{4}me pian^{2}yi^4!
How can you be so busy!
你怎么那么忙！ ni^3 zen^{3}me na^{4}me mang^2!

Remember, when using 多么, we would often drop the suffix 么 and use the exclamatory final 啊.

How nice!
多好啊！ duo^1 hao^3 a^4!
How interesting!
多有意思啊！ duo^1 you^3 yi^{4}si a^4!
Or
多有趣啊！ duo^1 you^3 qu^4 a^4!
Or
多好玩儿啊！ duo^1 hao^3 wan^2 a^4!
How beautiful!
多美啊！ duo^1 mei^3 a^4!
How pretty!
多漂亮啊！ duo^1 piao^{4}liang^4 a^4!

OK! By the way, we may also make an exclamation by using the word 真, although they essentially mean "real", "really", "true", and "truly".

He is really good, but in effect he is so good!
他真好！ ta^1 zhen^1 hao^3!
Chinese is so interesting!
汉语真有意思！ han^{4}yu^4 zhen^{1}you^3 yi^{4}si!
You are so great!
你真了不起！ ni^3 zhen^1 liao^{3}bu^{4}qi^3!
I'm so tired!
我真累！ wo^3 zhen^1 lei^4!

If you still want to keep the meaning of "really" or "truly", you can choose to use 真的 instead of 真.

He is really very good.
他真的很好！ ta^1 zhen^1 de hen^3 hao^3!
Chinese is really interesting.
汉语真的有意思！ han^{4}yu^4 zhen^1 de you^3 yi^{4}si!
You are so great.
你真的了不起！ ni^3 zhen^1 de liao^{3}bu^{4}qi^3!

I'm really tired!
我真的很累！ wo^{3} zhen^{1} de hen^{3} lei^{4}!

All right! If you don't remember something you have learned, you can say—

Sorry! I have forgotten it.
对不起，我忘了。dui^{4} bu^{4} qi^{3}, wo^{3} wang^{4} le.

Here the single-character word 忘 is the short form of the two-character word 忘记. So you can also say—

I have forgotten it.
我忘记了。wo^{3} wang^{4} ji^{4} le.
I have forgotten this word.
我忘记了这个词。wo^{3} wang^{4}ji^{4} le zhe^{4} ge^{4} ci^{2}.
I have forgotten the meaning of this word.
我忘记了这个词的意思。wo^{3} wang^{4}ji^{4} le zhe^{4} ge^{4} ci^{2} de yi^{4}si.
I can't think of it now.
想不起来了。xiang^{3} bu^{4} qi^{3}lai^{2} le.
Ah! I have called it back to mind.
啊！想起来了。a^{4}! xiang^{3} qi^{3}lai^{2} le.
Now I have called it back to mind.
现在想起来了。xian^{4}zai^{4} xiang^{3} qi^{3}lai^{2} le.
Now I have kept it in mind.
现在记住了！ xian^{4}zai^{4} ji^{4}zhu^{4} le!
Now I know it or I understand it.
现在知道了。xian^{4}zai^{4} zhi^{1}dao^{4} le.

As we see, the present perfect marker 了 may not always be related to the perfect tense. It is also a final particle that is understood according to the situation, such as "now", "for now", and "ok". For instance—

I understand now.
我懂了。wo^{3} dong^{3} le.
I don't understand now. I'm at a loss.
我不懂了。wo^{3} bu^{4} dong^{3} le.
Sorry! Or, I have to say sorry now.
对不起了。dui^{4} bu^{4} qi^{3} le.
I don't know more about this.
不知道了。bu^{4} zhi^{1}dao^{4} le.
All right now. Or, it's okay now.
好了。hao^{3} le.
Right.
对了。dui^{4} le.
I know now.

知道了。zhi^{1}dao^4 le.

I'm clear about it now.

明白了。ming^{2}bai^2 le.

Or

清楚了。qing^{1}chu^3 le.

In many cases, the function word 了 may carry no meaning other than suggesting that it is the end of the sentence or that some final conclusion is reached.

All right. Or, I'm ready.

好了。hao^3 le.

Right.

对了。dui^4 le.

Goodbye!

再见了！ zai^{4}jian^4 le.

Now, let's see more uses of this sentence final as we come to learn more useful words and expressions.

Too fast!

太快了！ tai^4 kuai^4 le!

Too slow!

太慢了！ tai^4 man^4 le!

It's too hard! Or, it's too difficult!

太难了！ tai^4 nan^2 le!

It's too easy!

太容易了！ tai^4 rong^{2}yi^4 le!

It's too simple!

太简单了！ tai^4 jian^{3}dan^1 le!

It's too much!

太多了！ tai^4 duo^1 le!

It's too little!

太少了！ tai^4 shao^3 le!

You speak too fast!

你说得太快了！ ni^3 shuo^1 de tai^4 kuai^4 le!

You read too slowly!

你读得太慢了！ ni^3 du^2 de tai^4 man^4 le!

Chinese is too difficult!

汉语太难了！ han^{4}yu^3 tai^4 nan^2 le!

This is too easy!

这个太容易了！ zhe^4 ge^4 tai^4 rong^{2}yi^4 le!

That is too simple!

那个太简单了！ na^4 ge^4 tai^4 jian^{3}dan^1 le!

You know too much!
你知道得太多了！ ni3 zhi1dao4 de tai4 duo1 le!
I have learned too little!
我学得太少了！ wo3 xue2 de tai4 shao3 le!
All right, let's now replace the word 太 with other adverbs.
You know enough already!
你知道得不少了！ ni3 zhi1dao4 de bu4 shao3 le!
I haven't learned much!
我学得不多。wo3 xue2 de bu4 duo1.
You know very much.
你知道得很多。ni3 zhi1dao4 de hen3 duo1.
I don't know much.
我知道得不多。wo3 zhi1dao4 de bu4 duo1.
I have learned very little.
我学得很少。wo3 xue2 de hen3 shao3.
He runs extremely fast.
他跑得极快。ta1 pao3 de ji2 kuai4.
Or
他跑得极其快。ta1 pao3 de ji2qi2 kuai4.
The word 极 or 极其 for "extremely" has a synonym that we also need to know. It is—
Literally, extraordinarily 非常 fei1chang2
This aircraft flies extraordinarily high. Or simply, it flies very high.
这飞机飞得非常高。zhe4 fei1ji1 fei1 de fei1chang2 gao1.
This book is written extraordinarily well.
这本书写得非常好。zhe4 ben3 shu1 xie3 de fei1chang2 hao3.
OK! Now let's do some practice. Listen and repeat.
What?
什么？ shen2me?
What do you say? Or, what did you say?
你说什么？ ni3 shuo1 shen2me?
Or
你说的是什么？ ni3 shuo1 de shi4 shen2me?
What do you mean?
你说的是什么意思？ ni3 shuo1 de shi4 shen2me yi4si?
Sorry! Or, pardon!
对不起！ dui4 bu4 qi3!
I don't understand what you're saying.
我不懂你说什么。wo3 bu4 dong3 ni3 shuo1 shen2me.
Please repeat.

请再说一遍。qing^{3} zai^{4} shuo^{1} yi^{1} bian^{4}.
Can you/ could you say it once more?
能不能再说一遍？neng^{2} bu^{4} neng^{2} zai^{4} shuo^{1} yi^{1} bian^{4}?
Sorry! I still don't understand.
对不起, 我还是不懂。dui^{4} bu^{4} qi^{3}, wo^{3} hai^{2}shi^{4} bu^{4} dong^{3}.
Still 还是 hai^{2}shi^{4}
I still don't understand.
我还是不懂。wo^{3} hai^{2}shi^{4} bu^{4} dong^{3}.
You speak too fast.
你说得太快了。ni^{3} shuo^{1} de tai^{4} kuai^{4} le.
Could you speak a little slowly?
能不能说慢一点？neng^{2} bu^{4} neng^{2} shuo^{1} man^{4} yi^{4} dian^{3}?
Words 单词 dan^{1}ci^{2}
I don't know many words.
我知道的单词不多。wo^{3} zhi^{1} dao^{4} de dan^{1}ci^{2} bu^{4} duo^{1}.
Grammar 语法 yu^{3}fa^{3}
I know very little grammar.
我知道的语法很少。wo^{3} zhi^{1}dao^{4} de yu^{3}fa^{3} hen^{3} shao^{3}.
Chinese grammar is very difficult.
中文语法很难。zhong^{1}wen^{2} yu^{3}fa^{3} hen^{3} nan^{2}.
Chinese character 汉字 han^{4}zi^{4}.
Chinese characters are too difficult.
汉字太难了。han^{4}zi^{4} tai^{4} nan^{2} le.
Sentence 句子 ju^{4}zi
I understand only short sentences.
我只懂短句子。wo^{3} zhi^{3} dong^{3} duan^{3} ju^{4}zi.
I don't understand long sentences.
我不懂长句子。wo^{3} bu^{4} dong^{3} chang^{2} ju^{4}zi.
Your sentence is too long.
你说的句子太长了。ni^{3} shuo^{1} de ju^{4}zi tai^{4} chang^{2} le.
Can you make it shorter?
能不能说短一点？neng^{2} bu^{4} neng^{2} shuo^{1} duan^{3} yi^{1}dian^{3}.
I have learned only a little.
我只学了一点。wo^{3} zhi^{3} xue^{2} le yi^{1}dian^{3}.
Not much or not many.
不多。bu^{4} duo^{1}.
Is my tone right?
我的声调对吗？wo^{3} de sheng^{1}diao^{4} dui^{4} ma^{1}.
No. It's not right.
不，不对。bu^{4}, bu^{4} dui^{4}.

Your tone is wrong.
你的声调不对。ni^{3} de sheng^{1}diao^{4} bu^{4} dui^{4}.
I remember too few words.
我记的单词太少了。wo^{3} ji^{4} de dan^{1}ci^{2} tai^{4} shao^{3} le.
Your sentence is too long.
你说的句子太长了。ni^{3} shuo^{1} de ju^{4}zi tai^{4} chang^{2} le.
It's wrong. 错了。cuo^{4} le.
All right! 好了。hao^{3} le.
Chinese grammar is too difficult.
汉语语法太难了。han^{4}yu^{3} yu^{3}fa^{3} tai^{4} nan^{2} le.
Can we speak English?
我们能不能说英语？wo^{3}men neng^{2} bu^{4} neng^{2} shuo^{1} ying^{1}yu^{3}?

LESSON 7 第七课

WE ARE LEARNING 我们在学习 WO^{3}MEN ZAI^{4} XUE^{2}XI^{2}

Although Chinese does not have the same tense changes as in English because it is not a language with inflection, there are nevertheless a few words that serve as tense markers. A tense marker may not only be placed at the end of a verb as the light-tone 了 as we have learned, but may also appear BEFORE the verb. One particular case of this is the continuous tense marker 在. This 在 is pronounced in the same fourth tone as the first word of 再见 for Goodbye but is completely a different word. Let's listen and repeat.

Be learning 在学 zai^{4} xue^{2}
Or
Be studying, or be learning 在学习 zai^{4} xue^{2}xi^{2}
We are studying, or learning Chinese.
我们在学中文。wo^{3}men zai^{4} xue^{2} zhong^{1}wen^{2}.
Or
我们在学汉语。wo^{3}men zai^{4} xue^{2} han^{4}yu^{3}.
Be listening
在听 zai^{4} ting^{1}
I'm listening.
我在听。wo^{3} zai^{4} ting^{1}.
I'm listening to music.
我在听音乐。wo^{3} zai^{4} ting^{1} yin^{1}yue^{4}.
I'm listening to you talking.
我在听你说。wo^{3} zai^{4} ting^{1} ni^{3} shuo^{1}.
Be speaking 在说 zai^{4} shuo^{1}
I'm speaking English.
我在说英语。wo^{3} zai^{4} shuo^{1} ying^{1}yu^{3}.
Be reading 在读 zai^{4} du^{2}
He is reading Chinese.
他在读中文。ta^{1} zai^{4} du^{2} zhong^{1}wen^{2}.

Or

He is reading a Chinese book.

他在读中文书。ta^{1} zai^{4} du^{2} zhong^{1}wen^{2}shu^{1}.

Be writing 在写 zai^{4} xie^{3}

I'm writing an email or the email.

我在写邮件。wo^{3} zai^{4} xie^{3} you^{2}jian^{4}.

Be thinking 在想 zai^{4} xiang^{3}

I'm thinking about this problem or this question.

我在想这个问题。wo^{3} zai^{4} xiang^{3} zhe^{4} ge^{4} wen^{4}ti^{2}.

I'm answering this question.

我在回答这个问题。wo^{3} zai^{4} hui^{2}da^{2} zhe^{4} ge^{4} wen^{4}ti^{2}.

Be looking 在看 zai^{4} kan^{4}

The children are seeing the movie.

孩子们在看电影。hai^{2}zimen zai^{4} kan^{4} dian^{4}ying^{3}.

Be doing, or be making 在做 zai^{4} zuo^{4}

What are you doing?

你在做什么？ni^{3} zai^{4} zuo^{4} shen^{2}me?

I'm working.

我在工作。wo^{3} zai^{4} gong^{1}zuo^{4}.

I'm resting.

我在休息。wo^{3} zai^{4} xiu^{1}xi.

I'm shopping.

我在购物。wo^{3} zai^{4} gou^{4}wu^{4}.

I'm in bed to sleep.

我在睡觉。wo^{3} zai^{4} shui^{4}jiao^{4}.

I'm eating.

我在吃饭。wo^{3} zai^{4} chi^{1} fan^{4}.

Breakfast 早饭 zao^{3}fan^{4}

I'm eating my breakfast.

我在吃早饭。wo^{3} zai^{4} chi^{1} zao^{3}fan^{4}.

Lunch 午饭 wu^{3}fan^{4}

I'm eating my lunch.

我在吃午饭。wo^{3} zai^{4} chi^{1} wu^{3}fan^{4}.

Dinner 晚饭 wan^{3}fan^{4}

I'm eating my dinner.

我在吃晚饭。wo^{3} zai^{4} chi^{1} wan^{3}fan^{4}.

Now we should know that the word for "do"— 做 (zuo^{4}) can be replaced by its synonym 干 (gan^{4}), which is more informal in style and more general in meaning.

What is he doing?

他在干什么？ta^{1} zai^{4} gan^{4} shen^{2}me?
What are they doing?
他们在干什么？ta^{1}men zai^{4} gan^{4} shen^{2}me?
Are they working?
他们在工作吗？ta^{1}men zai^{4} gong^{1}zuo^{4} ma^{1}?
Or
他们在不在工作？ta^{1}men zai^{4} bu^{4} zai^{4} gong^{1}zuo^{4}?
Yes. They are working.
是的，他们在工作。shi^{4} de, ta^{1}men zai^{4} gong^{1}zuo^{4}.
No. They are shopping.
不是的，他们在购物。bu^{4} shi^{4} de, ta^{1}men zai^{4} gou^{4}wu^{4}.
No. They are watching TV.
不，他们在看电视。bu^{4}, ta^{1}men zai^{4} kan^{4} dian^{4}shi^{4}.
They are seeing the movie.
他们在看电影。ta^{1}men zai^{4} kan^{4} dian^{4}ying^{3}.

For a synonym of 工作, the Chinese has 干活儿, which is more informal and colloquial.

Yes. They are working.
是的，他们在干活儿。shi^{4} de, ta^{1}men zai^{4} gan^{4}huo'r^{2}.
What work are they doing? (informal)
他们在做什么工作？ta^{1}men zai^{4} zuo^{4} shen^{2}me gong^{1}zuo^{4}?
What job are they doing? (informal)
他们在干什么活儿？ta^{1}men zai^{4} gan^{4} shen^{2}me huo'r^{2}?

In fact, Mandarin Chinese also has a very colloquial word for the interrogative word "what",

What?
啥？sha^{2}?
What do you do?
你干啥？ni^{3} gan^{4} sha^{2}?
What are you doing?
你在干啥？ni^{3} zai^{4} gan^{4} sha^{2}?
What do you say?
你说啥？ni^{3} shuo^{1} sha^{2}?
What are you saying?
你在说啥？ni^{3} zai^{4} shuo^{1} sha^{2}?
What is this?
这是啥？zhe^{4} shi^{4} sha^{2}?
What is the meaning?
啥意思？sha^{2} yi^{4}si?
What does this mean?

这是啥意思？ zhe^4 shi^4 sha^2 yi^4si?

What do you mean?

你说的是啥意思？ ni^3 $shuo^1$ de shi^4 sha^2 yi^4si?

What does this word mean?

这个词是啥意思？ zhe^4 ge^4 ci^2 shi^4 sha^2 yi^4si?

I'm doing my work. 我在干活儿。 wo^3 zai^4 $gan^4huo'r^2$.

I'm resting.

我在休息。 wo^3 zai^4 xiu^1xi.

I'm in bed to sleep.

我在睡觉。 wo^3 zai^4 $shui^4jiao^4$.

I'm eating.

我在吃饭。 wo^3 zai^4 chi^1 fan^4.

I'm working.

我在工作。 wo^3 zai^4 $gong^1zuo^4$.

I'm shopping.

我在购物。 wo^3 zai^4 gou^4wu^4.

The continuous tense marker 在 can also be replaced by a two-character word 正在, in which the first single-character 正 means "just" or "right".

I'm eating my breakfast.

我们正在吃早饭。 wo^3men $zheng^4zai^4$ chi^1 zao^3fan^4.

They are eating their lunch.

他们正在吃午饭。 ta^1men $zheng^4zai^4$ chi^1 wu^3fan^4.

You are eating your dinner.

你们正在吃晚饭。 ni^3men $zheng^4zai^4$ chi^1 wan^3fan^4.

Of course we can also use the time adverbial for "now" along with the present tense, which has a character pronounced exactly the same with the tense marker 在.

Now 现在 $xian^4zai^4$

We should know that time words are always placed before the verb or the sentence, never at the end of the sentence as in English.

What are you doing now?

你现在正在干什么？ ni^3 $xian^4zai^4$ $zheng^4zai^4$ gan^4 $shen^2me$?

现在你正在干什么？ $xian^4zai^4$ ni^3 $zheng^4zai^4$ gan^4 $shen^2me$?

I'm resting now.

我现在正在休息。 wo^3 $xian^4zai^4$ $zheng^4zai^4$ xiu^1xi.

现在我正在休息。 $xian^4zai^4$ wo^3 $zheng^4zai^4$ xiu^1xi.

He is sleeping now.

他现在正在睡觉。 ta^1 $xian^4zai^4$ $zheng^4zai^4$ $shui^4jiao^4$.

现在他正在睡觉。 $xian^4zai^4$ ta^2 $zheng^4zai^4$ $shui^4jiao^4$.

You are speaking now.
你现在正在说话。ni3 xian4zai4 zheng4zai4 shuo1hua4.
现在你正在说话。xian4zai4 ni3 zheng4zai4 shuo1hua4.

When other adverbs are used, they are usually placed immediately before the 在 or 正在. Let's take three adverbs for practice.

Also, too 也 ye3
I am also resting.
我也在休息。wo3 ye3 zai4 xiu1xi.
They are learning Chinese, too.
他们也正在学汉语。ta1men ye3 zheng4zai4 xue2 han4yu3.
Still, yet 还 hai2
I'm still working.
我还在工作。wo3 hai4 zai4 gong1zuo4.
He is still looking for a job.
他还在找工作。ta1 hai2 zai4 zhao3 gong1zuo4.
All or both 都 dou1
We are all working.
我们都在工作。wo3men dou1zai4 gong1zuo4.
Both he and she are looking for a job.
他和她都在找工作。ta1 he2 ta1 dou1 zai4 zhao3 gong1zuo4.
He and she 他和她 ta1 he2 ta1
Both he and she are looking for a job.
他和她都在找工作。ta1 he2 ta1 dou1 zai4 zhao3 gong1zuo4.
They are looking for a job, and also studying.
他们在找工作，也在学习。ta1men zai4 zhao3 gong1zuo4, ye3 zai4 xue2xi2.

As we see, the connector 和 in Chinese are used only between nominal words, while 也 and 还 are used between verbs.

I'm learning, and teaching too.
我在学习，也在教学。wo3 zai4 xue2xi2, ye3 zai4 jiao4xue2.
Or
我在学习，还在教学。wo3 zai4 xue2xi2, hai2 zai4 jiao4xue2.

Now, we should know that the word 在 is different from 正在 in that it is not only a continuous tense marker, but also a preposition used before a word giving the place or location of the action. It is originally a verb that means "to exist, lie, stay", or "to be present", but when functioning as a preposition, it is like the English "at", "in" or "on". Now let's listen and learn.

I'm here, I'm in, or I'm online, depending on the context.
我在 wo3 zai4

I'm here, or in here.
我在这里 wo3zai4 zhe4li3.
There, or in there 在那里 zai4 na4li3
Where or in which place 在哪里 zai4 na3li3.
Where are you?
你在哪里？ ni3 zai4 na3li3?
I'm at home.
我在家 wo3 zai4 jia1.
Or
我在家里 wo3 zai4 jia1 li3.
Online 在线 zai4xian4
On the internet 在网上 zai4 wang2shang4
At the post office 在邮局 zai4 you2ju2
At the bank 在银行 zai4 yin2hang2
At the hotel 在宾馆 zai4 bin1guan3
At the shop or store 在商店 zai4 shang1dian4
At the airport 在机场 zai4 ji1chang3
At the railway station 在火车站 zai4 huo3che1zhan4
At the bus stop 在汽车站 zai4 qi4che1zhan4
On the way, on the road 在路上 zai4 lu4shang4
In the school 在学校 zai4 xue2xiao4
In the company 在公司 zai4 gong1si1
In the library 在图书馆 zai4 tu2shu1guan3
In the dorm 在宿舍 zai4 su4she4

It should be noted that prepositional phrases are usually used before the verb in sentences, and sometimes the tense should be understood according to the context.

Where do you work or are you working?
你在哪里工作？ ni3 zai4 na3li3 gong1zuo4?
I work or I'm working in the bank.
我在银行工作。wo3 zai4 yin2hang2 gong1zuo4.
Where do you take a rest or where are you resting?
你在哪里休息？ ni3 zai4 na3li3 xiu1xi?
I rest at home or I'm resting at home.
我在家里休息。wo3 zai4 jia1li3 xiu1xi.
Where do you chat or are you chatting?
你们在哪里聊天？ ni3men zai4 na3li3 liao2tian1?
We chat or we're chatting on the net.
我们在网上聊天。wo3men zai4 wang3shang4 liao2tian1.
Where are we going to wait for him?

我们在哪里等他？wo^{3}men zai^4 na^{3}li^3 deng^3 ta^1?
We will wait for him at the airport.
我们在机场等他。wo^{3}men zai^4 ji^{1}chang^3 deng^3 ta^1.
Are you online chatting?
你在线聊天吗？ni^3 zai^{4}xian^4 liao^{2}tian^1 ma^1?
Yes. I'm chatting online.
是的，我在线聊天。shi^4 de, wo^3 zai^{4}xian^4 liao^{2}tian^1.
Let's do more practice.
I'm driving.
我在开车。wo^3 zai^4 kai^{1}che^1.
I'm on the road, or I'm on my way.
我在路上。wo^3 zai^4 lu^{4}shang.
I'm driving on the road.
我在路上开车。wo^3 zai^4 lu^{4}shang^4 kai^{1}che^1.
He is at home.
他在家里。ta^1 zai^4 jia^{1}li^3.
He is writing characters.
他在写字。ta^1 zai^4 xie^{3}zi^4.
He writes, or is writing characters at home.
他在家里写字。ta^1 zai^4 jia^1 li^3 xie^{3}zi^4.
My younger brother is in the school.
我弟弟在学校。wo^3 di^{4}di zai^4 xue^{2}xiao^4.
My younger brother is studying in the school.
我弟弟在学校学习。wo^3 di^{4}di zai^4 xue^{2}xiao^4 xue^{2}xi^2.
I learn or I'm learning Chinese in the school.
我在学校学汉语。wo^3 zai^4 xuc^{2}xiao^4 xuc^2 han^{4}yu^3.
Now let's change the simple present tense into continuous tense.
He or she listens.
他/她听。ta^1 ting^1.
He is listening.
他/她在听。ta^1 zai^4 ting^1.
He or she speaks.
他/她说。ta^1 shuo^1.
He or she is speaking.
他/她在说。ta^1 zai^4 shuo^1.
They read.
他们读。ta^{1}men du^2.
They are reading.
他们在读。ta^{1}men zai^4 du^2.
You (in singular) learn, or you study.

你学 ni^3 xue^2.
You (in singular) are learning.
你在学。ni^3 zai^4 xue^2.
You (plural) learn, or you study.
你们学。ni^{3}men xue^2.
You (plural) are learning.
你们在学。ni^{3}men zai^4 xue^2.
You (in plural) write.
你们写。ni^{3}men xie^3.
You (in plural) are writing.
你们在写。ni^{3}men zai^4 xie^3.
I think.
我想。wo^3 xiang^3.
I’m thinking.
我在想。wo^3 zai^4 xiang^3.
We are thinking.
我们在想。wo^{3}men zai^4 xiang^3.
I look.
我看。wo^3 kan^4.
I’m looking.
我在看。wo^3 zai^4 kan^4.
We look.
我们看。wo^{3}men kan^4.
We’re looking.
我们在看。wo^{3}men zai^4 kan^4.
Is the manager in the company?
经理在不在公司？jing^{1}li^3 zai^4 bu^4 zai^4 gong^{1}si^1?
No. He is at home.
不在。他在家里。bu^4 zai^4. ta^1 zai^4 jia^1 li^3.
What is he doing at home?
他在家干什么？ta^1 zai^4 jia^1 gan^4 shen^{2}me?
He is sleeping.
他在睡觉。ta^1 zai^4 shui^{4}jiao^4.
Where are they?
他们在哪里？ta^{1}men zai^4 na^{3}li^3?
They are in the restaurant.
他们在饭店。ta^{1}men zai^4 fan^{4}dian^4.
What are they doing in the restaurant?
他们在饭店干什么？ta^{1}men zai^4 fan^{4}dian^4 gan^4 shen^{2}me?
They are eating in the restaurant.

他们在饭店吃饭。ta^{1}men zai^4 fan^{4}dian^4 chi^1 fan^4.

Is your son in the school?

你儿子在不在学校？ni^3 er^{2}zi zai^4 bu^4 zai^4 xue^{2}xiao^4?

Yes. He is now in the library.

在，他现在在图书馆。zai^4, ta^1 xian^{4}zai^4 zai^4 tu^{2}shu^{1}guan^3.

Is your boss in the factory?

你们的老板在不在工厂？ni^{3}men^2 de lao^{3}ban^3 zai^4 bu^4 zai^4 gong^1 chang^3?

No. He is in the office.

不在，他在办公室。bu^4 zai^4, ta^1 zai^4 ban^{4}gong^{1}shi^4.

What is he doing in the office?

他在办公室干什么？ta^1 zai^4 ban^{4}gong^{1}shi^4 gan^4 shen^{2}me?

He is writing there.

他在那里写东西。ta^1 zai^4 na^{4}li^3 xie^3 dong^{1}xi.

OK! Here we have encountered a very special and important word in Chinese—

东西 dong^{1}xi

It actually means a thing, something, or anything material or non-material. For instance—

What thing? Or, what is it?

啥东西？sha^2 dong^{1}xi?

What is this?

这是什么东西？zhe^4 shi^4 shen^{2}me dong^{1}xi?

Something good.

好东西。hao^3 dong^{1}xi.

Shopping for something 买东西 mai^3 dong^{1}xi

Eating something 吃东西 chi^1 dong^{1}xi

What else?

还有什么东西？hai^2 you^3 shen^{2}me dong^{1}xi?

It should be noted that the two characters in this word originally mean "east" and "west" respectively. However, when used for real direction, the two characters will be pronounced in their original tones, and not with the second changed into the light tone. Let's compare.

East and west 东西 dong^{1}xi^1

East, west, south and north 东西南北 dong^1 xi^1 nan^2 bei^3

A thing, something or anything 东西 dong^{1}xi

Look for east and west, look for direction 找东西 zhao^3 dong^{1}xi^1

Look for something 找东西 zhao^3 dong^{1}xi

What is he doing at home?

他在家干什么？ta^1 zai^{4}jia^1 gan^4 shen^{2}me?

He is looking for something at home.
他在家找东西。ta^{1} zai^{4}jia^{1} zhao^{3} dong^{1}xi.
What is he looking for?
他在找什么东西？ta^{1} zai^{4} zhao^{3} shen^{2}me dong^{1}xi?
He is looking for something important.
他在找重要的东西。ta^{1} zai^{4} zhao^{3} zhong^{4}yao^{4} de dong^{1}xi.
What are you doing?
你在干什么？ni^{3} zai^{4} gan^{4} shen^{2}me?
I am resting.
我在休息。wo^{3} zai^{4} xiu^{1}xi.
Is your wife resting too?
你妻子也在休息吗？ni^{3} qi^{1}zi ye^{3} zai^{4} xiu^{1}xi ma^{1}?
Yes. We are both resting.
是的，我们都在休息。shi^{4} de, wo^{3}men dou^{1} zai^{4} xiu^{1}xi.
What are the children doing?
孩子们都在干什么？hai^{2}zimen dou^{1} zai^{4} gan^{4} shen^{2}me?
The children are all sleeping.
孩子们都在睡觉。hai^{2}zimen dou^{1} zai^{4} shui^{4}jiao^{4}.

LESSON 8 第八课

I WANT...; I NEED... 我想要……；我需要…… WO^{3} XIANG^{3}YAO^{4}...; WO^{3} XU^{1}YAO^{4}...

In this lesson, we'll learn how to ask for something and express our needs.

In this regard, the first word we need to know is 要, which is often interchangeable with the two-character word 想要. These two words basically mean "ask for", "need" or "wish to have" and the particular meaning can be understood according to the context in which they are used.

What do you want?
你要什么？ni^{3} yao^{4} shen^{2}me?
Or
你想要什么？ni^{3} xiang^{3}yao^{4} shen^{2}me?
I want 我要 wo^{3} yao^{4}
Or
我想要 wo^{3} xiang^{3}yao^{4}
I want this.
我要这个。wo^{3} yao^{4} zhe^{4} ge^{4}.
我想要这个。wo^{3} xiang^{3}yao^{4} zhe^{4} ge^{4}.
I want that.
我要那个。wo^{3} yao^{4} na^{4} ge^{4}.
我想要那个。wo^{3} xiang^{3}yao^{4} na^{4} ge^{4}.
I want this and that.
我要这个和那个。wo^{3} yao^{4} zhe^{4} ge^{4} he^{2} na^{4} ge^{4}.
I want some bread and milk.
我要 些面包和牛奶。wo^{3} yao^{4} yi^{1}xie^{1} mian^{4}bao^{1} he^{2} niu^{2}nai^{3}.
I want some water.
我想要一点水。wo^{3} xiang^{3}yao^{4} yi^{1}dian^{3} shui^{3}.
I want some food, or I want something to eat.

我想要一点吃的。wo3 xiang3yao4 yi1dian3 chi1 de.
I want some drink.
我要一点喝的。wo3 yao4 yi1dian3 he1 de.
I want something to eat and drink.
我要一点吃的和喝的。wo3 yao4 yi1dian3 chi1 de he2 he1 de.
I want some fruit.
我想要一些水果。wo3 xiang3yao4 yi1xie1 shui3guo3.
I want some Chinese dish.
我要一些中国菜。wo3 yao4 yi1xie1 zhong1guo2 cai4.
I want some potatoes.
我要一些土豆。wo3 yao4 yi1xie1 tu3dou4.
I want some rice.
我要一些米饭。wo3 yao4 yi1xie1 mi3fan4.
I want some milk.
我要一些牛奶。wo3 yao4 yi1xie1 niu2nai3.
I want a little sugar.
我要一些砂糖。wo3 yao4 yi1xie1 sha1tang2.
I want a little cheese.
我要一点奶酪。wo3 yao4 yi1dian3 nai3lao4.

As we see, in Chinese, 一点 and 一些 respectively mean "a little" and "some".

In casual and informal speech, the first character 一 is often omitted, and the pronunciation of 点 is changed by adding the retroflex "r" as in the pronunciation of "worker" and "farmer" in American English. So let's listen to the changes.

I want a little water.
我想要一点水。wo3 xiang3yao4 yi1dian3 shui3.
我想要点儿水。wo3 xiang3yao4 dian'r3 shui3.
I want a little food.
我想要一点吃的。wo3 xiangyao4 yi1dian3 chi1 de.
我想要点儿吃的。wo3 xiang3yao4 dian'r3 chi1 de.
I want a little drink.
我想要一点喝的。wo3 xiang3yao4 yi1dian3 he1 de.
我想要点儿喝的。wo3 xiang3yao4 dian'r3 he1 de.
I want something to eat and drink.
我要一点吃的和喝的。wo3 yao4 yi1dian3 chi1 de he2 he1 de.
我要点儿吃的和喝的。wo3 yao4 dian'r3 chi1 de he2 he1 de.
I want some fruit.
我想要一些水果。wo3 xiang3yao4 yi1xie1 shui3guo3.
我想要些水果。wo3 xiang3yao4 xie1 shui3guo3.

I want some rice.
我要一些米饭。wo^{3} yao^{4} yi^{1}xie^{1} mi^{3}fan^{4}.
我要些米饭。wo^{3} yao^{4} xie^{1} mi^{3}fan^{4}.
I want a little sugar.
我想要一些砂糖。wo^{3} xiang^{3}yao^{4} yi^{1}xie^{1} sha^{1}tang^{2}.
我想要些砂糖。wo^{3} xiang^{3}yao^{4} xie^{1} sha^{1}tang^{2}.
I want a little milk.
我要一点牛奶。wo^{3} yao^{4} yi^{1}dian^{3} niu^{2}nai^{3}.
我要一点儿牛奶。wo^{3} yao^{4} yi^{1}dian'r^{3} niu^{2}nai^{3}.
我要点儿牛奶。wo^{3} yao^{4} dian'r^{3} niu^{2}nai^{3}.
I want a little cheese.
我要一点奶酪。wo^{3} yao^{4} yi^{1}dian^{3} nai^{3}lao^{4}.
我要点儿奶酪。wo^{3} yao^{4} dian'r^{3} nai^{3}lao^{4}.

If the thing you want is given in fixed portion, you can simply say—
一份 yi^{1} fen^{4}
I want a breakfast.
我要一份早餐。wo^{3} yao^{4} yi^{1} fen^{4} zao^{3}can^{1}.
We want two lunches.
我们要两份午餐。wo^{3}men yao^{4} liang^{3} fen^{4} wu^{3}can^{1}.
They need three dinners.
他们要三份晚餐。ta^{1}men yao^{4} san^{1} fen^{4} wan^{3}can^{1}.
I want a dish.
我想要一份菜。wo^{3} xiang^{3}yao^{4} yi^{1} fen^{4} cai^{4}.
I want a salad.
我要一份色拉。wo^{3} yao^{4} yi^{1} fen^{4} se^{4} la^{1}.
I want one fried rice.
我要一份炒饭。wo^{3} yao^{4} yi^{1} fen^{4} chao^{3}fan^{4}.
I want a steak.
我要一份肉排。wo^{3} yao^{4} yi^{1} fen^{4} rou^{4}pai^{2}.

Now we have come to a very important matter in Chinese— that is, the combination of a number and a measure word. In Chinese there are quite many measure words and their uses are highly customary, but the most important measure word is—

个 ge^{4}

This measure word can be used before a noun that refers to people.
One man, one person 一个人 yi^{1} ge^{4} ren^{2}
Two sons 两个儿子 liang^{3} ge^{4} er^{2}zi
Three daughters 三个女儿 san^{1} ge^{4} nv^{3}er^{2}
Four children 四个孩子 si^{4} ge^{4} hai^{2}zi

Five workers 五个工人 wu^{3} ge^{4} gong^{1}ren
Six students 六个学生 liu^{4} ge^{4} xue^{2}sheng^{1}

Depending on what people are being referred to, the Chinese may use two other words in place of 个, namely 位 and 名. The word 位 literally means "position" or "seat" and the word 名 means "name".

Four professors 四位教授 si^{4} wei^{4} jiao^{4}shou^{4}
Five leaders 五位领导 wu^{3} wei^{4} ling^{3}dao^{3}

"名" and "位" are used for persons only, with the latter more respectful.

Several gentlemen 几位先生 ji^{3} wei^{4} xian^{1}sheng

The measure word 个 is also used for many things that can be counted one by one.

Six apples 六个苹果 liu^{4} ge^{4} ping^{2}guo^{3}
Seven bananas 七个香蕉 qi^{1} ge^{4} xiang^{1}jiao^{1}
Eight oranges 八个橙子 ba^{1} ge^{4} cheng^{2}zi
Nine eggs 九个鸡蛋 jiu^{3} ge^{4} ji^{1}dan^{4}

In addition, nouns that refer to something abstract or non-material can also take this measure word.

Seven questions 七个问题 qi^{1} ge^{2} wen^{4}ti^{2}
Eight answers 八个答案 ba^{1} ge^{4} da^{2}an^{4}
Nine exercises 九个练习 jiu^{3} ge^{4} lian^{4}xi^{2}
Ten ideas 十个想法 shi^{2} ge^{4} xiang^{3}fa^{3}

However, on the whole, the use of the measure word 个 is highly customary and should be learned gradually from the native speakers. For example, it is right to use it before "month", "week" and "hour" but not before "year", "day", and "minute".

A month 一个月 yi^{1} ge^{4} yue^{4}
Two months 两个月 liang^{3} ge^{4} yue^{4}
A week 一个星期 yi^{1} ge^{4} xing^{1}qi^{1}
Two or three weeks 两、三个星期 liang^{3} san^{1} ge^{4} xing^{1}qi^{1}
Four hours 四个小时 si^{4} ge^{4} xiao^{3}shi^{2}
A year 一年 yi^{1} nian^{2}
Two years 两年 liang^{3} nian^{2}
A day 一天 yi^{1} tian^{1}
Five days 五天 wu^{3} tian^{1}
Six or seven minutes 六七分钟 liu^{4} qi^{1} fen^{1}zhong^{1}

All right! Please don't be discouraged by this, because many Chinese measure words use something concrete and material as means of measure, just as in English.

A cup 一杯 yi^{1} bei^{1}

I want a cup of coffee.
我想要一杯咖啡。wo^3 xiang^{3}yao^4 yi^1 bei^1 ka^{1}fei^1.
We want two cups of tea.
我们想要两杯茶。wo^{3}men xiang^{3}yao^4 liang^3 bei^1 cha^2.
They want three glasses of red wine.
他们想要三杯红酒。ta^{1}men xiang^{3}yao^4 san^1 bei^1 hong^{2}jiu^3.

As we see, the Chinese 杯 can be both the "cup" and the "glass" in English. If you want to indicate that it is a glass cup, then you can say—
玻璃杯 bo^{1}li^{2}bei^1

Another thing we should know is that the English expression "I'd like to have" is also translated as "我要" or "我想要".

I'd like to have a glass of brandy.
我要一杯白兰地。wo^3 yao^4 yi^1 bei^1 bai^{2}lan^{2}di^4.
I'd like to have a cup of whisky.
我想要一杯威士忌。wo^3 xiang^{3}yao^4 yi^4 bei^1 wei^{1}shi^{4}ji^4.
I'd like to have a cup of green tea.
我要一杯绿茶。wo^3 yao^4 yi^1 bei^1 lv^{4}cha^2.
We'd like to have two cups of black tea.
我们想要两杯红茶。wo^{3}men xiang^{3}yao^4 liang^3 bei^1 hong^{2}cha^2.
We'd like to have four glasses of coke.
我们想要四杯可乐。wo^{3}men xiang^{3}yao^4 si^4 bei^1 ke^{3}le^4.

Have you found something puzzling here? While "green tea" literally translates into Chinese as 绿茶, the translation of "black tea" is changed to 红茶, which actually means "red tea". This is perhaps because in English the color is of the tea leaves while in Chinese it is of the tea served.

OK! Now let's go on and learn an important word that is often interchangeable with 要 or 想要.

Need 需要 xu^{1}yao^4
We need 我们需要 wo^{3}men xu^{1}yao^4
We need four glasses of orange juice.
我们需要四杯橙汁。wo^{3}men xu^{1}yao^4 si^4 bei^1 cheng^2 zhi^1.
They need 他们需要 ta^{1}men xu^{1}yao^4
They need five glasses of apple juice.
他们需要五杯苹果汁。ta^{1}men xu^{1}yao^4 wu^3 bei^1 ping^{2}guo^{3}zhi^1.
We need six bottles of beer.
我们需要六瓶啤酒。wo^{3}men xu^{1}yao^4 liu^4 ping^2 pi^{2}jiu^3.
Bottle 瓶 ping^2
Six bottles of beer 六瓶啤酒 liu^4 ping^2 pi^{2}jiu^3
One bottle of coke 一瓶可乐 yi^1 ping^2 ke^{3}le^4
One big bottle of coke 一大瓶可乐 yi^1 da^4 ping^2 ke^{3}le^4

OK! Please remember if the measure of something is not a specified container, we can simply use the word 份, which literally means a given appropriation of something. It is usually interchangeable with the most generally used measure word of 个.

A drink 一份饮料 yi^{1} fen^{4} yin^{3}liao^{4}

I want a drink.

我要一份饮料。wo^{3} yao^{4} yi^{1} fen^{4} yin^{3}liao^{4}

An ice cream 一份冰淇淋 yi^{2} fen^{4} bing^{1}qi^{2}lin^{2}

I'd like to have an ice cream.

我要一份冰淇淋。wo^{3} yao^{4} yi^{1} fen^{4} bing^{1}qi^{2}lin^{2}.

I'd like to have a breakfast.

我要一份早餐。wo^{3} yao^{4} yi^{1} fen^{4} zao^{3}can^{1}.

I'd like to have a dish.

我想要一份菜。wo^{3} xiang^{3}yao^{4} yi^{1} fen^{4} cai^{4}.

I want, or I'd like to have a salad.

我想要一份色拉。wo^{3} xiang^{3}yao^{4} yi^{1} fen^{4} se^{4}la^{1}.

I want one fried rice.

我要一份炒饭。wo^{3} yao^{4} yi^{1} fen^{4} chao^{3}fan^{4}.

I want a steak.

我要一份肉排。wo^{3} yao^{4} yi^{1} fen^{4} rou^{4}pai^{2}.

In fact, the use of 份 as a measure word is also customary and should be learned by following the native speakers. However, if you are not sure which measure word to use, you probably can try to use 个. Listen and repeat the following:

I want that job.

我想要那份工作。wo^{3} xiang^{3}yao^{4} na^{4} fen^{4} gong^{1}zuo^{4}.

我想要那个工作。wo^{3} xiang^{3}yao^{4} na^{4} ge^{4} gong^{1}zuo^{4}.

I need this newspaper.

我需要这份报纸。wo^{3} xu^{1}yao^{4} zhe^{4} fen^{4} bao^{4}zhi^{3}.

我想要这个报纸。wo^{3} xiang^{3}yao^{4} zhe^{4} ge^{4} bao^{4}zhi^{3}.

I want this magazine.

我想要这份杂志。wo^{3} xiang^{3}yao^{4} zhe^{4} fen^{4} za^{2}zhi^{4}.

我想要这个杂志。wo^{3} xiang^{3}yao^{4} zhe^{4} ge^{4} za^{2}zhi^{4}.

OK! Now let's learn a few more words that use different containers as the unit of measurement.

A small box, a case or packet 盒 (he^{2})

I want a box of chocolate.

我要一盒巧克力。wo^{3} yao^{4} yi^{1} he^{2} qiao^{3}ke^{4}li^{4}.

I want a packet of cigarettes.

我想要一盒香烟。wo^{3} xiang^{3}yao^{4} yi^{1} he^{2} xiang^{1}yan^{1}.

A package, a packet, or a parcel 包 bao1

I need a packet of paper napkins.

我需要一包餐巾纸。wo3 xu1yao4 yi1 bao1 can1jin1zhi3.

I need a packet of tissues.

我需要一包手纸。wo3 xu1yao4 yi1 bao1 shou3zhi3.

A tray, a dish 盘 pan2

I need a dish of salad.

我需要一盘色拉。wo3 xu1yao4 yi1 pan2 se4la1.

I want a tray of peanuts.

我要一盘花生。wo3 yao4 yi1pan2 hua1sheng1.

A bowl 碗 wan3

I'd like to have a bowl of rice.

我想要一碗米饭。wo3 xiang3yao4 yi1 wan3 mi3fan4.

I'd like to have a bowl of fried noodles.

我要一碗炒面。wo3 yao4 yi1 wan3 chao3mian4.

Good! Now let's come back to the question to ask if someone wants anything.

What do you want?

你要什么？ni3 yao4 shen2me?

Or

What do you want to ask for?

你想要什么？ni3 xiang3yao4 shen2me?

The same questions can also be asked in a more informal and casual way, as the following:

你想要点儿什么？ni3 xiang3yao4 dian'r3 shen2me?

你要点儿什么？ni3 yao4 dian'r3 shen2me?

Here, please remember that 点儿 is changed from 一点 through the pronunciation change called Er-hua, that is, by adding the retroflex sound of Er as in the American English pronunciation of "worker" and "farmer".

你想要点儿什么？ni3 xiang3yao4 dian'r3 shen2me?

你要点儿什么？ni3 yao4dian'r3 shen2me?

I'd like to have a salad and a steak.

我要一盘色拉和一份肉排。wo3 yao4 yi1 pan2 se4la1 he2 yi1 fen4 rou4pai2.

I'd like to have fried noodles and a drink.

我要一碗炒面和一份饮料。wo3 yao4 yi1 wan3 chao3mian4 he2 yi1 fen4 yin3liao4.

What about him?

他呢？ta1 ne?

He'd like to have one fried rice, one dish and a bottle of beer.

他要一份炒饭，一份菜和一瓶啤酒。ta^1 yao^4 yi^1 fen^4 chao^{3}fan^4, yi^1 fen^4 cai^4, he^2 yi^1 ping^2 pi^{2}jiu^3.

Now we should remember that there is a difference between 一点 or 一点儿 and 一些. This is: 一点 or 一点儿 means "a little", while 一些 means "some". The thing to know is that, the character 一 can be omitted.

What would you like to have? (you in the plural)

你们要些什么？ni^{3}men yao^4 xie shen^{2}me?

Then you can choose from the following list:

A cup of coffee 一杯咖啡 yi^1 bei^1 ka^{1}fei^1

Two cups of tea 两杯茶 liang^3 bei^1 cha^2

One green tea and another black tea 一杯绿茶和一杯红茶 yi^1 bei^1 lv^{4}cha^2 he^2 yi^1 bei^1 hong^{2}cha^2

Three glasses of red wine 三杯红酒 san^1 bei^1 hong^{2}jiu^3

A glass of brandy 一杯白兰地 yi^1 bei^1 bai^{2}lan^{2}di^4

A cup of whisky 一杯威士忌 yi^1 bei^1 wei^{1}shi^{4}ji^4

Four glasses of coke 四杯可乐 si^{4}bei^1 ke^{3}le^4

Anything else?

还要什么吗？hai^2 yao^4 shen^{2}me ma^1?

Oh, yes. And a packet of cigarettes and a packet of paper napkins.

哦，还要一包香烟和一包餐巾纸。o^4 hai^2 yao^4 yi^1 bao^1 xiang^{1}yan^1 he^2 yi^1 bao^1 can^{1}jin^{1}zhi^3.

Anything more?

还有吗？hai^2 you^3 ma^1?

Nothing more.

没有了。mei^2 you^3 le.

All right! Now you have learned quite many useful expressions to express what you want and need. If you are not sure you have already learned them by heart, just go through it once more. If you do, you can go on to the next lesson.

LESSON 9 第九课

HOW MUCH IS IT?
多少？DUO^{1}SHAO^{3}?

In Chinese, many words are formed by two characters that have opposite meanings. Here we have an example.

Many or much 多 duo^{1}

Few or little 少 shao^{3}

How many or how much?

多少？duo^{1}shao^{3}?

Literally, how much money? Or simply, how much?

多少钱？duo^{1}shao^{3} qian^{2}?

To answer this question, we need to use combinations of numbers and words of the Chinese money unit. Now, let's first learn the basic numbers.

1, 2, 3, 4 一 yi^{1}, 二 er^{4}, 三 san^{1}, 四 si^{4}

5, 6, 7, 8, 五 wu^{3}, 六 liu^{4}, 七 qi^{1}, 八 ba^{1}

9, 10, 0, 九 jiu^{3}, 十 shi^{2}, 零 ling^{2}

11, 12, 13 十一 shi^{2}yi^{1}, 十二 shi^{2} er^{4}, 十三 shi^{2} san^{1}

14, 15, 16 十四 shi^{2} si^{4}, 十五 shi^{2}wu^{3}, 十六 shi^{2}liu^{4}

60, 50, 40 六十 liu^{4}shi^{2}, 五十 wu^{3}shi^{2}, 四十 si^{4}shi^{2}

77, 88, 99 七十七 qi^{1}shi^{2}qi^{1}, 八十八 ba^{1}shi^{2}ba^{1}, 九十九 jiu^{3}shi^{2}jiu^{3}

100 一百 yi^{1} bai^{3}

1,000 一千 yi^{1} qian^{1}

10,000 一万 yi^{1} wan^{4}

100,000 十万 shi^{2} wan^{4}

A million 一百万 yi^{1} bai^{3}wan^{4}

As we see in the above, Chinese is different from the English in that it has ten thousand as an independent unit, 万 which does not exist in English.

All right! Now we need to know the Chinese money unit.

Money 钱 qian^{2}

The Chinese dollar 元 yuan^{2}

The Chinese dime 角 jiao^{3}

The Chinese cent 分 fen^1

It should be noted that both the Chinese dollar 元 and dime 角 have a more frequently used informal word. They are—

块 kuai^4

毛 mao^2

Now let's say the following as a practice.

One yuan, a Chinese dollar 一块 yi^1 kuai^4

￥1.23 一块两毛三分 yi^1 kuai^4 liang^3 mao^2 san^1 fen^1

￥2.32 两块三毛二分 liang^3 kuai^4 san^1 mao^2 er^4 fen^1

￥3.45 三块四毛五 san^1 kuai^4 si^4 mao^2 wu^3

￥5.67 五块六毛七 wu^3 kuai^4 liu^4 mao^2 qi^1

￥7.89 七块八毛九 qi^1 kuai^4 ba^1 mao^2 jiu^3

￥10.10 十块一毛 shi^2 kuai^4 yi^1 mao^2

￥10.01 十块零一分 shi^2 kuai^4 ling^2 yi^1 fen^1

￥11.98 十一块九毛八 shi^2 yi^1 kuai^4 jiu^3 mao^2 ba^1

￥12.89 十二块八毛九 shi^2 er^4 kuai^4 ba^1 mao^2 jiu^3

￥23.76 二十三块七毛六 er^4 shi^2 san^1 kuai^4 qi^1 mao^2 liu^4

￥32.54 三十二块五毛四 san^1 shi^2 er^4 kuai^4 wu^3 mao^2 si^4

￥43.32 四十三块三毛二 si^4 shi^2 san^1 kuai^4 san^1 mao^2 er^4

￥54.23 五十四块两毛三 wu^3 shi^2 si^4 kuai^4 liang^3 mao^2 san^1

Do you notice that we have so far used two different words for the number two? Yes! They are 二 and 两, which are the same in meaning but are used in different contexts, while 二 is normally used along with other numbers, 两 often goes with a measure word; but on the whole, the choice is still customary. Let's listen again.

￥1.23 一块两毛三分 yi^1 kuai^4 liang^3 mao^2 san^1 fen^1

￥2.32 两块三毛二分 liang^3 kuai^4 san^1 mao^2 er^4 fen^1

￥23.76 二十三块七毛六 er^4 shi^2 san^1 kuai^4 qi^1 mao^2 liu^4

￥32.54 三十二块五毛四 san^1 shi^2 er^4 kuai^4 wu^3 mao^2 si^4

￥54.23 五十四块两毛三 wu^3 shi^2 si^4 kuai^4 liang^3 mao^2 san^1

Please note another important difference between 二 and 两. That is, while 二 is always used as a number, the word 两 can serve as a Chinese measure unit too, it is a tenth of the measurement 斤 (jin^1) that equals to half a kilogram. That is to say, a 斤 is 500 grams and a 两 50 grams. Let's listen!

50 grams 一两 yi^1 liang^3

100 grams 二两 er^4 liang^3

Although the measurement of 斤 and 两 are used generally as national standard units, the international metric system is also adopted.

One kilogram 一公斤 yi^1 gong^{1}jin^1

One gram 一克 yi1 ke4
One kilogram is 1,000 grams.
一公斤是一千克。yi1 gong1jin1 shi4 yi1 qian1 ke4.
One kilogram is two Chinese *jin*.
一公斤是两市斤。yi1 gong1jin1 shi4 liang2 shi4jin1.
One Chinese *jin* is 500 grams.
一市斤是五百克。yi2 shi4jin1 shi4 wu3 bai3 ke4.
One Chinese *jin* is half a kilogram.
一市斤是半公斤。yi2 shi4jin1 shi4 ban4gong1jin1.
Half a kilogram is one Chinese *jin*.
半公斤是一市斤。ban4gong1 jin1 shi4 yi1 shi4jin1.
One Chinese *jin* is ten Chinese *liang*.
一市斤是十两。yi1 shi4jin1 shi4 shi2 liang3.
One kilogram is 20 Chinese *liang*.
一公斤是二十两。yi1 gong1jin1 shi4 er4 shi2 liang3.
One Chinese *liang* is 50 grams.
一两是五十克。yi1 liang3 shi4 wu3 shi2 ke4.
Half a Chinese *liang* is 25 grams.
半两是二十五克。ban4 liang3 shi4 er4 shi2 wu3 ke4.

In the above, we have also learned the word for half, namely, 半. Then there is another word that we need to learn.

Each or per 每 mei3
Each one 每个 mei3 ge4
Each person 每个人 mei3 ge4 ren2
Each kilogram, per kilogram 每公斤 mei3 gong1jin1

All right! Now we will learn what to say when going shopping in the market. Let's listen and repeat.

What do you want? Or, what can I do for you?
你要什么？ni3 yao4 shen2me?
I'd like to have ... 我想要……wo3 xiang3yao4...
Six apples 六个苹果 liu4 ge4 ping2guo3
Seven bananas 七个香蕉 qi1 ge4 xiang1jiao1
Eight oranges 八个橙子 ba1 ge4 cheng2zi
Nine eggs 九个鸡蛋 jiu3 ge4 ji1dan4
How much are these?
这些多少钱？zhe4 xie1 duo1shao3 qian2?
These are all sold by weight.
这些都按重量卖。zhe4 xie1 dou1 an4 zhong4liang4 mai4.
By weight 按重量 an4 zhong4liang4
Not by quantity 不按数量 bu4 an4 shu4laing4

The word 重量 literally translates into English as "weight measure" or "weight amount".

How much is the weight?

重量是多少？zhong^{4}liang^4 shi^4 duo^{1}shao^3?

Not too heavy

不太重 bu^4 tai^4 zhong^4

Very heavy 很重 hen^3 zhong^4

Very light 很轻 hen^3 qing^2

When asking about the price, the following expressions will be used.

How much money?

多少钱？duo^{1}shao^3 qian^2?

What is the price?

什么价钱？shen^{2}me jia^{4}qian^2?

Or 价钱是多少？jia^{4}qian^2 shi^4 duo^{1}shao^3?

Literally, how is it sold?

怎么卖？zen^{3}me mai^4?

Now we have learned the Chinese for "sell" is 卖 (mai^4), we also need to know the word for "buy". It is a word with the same pronunciation but said in a different tone. Listen and repeat.

买 mai^3

These two words can combine to form a new word.

Buying and selling. Or, simply business 买卖 mai^{3}mai^4

Do business 做买卖 zuo^4 mai^{3}mai^4

In fact, the word 价钱 for price can be pronounced either in the original two second tones or with 钱 changed to the light tone.

价钱 (originals) jia^{4}qian^2

价钱 (changed light tone ending) jia^{4}qian

So, let's listen and repeat.

What price is this?

这是什么价钱？zhe^4 shi^4 shen^{2}me jia^{4}qian?

What's the price of this?

这个价钱是多少？zhe^4 ge^4 jia^4 qian shi^4 duo^{1}shao^3?

What prices are these?

这些是什么价钱？zhe^4 xie^1 shi^4 shen^{2}me jia^{4}qian?

How is that sold?

那个怎么卖？na^4 ge^4 zen^{3}me mai^4?

How much is that?

那个是多少钱？na^4 ge^4 shi^4 duo^{1}shao^3 qian^2?

How much is this?

这个是多少钱？zhe^4 ge^4 shi^4 duo^{1}shao^3 qian^2?

When giving the price of an item, the seller may choose to say either the measurement unit or the money first.

Six yuan per kilo.
一公斤六块钱。yi^{1} gong^{1}jin^{1} liu^{4} kuai^{4} qian^{2}.
Six yuan per kilo.
六块钱一公斤。liu^{4} kuai^{4} qian^{2} yi^{1} gong^{1}jin^{1}.
Twelve yuan per kilo.
一公斤十二块。yi^{1} jin^{1} shi^{2} er^{4} kuai^{4}.
Twelve yuan per kilo.
十二块钱一公斤。shi^{2} er^{4} kuai^{4} qian^{2} yi^{1} jin^{1}.

To make a bargain, you will find the following expressions very useful.

It's too expensive.
太贵了。tai^{4} gui^{4} le.
Would you make it a little cheaper?
便宜点儿好吧？pian^{2}yi^{4} dian'r^{3} hao^{3} ba?
Make it still cheaper.
再便宜点儿吧。zai^{4} pian^{2}yi^{4} dian'r^{3} ba.
Can you make it a little cheaper still?
能不能再便宜一点？neng^{2} bu^{4} neng^{2} zai^{4} pian^{2}yi^{4} yi^{4} dian^{3}?
Please give me a discount.
给我打个折吧。gei^{3} wo^{3} da^{3} ge^{4} zhe^{2} ba.
It's still too expensive.
还是太贵了。hai^{2}shi^{4} tai^{4} gui^{4} le.

In the meantime, you should understand what the seller may probably say.

This is not expensive.
这不贵。zhe^{4} bu^{4} gui^{4}.
This is really not expensive.
这真的不贵。zhe^{4} zhen^{1} de bu^{4} gui^{4}.
It's already very cheap.
已经很便宜了。yi^{3}jing^{1} hen^{3} pian^{2}yi^{4} le.
It really can't be cheaper.
真的不能再便宜了。zhen^{1} de bu^{4} neng^{2} zai^{4} pian^{2}yi^{4} le.
It's already the bottom price.
这已经是最低价了。zhe^{4} yi^{3}jing^{1} shi^{4} zui^{4} di^{1} jia^{4} le.

Now we have learned the Chinese superlative adverb 最, we need to know the word for the comparative degree: 更 (geng^{4}). It's in the fourth tone too, as the superlative.

Lower 更低 geng^{4} di^{1}
Lowest 最低 zui^{4} di^{1}

More expensive 更贵 geng4 gui4
Most expensive 最贵 zui4 gui4
Cheaper 更便宜 geng4 pian2yi4
Cheapest 最便宜 zui4 pian2yi4
Better 更好 geng4 hao3
Best 最好 zui4 hao3

OK! Now, after learning the two sentence finals 吧 and 了, we need to know that while 吧 is used for adding a tone of suggestion or pleading, 了 indicates an affirmative end of the sentence, meaning that the speaker has a firm opinion or attitude. For emphasis, the affirmative tone could be made even stronger by changing 了 into 啦.

It's too expensive.
太贵啦！ tai4 gui4 la1!
It's still too expensive.
还是太贵啦！ hai2shi4 tai4 gui4 la1!
It's already very cheap.
已经很便宜啦！ yi3 jing1 hen3 pian2yi4 la1!
Come on! It can't be made cheaper.
好啦！不能再便宜啦！ hao3 la1! bu4 neng2 zai4 pian2yi4 la1!

All right! Now let's go on to listen to some sentences using the expressions we have learned.

How much is for a *jin* or half a kilo of apples?
苹果多少钱一斤？ ping2guo3 duo1shao3 qian2 yi1 jin1?
￥2.85 for a Chinese *jin*.
每斤两块八毛五。mei3 jin1 liang3 kuai4 ba1 mao2 wu3.
It is 2.2 *jin*.
这是两斤二两。zhe4 shi4 liang3 jin1 er4 liang3.
It's worth ￥6.27.
需要六块两毛七。xu1yao4 liu4 kuai4 liang3 mao2 qi1.
How about the bananas and orange?
香蕉和橙子呢？ xiang1jiao1 he2 cheng2zi ne?
Banana is ￥3.50 for half a kilogram.
香蕉是一斤三块五。xiang1 jiao1 shi4 yi1 jin1 san1 kuai4 wu3.
This is one kilogram and a half, three Chinese *jin*.
这是一公斤半。zhe4 shi4 yi1 gong1jin2 ban4.
Is one kilogram and half two and half Chinese *jin*?
一公斤半是两斤半吗？ yi1 gong1jin1 ban4 shi4 laing3 jin1 ban4 ma1?
No. It is three Chinese *jin*.
不是，是三斤。bu4 shi4 shi4 san1 jin1.
Then, how much is it?

那么，是多少钱呢？na^{4}me shi^4 duo^{1}shao^3 qian^2 ne?

Three Chinese *jin* is for ￥10.50.

三斤是十块零五毛钱。san^1 jin^1 shi^4 shi^2 kuai^4 ling^2 wu^3 mao^2 qian^2.

How about the oranges?

橙子呢？cheng^{2}zi ne?

Oranges are￥4.65 for half a kilogram.

橙子是四块六毛五一斤。cheng^{2}zi shi^4 si^4 kuai^4 liu^4 mao^2 wu^3 yi^1 jin^1.

How much is the weight?

重量是多少？zhong^{4}liang^4 shi^4 duo^{1}shao^3?

It weighs two kilograms, or four Chinese *jin*.

重量是两公斤，四斤。zhong^{4}liang^4 shi^4 liang^3 gong^{1}jin^1, si^4 jin^1.

How much money?

多少钱？duo^{1}shao^3 qian^2?

Four Chinese *jin* are for ￥18.60.

两公斤是十八块六。liang^3 gong^{1}jin^1 shi^4 shi^2 ba^1 kuai^4 liu^4.

How about the nine eggs?

九个鸡蛋呢？jiu^3 ge^4 ji^{1}dan^4 ne?

Eggs are at ￥3.70 for half a kilogram.

鸡蛋的价钱是每斤三块七。ji^{1}dan^4 de jia^{4}qian shi^4 mei^3 jin^1 san^1 kuai^4 qi^1.

9 eggs are 550 grams, for ￥4.07.

九个鸡蛋是一斤一两，要四块零七分。jiu^3 ge^4 ji^{1}dan^4 shi^4 yi^1 jin^1 yi^1 liang^3 yao^4 si^4 kuai^4 ling^2 qi^1 fen^1.

Do you want anything else?

还要别的吗？hai^2 yao^4 bie^2 de ma^1?

Other or else 别的 bie^2 de

Anything else?

还要别的吗？hai^2 yao^4 bie^2 de ma^1?

Oh, yes! I need some other things.

哦，对了！还要一些东西。o^4, dui^4 le! hai^2 yao^4 yi^1 xie^1 dong^{1}xi.

What? 什么？shen^{2}me?

Vegetable, meat, and fish. 蔬菜、肉和鱼。shu^{1}cai^4 rou^4 he^2 yu^2.

What vegetable?

什么蔬菜？shen^{2}me shu^{1}cai^4?

Carrot, onion, and cabbage.

胡萝卜、洋葱、白菜。hu^2 luo^{2}bo yang^{2}cong^1 bai^{2}cai^4.

Anything else?

还有吗？hai^2 you^3 ma^1?

And cucumber and tomato.

还有黄瓜和西红柿。hai^2 you^3 huang^{2}gua^1 he^2 xi^{1}hong^{2}shi^4.

What about meat and fish?
肉和鱼呢？ rou^4 he^2 yu^2 ne?
This kind of fish and that kind of meat.
这种肉，那种鱼。zhe^4 zhong^3 rou^4 na^4 zhong^3 yu^2.
Is that all?
就这些了吧？ jiu^4 zhe^4 xie^1 le ba?
Yes. That's all.
是的。就这些了。shi^4 de jiu^4 zhe^4 xie^1 le.
How much is the total?
一共多少钱？ yi^1 gong^4 duo^{1}shao^3 qian^2?
How much is the total?
总共多少钱？ zong^{3}gong^4 duo^{1}shao^3 qian^2?
Oh, let me see.
哦，让我看看。o^4, rang^4 wo^3 kan^4 kan.
Or literally, let me calculate.
让我算算。rang^4 wo^3 suan^4 suan.
The total is ￥135.02.
一共是一百三十五元零二分。yi^1 gong^4 shi^4 yi^1 bai^3 san^1 shi^2 wu^3 yuan^2 ling^2 er^4 fen^1
Here is ￥150.00.
这是一百五十块。zhe^4 shi^4 yi^1 bai^3 wu^3 shi^2 kuai^4.
All right! Here is your change, ￥14.98.
这是找给您的，十四块九毛八。zhe^2 shi^4 zhao^3 gei^3 nin^2 de shi^2 si^4 kuai^4 jiu^3 mao^2 ba^1.
Thank you!
谢谢！ xie^{4}xie!
Not at all.
没什么。mei^2 shen^{2}me.

LESSON 10 第十课

PLEASE
请……QING^3...

The third-tone word 请 (qing^3) basically means "please". We can use it before a verb to ask somebody to do something politely.

Please enter, or please come in or go in.
请进。qing^3 jin^4.
Please sit, or please take a seat.
请坐。qing^3 zuo^4.
Please listen or hear.
请听。qing^3 ting^1.
Please speak, or please say it.
请说。qing^3 shuo^1.
Please read.
请读。qing^3 du^2.
Please write.
请写。qing^3 xie^3.
Please look.
请看。qing^3 kan^4.
Please ask.
请问。qing^3 wen^4.
Or
Please allow me to ask...
请问……qing^3 wen^4...

Here we have a very special case, that is, 请问 can mean both "please ask" and "please allow me to ask", depending on the context. Besides, 请 also means "to invite" or "to ask". When used to the second person as a request, the personal pronoun can be omitted. Let's learn its different uses with more examples.

Please come in.
请进来。qing^3 jin^{4}lai^2.
Ask him to come in, or invite him in.

请他进来。qing^3 ta^1 jin^{4}lai^2.
I ask you to answer, or invite you to give an answer.
请你回答。qing^3 ni^3 hui^{2}da^2.
I want to invite you for a coffee.
我想请你喝咖啡。wo^3 xiang^3 qing^3 ni^3 he^1 ka^{1}fei^1.
I want to invite you for dinner, or I want to treat you to dinner.
我想请你吃饭。wo^3 xiang^3 qing^3 ni^3 chi^1 fan^4.
I want to invite you for dinner, or treat you to dinner.
我想请你吃饭。wo^3 xiang^3 qing^3 ni^3 chi^1 fan^4.
I ask you, or invite you to translate it.
请你翻译。qing^3 ni^3 fan^{1}yi^4.
Ask him to translate.
请他翻译。qing^3 ta^1 fan^{1}yi^4.
Ask the teacher to explain.
请老师解释。qing^3 lao^{3}shi^1 jie^{3}shi^4.
Please say it once more.
请再说一遍。qing^3 zai^4 shuo^1 yi^1 bian^4.
Please ask him to say it again.
请他再说一遍。qing^3 ta^1 zai^4 shuo^1 yi^1 bian^4.
Or
Please ask him to repeat once.
请他再重复一遍。qing^3 ta^1 zai^4 chong^{2}fu^4 yi^1 bian^4.
Please ask him to wait a while.
请他等一下。qing^3 ta^1 deng^3 yi^1 xia^4.
Please ask him to wait just a short while.
请他稍等。qing^3 ta^1 shao^1 deng^3.
I ask or invite you to listen.
我请你听。wo^3 qing^3 ni^3 ting^1.
I ask or invite you to listen. (Formal)
我请您听。wo^3 qing^3 nin^2 ting^1
I ask or invite you to wait.
请您等等。qing^3 nin^2 deng^3 deng^3.
Ask him to speak or say.
请他说。qing^3 ta^1 shuo^1.
You ask or invite him to speak or say.
你请他说。ni^3 qing^3 ta^1 shuo^1.
Ask or invite her to read.
请她读。qing^3 ta^1 du^2.
I ask her or invite her to read.
我请她读。wo^3 qing^3 ta^1 du^2.

I ask you, or invite you to write.
请你写。qing^3 ni^3 xie^3.
I ask you to write.
我请你写。wo^3 qing^3 ni^3 xie^3.
I ask you, or invite you to look.
请你看。qing^3 ni^3 kan^4.
I ask you to look.
我请你看。wo^3 qing^3 ni^3 kan^4.
I ask you, or invite you to ask.
请你问。qing^3 ni^3 wen^4.
Or, simply—
Please ask.
请问。qing^3 wen^4.
I ask you or invite you to ask.
我请你问。wo^3 qing^3 ni^3 wen^4.
Please begin.
请开始。qing^3 kai^{1}shi^3.
Ask him to begin.
请他开始。qing^3 ta^1 kai^{1}shi^3.
Please remember.
请记住。qing^3 ji^{4}zhu^4.
I ask you to remember.
请你记住。qing^3 ni^3 ji^{4}zhu^4.

All right! Let's now look at a special difference between two expressions of the same meaning.

Please enter.
请进。qing^3 jin^4.
Please come in.
请进来。qing^3 jin^{4}lai.

The word 进 literally translates as the English "enter", and 进来 reverses the word order of "come in". The word for "come"— 来 is actually used as a verbal complement to 进. Let's listen to more such constructs that reverse the word order of the English literal translation.

Please come in.
请进来。qing^3 jin^{4}lai.
Please go in.
请进去。qing^3 jin^{4}qu^4.
Please come out.
请出来。qing^3 chu^{1}lai.

Please go out.
请出去。qing^3 chu^{1}qu.
Please come over, or please come here.
请过来。qing^3 guo^{4}lai.
Please go over, or please go there.
请过去。qing^3 guo^{4}qu.
Please go up.
请上去。qing^3 shang^{4}qu.
Please come up.
请上来。qing^3 shang^{4}lai.
Please go down.
请下去。qing^3 xia^{4}qu.
Please come down.
请下来。qing^3 xia^{4}lai.

In the examples above, the words 上 and 下 can also be used as verbal complements. Let's listen to some examples.

Please close the window, or literally, please "shut up" the window.
请关上窗。qing^3 guan^{1}shang^4 chuang^1.
Please sit down.
请坐下。qing^3 zuo^{4}xia^4.
Please lie down.
请躺下。qing^3 tang^{3}xia^4.
Please stop.
请停下。qing^3 ting^{2}xia^4.
Please close the door.
请关上门。qing^3 guan^1 shang^4 men^2.
Please sit down.
请坐下。qing^3 zuo^{4}xia^4.
Or
请坐下来。qing^3 zuo^{4}xia^{4}lai.

In the examples above, 下来 acts as a verbal complement with basically the same meaning as the single-syllable word 下. However, it is important to note that its antonym 下去 makes a special construct that has an even more important adverbial function. Let's listen to the following:

Go on listening... Or, as I go on listening...
听下去…… ting^1 xia^{4}qu...
Keep on watching... Or, as I carry on watching...
看下去…… kan^4 xia^{4}qu...
Keep on talking... Or, as I go on talking...
说下去…… shuo^1 xia^{4}qu…

Go on learning or studying… Or, as I carry on studying it...

学下去…… xue2 xia4qu…

I will carry on listening.

我要听下去。wo3 yao4 ting1 xia4qu.

I want to carry on reading.

我想读下去。wo3 xiang3yao4 du4 xia4qu.

Please note that this structure equally applies to 上去, but with a change in the meaning.

It sounds... Or, as I come to listen to it...

听上去…… ting1 shang4qu...

It looks… Or, as I come to look at it...

看上去…… kan4 shang4qu...

Mandarin Chinese sounds beautiful.

汉语听上去很美。han4yu3 ting1 shang4qu4 hen3 mei3.

This book looks very good.

这本书看上去很好。zhe4 ben3 shu1 kan4 shang4qu4 hen3 hao3.

All right! With these examples, we have learned the use of 上去 and 下去 as verbal complements. Now, it may be necessary to know another verbal complement that is opposite in meaning to 下去. This is:

起来 qi3lai

This verb primarily means "to rise" or "to get up", but here it acts as a verbal complement, meaning that the action of the preceding verb is starting. And, as a complement, it would use the light tone.

Start to learn, or as we start to learn...

学起来 xue2 qi3lai.

Chinese is not difficult when we begin.

中文学起来不难。zhong1wen2 xue2 qi3lai2 bu4 nan2.

But it is not easy to carry on with it or go deeper.

但是学下去不容易。dan4shi4 xue2 xia4qu bu4 rong2yi4.

But it's not easy.

但是，不容易。dan4shi4, bu4 rong2yi4.

Go on learning, carry on with it, or go further in learning it.

学下去…… xue2 xia4qu...

But it's not easy to carry on, or go deeper.

但是学下去不容易。dan4shi4 xue2 xia4qu bu4 rong2yi4.

Chinese is easy to speak, but hard to read.

中文说起来容易读起来难。zhong1wen2 shuo1 qi3lai rong2yi4 du2 qi3lai nan2.

It's easier to say than to do, or it is easier said than done.

说起来容易做起来难。shuo1 qi3lai2 rong2yi4 zuo4 qi3lai nan2.

It is easier to start than to carry on.
做起来容易做下去难。zuo4 qi3lai rong2yi4 zuo4 xia4qu nan2.
Chinese characters are easy to read, but hard to write.
汉字读起来容易写起来难。han4zi4 du2 qi3lai rong2yi4 xie3 qi3lai nan2.
It's a long story to tell.
说起来话长。shuo1 qi3lai hua4 chang2.
I'm happy to think of it.
我想起来就愉快。Wo3 xiang3 qi3lai jiu4 yu2kuai4.

OK! After learning so many verbs and verbal phrases while practicing, we probably need to know another word to substitute for the word 请 which we can use when there is no need to stand on ceremony. This word means "let" or "allow". Let's listen and repeat it:

让 rang4
Let him in.
让他进来。rang4 ta1 jin4lai2.
Let him come over.
让他过来。rang4 ta1 guo4lai2.
Let him go, or let him leave.
让他走。rang4 ta1 zou3.
I ask you to answer.
我让你回答。wo3 rang4 ni3 hui2da2.
Let me think, or let me see.
让我想想。rang4 wo3 xiang3 xiang3.
The teacher asked me to think for a while.
老师让我想一想。lao3shi1 rang4 wo3 xiang3yi1 xiang3.
Or
老师让我想想。lao3shi1 rang4 wo3 xiang3xiang3

In fact, 让 and 请 can be used together in a sentence to form a typical verbal chain in Chinese, as in the following:

He asks me to ask you to wait a while.
他让我请你等等。ta1 rang4 wo3 qing3 ni3 deng3deng3.
I ask you to invite the guest to sit down.
我让你请朋友坐下。wo3 rang4 ni3 qing3 peng2you3 zuo4 xia4.

Interestingly, the word order in this chain can be changed.

He asks me to ask you to wait a while.
他请我让你等等。ta1 qing3 wo3 rang4 ni3 deng3deng3.
I ask you to invite the guest to sit down.
我请你让朋友坐下。wo3 qing3 ni3 rang4 peng2you3 zuo4 xia4.

In the above cases, the order of 让 and 请 are often interchangeable.

He asks me to ask you to wait a while.

他请我让你等等。ta^{1} qing^{3} wo^{3}rang^{4} ni^{3} deng^{3}deng^{3}.

I ask you to invite the guest to sit down.

我请你让朋友坐下。wo^{3} qing^{3} ni^{3}rang^{4} peng^{2}you^{3} zuo^{4} xia^{4}.

When asking somebody not to do something, we can directly use 不要 after the word 请.

Please don't...

请不要…… qing^{3} bu^{1}yao^{4}...

Please don't talk.

请不要说话。qing^{3} bu^{1}yao^{4} shuo^{1}hua^{4}.

Please don't go.

请不要走。qing^{3} bu^{1}yao^{4} zou^{3}.

Please don't go there.

请不要去那里。qing^{3} bu^{1}yao^{4} qu^{4} na^{4}li^{3}.

Please don't come.

请不要来。qing^{3} bu^{1}yao^{4} lai^{2}.

Please don't come here.

请不要来这里。qing^{3} bu^{1}yao^{4} lai^{2} zhe^{4}li^{3}.

Please don't stop.

请不要停。qing^{3} bu^{1}yao^{4} ting^{2}.

Please don't listen.

请不要听。qing^{3} bu^{1}yao^{4} ting^{1}.

Please don't smoke here.

请不要在这里吸烟。qing^{3} bu^{1}yao^{4} zai^{4} zhe^{4}li^{3} xi^{1}yan^{1}.

Please don't ask him.

请不要问他。qing^{3} bu^{1}yao^{4} wen^{4} ta^{1}.

All right! Now we should also know that there are two other single-character words in Chinese for expressing the same meaning of 不要.

The first one is relatively informal. It is:

别 bie^{2}

Please don't talk.

请别说话。qing^{3} bie^{2} shuo^{1}hua^{4}.

Please don't smoke.

请别吸烟。qing^{3} bie^{2} xi^{1}yan^{1}.

Don't go, or don't leave.

别走。bie^{2} zou^{3}.

Don't ask.

别问。bie^{2} wen^{4}.

Don't go there.

别去那里。bie^{2} qu^{4} na^{4}li^{3}.

Please don't come in.

请别进来。qing^3 bie^2 jin^{4}lai^2.

Don’t stop.

别停下。bie^2 ting^{2}xia^4.

The second word to use for the same meaning of 不要 is the single-syllable word— 勿 (wu^4). It is very formal and mainly used in writing, especially in public signs and posters. For example:

No smoking.

请勿吸烟。qing^3 wu^4 xi^{1}yan^1.

Keep clear distance, or literally, please don’t get close.

请勿靠近。qing^3 wu^4 kao^{4}jin^4.

No photos, or literally, no shooting photographs.

请勿拍照。qing^3 wu^4 pai^{1}zhao^4.

Of course, in places where public signs like the above are used, you may also find another word in use for the same effect. This is:

To prohibit

禁止 jin^{4}zhi^3

No smoking.

禁止吸烟。jin^{4}zhi^3 xi^{1}yan^1.

No photos.

禁止拍照。jin^{4}zhi^3 pai^{1}zhao^4.

No parking, or no stopping.

禁止停车。Jin^{4}zhi^3 ting^{2}che^1.

Or, to mean only “No parking” and not “No stopping”, we can say—

禁止泊车。Jin^{4}zhi^{3}po^{1}che^1.

OK! Now, after learning these expressions of the negative request, we should remember that when asking somebody for information, we can begin the question by saying 请问, simply to show courtesy.

Excuse me...

请问……qing^3 wen^4...

Excuse me. May I ask who he is?

请问，他是谁？qing^3 wen^4, ta^1 shi^4 shui^2?

Let’s compare the two different explanations of the same word 请问。

If you have questions, please ask.

如果你有问题，请问。ru^{2}guo^3 ni^3 you^3 wen^{4}ti^2, qing^3 wen^4.

May I ask what your name is?

Or

Excuse me, what’s your name?

请问，您叫什么名字？qing^3 wen^4, nin^2 jiao^4 shen^{2}me ming^{2}zi?

May I ask what your phone number is? Or, excuse me, what’s your phone number?

请问，您的电话是什么？qing^3 wen^4, nin^2 de dian^{4}hua^4 shi^4 shen^{2}me?

May I ask where you live?

请问，您住在哪里？qing^3 wen^4, nin^2 zhu^4 zai^4 na^{3}li^3?

Another point to remember is that in Chinese there is often the need to use a measure word as a complement of the main verb, just to make a sentence feel complete, such as the following:

Literally, once 一下 yi^1 xia^4

Or

一次 yi^1 ci^4

Or

一遍 yi^1 bian^4

Among these three expressions, 一下 and 一次 have basically the same meaning and are interchangeable; but 一遍 also implies an act of "going through" or "going from beginning to end". Let's listen to more examples as we review:

I ask you, or invite you to listen.

请你听一下。qing^3 ni^3 ting^1 yi^1 xia^4.

I ask you, or invite you to read.

请你读一下。qing^3 ni^3 du^2 yi^1 xia^4.

I ask you, or invite you to wait a moment or a while.

请您等一下。qing^3 nin^2 deng^3 yi^1 xia^4.

I ask you, or invite you to listen once more.

请你再听一遍。qing^3 ni^3 zai^4 ting^1 yi^1 bian^4.

I ask you to read it once more.

我请你再读一遍。wo^3 qing^3 ni^3 zai^4 du^2 yi^1 bian^4.

I ask you, or invite you to it again.

请你再说一遍。qing^3 ni^3 zai^4 shuo^1 yi^1 bian^4.

I ask you to say it once more.

我请你再说一遍。wo^3 qing^3 ni^3 zai^4 shuo^1 yi^1 bian^4.

I ask you, or invite you to repeat it once.

请你重复一遍。qing^3 ni^3 chong^{2}fu^4 yi^1 bian^4.

I ask you to repeat it once again.

我请你再重复一遍。wo^3 qing^3 ni^3 zai^4 chong^{2}fu^4 yi^1 bian^4.

They ask you to repeat twice.

他们请你重复两遍。ta^{1}men qing^3 ni^3 chong^{2}fu^4 liang^3 bian^4.

We ask you to translate it.

我们请你翻译一下。wo^{3}men qing^3 ni^3 fan^{1}yi^4 yi^1 xia^4.

We ask you to translate it once.

我们请你翻译一遍。wo^{3}men qing^3 ni^3 fan^{1}yi^4 yi^1 bian^4.

I ask you, or invite you to give an explanation. Or simply, please explain.

请你解释一下。qing^{3} ni^{3} jie^{3}shi^{4} yi^{1} xia^{4}.

We ask you to give an explanation.

我们请你解释一下。wo^{3}men qing^{3} ni^{3} jie^{3}shi^{4} yi^{1} xia^{4}.

We ask you to explain again.

我们请你再解释一遍。wo^{3}men qing^{3} ni^{3} zai^{4} jie^{3}shi^{4} yi^{1} bian^{4}.

I ask you, or invite you to say it again.

请你再说一次。qing^{3} ni^{3} zai^{4} shuo^{1} yi^{1} ci^{4}.

I ask you, or invite you to review this lesson.

请你把这一课复习一下。qing^{3} ni^{3} ba^{3} zhe^{4} yi^{1} ke^{4} fu^{4}xi^{2} yi^{1} xia^{4}.

I ask you to say it again, or I ask you to repeat.

我请你再说一遍。wo^{3} qing^{3} ni^{3} zai^{4} shuo^{1} yi^{1} bian^{4}.

The Chinese measure words can be very changeable. For instance, if a two-syllable verb is composed of a verb plus an object, then we can insert a measure word between them, as in the following:

Read, or read the book 看书 kan^{4} shu^{1}

Read for a while 看一会儿书 kan^{4} yi^{1} hui^{3}er shu^{1}

Chat 聊天 liao^{2} tian^{1}

Chat for a while 聊一会儿天 liao^{2} yi^{1} hui^{3}er tian^{1}

Talk or speak 说话 shuo^{1} hua^{4}

Talk or speak for a while 说一会儿话 shuo^{1} yi^{1} hui^{3}er hua^{4}

Eat or have a meal 吃饭 chi^{1} fan^{4}

Have dinner or eat dinner 吃一顿饭 chi^{1} yi^{1} dun^{4} fan^{4}

Get on the internet or use the internet 上网 shang^{4} wang^{3}

Use the internet for a while 上一会儿网 shang^{4} yi^{1}hui^{3}er wang^{3}

Play a ball game 打球 da^{3} qiu^{2}

Play "a round of" a ball game 打一场球 da^{3} yi^{1} chang^{3} qiu^{2}

Have a meeting or conference 开会 kai^{1} hui^{4}

Have a meeting, or literally, have a time of meeting 开一次会 kai^{1} yi^{1} ci^{4} hui^{4}

Have a class 上课 shang^{4} ke^{4}

Have a class, or literally, have one period of a class 上一节课 shang^{4} yi^{1} jie^{2} ke^{4}

This general rule also applies to the verbal phrase that has an object word consisting of more than one syllable. Let's take a basic Chinese verb and see how this rule works:

打 da^{3}

Although this verb has the meaning "to beat", "to strike", or "to attack", we can also use it to mean "to play".

Play poker
打扑克牌 da3 pu1ke4pai2
Or
打扑克 da3 pu1ke4
Play poker for a while
打一会儿扑克 da3 yi1hui3er pu1ke4
打一会儿扑克牌 da3 yi1hui3er pu1ke4pai2
Play basketball
打篮球 da3 lan2qiu2
Play basketball for a while
打一会儿篮球 da3 yi1hui3er lan2qiu2
Play "a round of" basketball
打一场篮球 da3 yi1 chang3 lan2qiu2
Play tennis
打网球 da3 wang3qiu2
Play "a round of" tennis
打一场网球 da3 yi1 chang3 wang3qiu2
Play golf
打高尔夫 da3 gao1er3fu1
Play golf for a while
打一会儿高尔夫 da3 yi1 hui3er gao1er3fu1
Play football, or literally, kick football
踢足球 ti1 zu2qiu2
Play football, or literally, kick football for a while
踢一会儿足球 ti1 yi1 hui3er zu2qiu2
Listen to a concert
听音乐会 ting1 yin1yue4hui4
Listen to a concert, or literally, "a round of" concert
听一场音乐会 ting1 yi1 chang3 yin1yue4hui4
See a movie
看电影 kan4 dian4ying3
See a movie, or literally, see "a round of" movie
看一场电影 kan4 yi1 chang3 dian4ying3
Watch a video
看视频 kan4 shi4pin2
Watch a video, or watch a video for a while.
看一会儿视频 kan4 yi1 hui3er shi4pin2
Watch a football game, or literally, watch a football game
看一会儿足球比赛 kan4 yi1 hui3er zu2qiu2 bi3sai4

All right! Now that you have a good understanding of the measure word, let's come back to the uses of 请. With this word, we can express our willingness to treat somebody to food or something enjoyable. Here are some examples.

Literally, invite a guest, or give somebody a treat

请客 qing^{3} ke^{4}

I'll give it as a treat, or I'll pay for it as a treat, or it's on me.

我请客。wo^{3} qing^{3} ke^{4}.

I'll give you a treat, or it's my treat.

我请你。wo^{3} qing^{3} ni^{3}.

Literally, eat a meal, or simply, eat

吃饭 chi^{1} fan^{4}

I'll treat you to a meal.

我请你吃饭。wo^{3} qing^{3} ni^{3} chi^{1} fan^{4}.

Drink tea

喝茶 he^{1} cha^{2}

I'll treat you to some tea.

我请你喝茶。wo^{3} qing^{3} ni^{3} he^{1} cha^{2}.

Drink coffee

喝咖啡 he^{1} ka^{1}fei^{1}

I'll treat you to a coffee.

我请你喝咖啡。wo^{3} qing^{3} ni^{3} he^{1} ka^{1}fei^{1}.

See a movie

看电影 kan^{4} dian^{4}ying^{3}

I'll treat you to a movie.

我请你看电影。wo^{3} qing^{3} ni^{3} kan^{4} dian^{4}ying^{3}.

I would like to invite you to a movie as a treat.

我想请你看一场电影。wo^{3} xiang^{3} qing^{3} ni^{3} kan^{4} yi^{1} chang^{3} dian^{4}ying^{3}.

Literally, I would like to invite you to play "a round of" basketball as a treat.

我想请你打一场篮球。wo^{3} xiang^{3} qing^{3} ni^{3} da^{3} yi^{1} chang^{3} lan^{2}qiu^{2}.

Literally, I would like to invite you to play "a round of" football as a treat.

我要请你踢一场足球。wo^{3} yao^{4} qing^{3} ni^{3} ti^{1} yi^{1} chang^{3} zu^{2}qiu^{2}.

I'll invite you to see a football game as a treat, or I'll treat you to a football game.

我要请你看一场足球比赛。wo^{3} yao^{4} qing^{3} ni^{3} kan^{4} yi^{1} chang^{3} zu^{2}qiu^{2} bi^{3}sai^{4}.

As we know, the Chinese measure words are highly customary and should be gradually learned following the example of the native speaker. Let's hear more such words.

I'd like to offer you a cup of tea.
我要请你喝一杯茶。wo^{3} yao^{4} qing^{3} ni^{3} he^{1} yi^{1} bei^{1} cha^{2}.
I'd like to offer you a cigarette.
我要请你抽一只烟。wo^{3} yao^{4} qing^{3} ni^{3} chou^{1} yi^{1} zhi^{1} yan^{1}.
In the above, "to take a cigarette" is—
抽一只烟 chou^{1} yi^{1} zhi^{1} yan^{1}

The word 抽 literally means "draw", which is interchangeable with the word "inhale"— 吸 (xi^{1}); 只 is a measure word for something that appears thin and long.

I'd like to offer you a cigarette.
我要请你抽一只烟。wo^{3} yao^{4} qing^{3} ni^{3} chou^{1} yi^{1} zhi^{1} yan^{1}.
我要请你吸一只烟。wo^{3} yao^{4} qing^{3} ni^{3} xi^{1} yi^{1} zhi^{1} yan^{1}.
I'd like to treat you to a glass of wine.
我要请你喝一杯酒。wo^{3} yao^{4} qing^{3} ni^{3} he^{1} yi^{1} bei^{1} jiu^{3}.
I'd like to treat you to a meal.
我要请你吃一顿饭。wo^{3} yao^{4} qing^{3} ni^{3} chi^{1} yi^{1} dun^{4} fan^{4}.
I'd like to invite you to see an opera.
我要请你看一台京剧。wo^{3} yao^{4} qing^{3} ni^{3} kan^{4} yi^{1} tai^{2} jing^{1}ju^{4}.

Being highly customary, the use of measure words can be hard for learners of Chinese. However, if you can't be sure which word to use, you could at least try the most general word 一个, and drop the number 一.

I'd like to offer you a cup of tea.
我要请你喝个茶。wo^{3} yao^{4} qing^{3} ni^{3} he^{1} ge^{4} cha^{2}.
I'd like to offer you a cigarette.
我要请你抽个烟。wo^{3} yao^{4} qing^{3} ni^{3} chou^{1} ge^{4} yan^{1}.
I'd like to treat you to a glass of wine.
我要请你喝个酒。wo^{3} yao^{4} qing^{3} ni^{3} chou^{1} ge^{4} jiu^{3}.
I'd like to treat you to dinner.
我要请你吃个饭。wo^{3} yao^{4} qing^{3} ni^{3} chi^{1} ge^{4} fan^{4}.

Of course, we still remember the word 请 can mean "ask", "invite", "treat", or simply "please". Its particular meaning should be understood in the particular context of use. Let's hear the following:

I ask you, or invite you to come in.
请你进来。qing^{3} ni^{3} jin^{4}lai^{2}.
I ask you, or invite you to come in and sit for a while.
请你进来坐坐。qing^{3} ni^{3} jin^{4}lai^{2} zuo^{4}zuo.
Ask him to come up.

请他过来。qing^{3} ta^{1} guo^{4}lai^{2}.

Ask him to come up and chat for a while.

请他过来聊聊。qing^{3} ta^{1} guo^{4}lai^{2} liao^{2}liao.

Or

请他过来聊聊天。qing^{3} ta^{1} guo^{4}lai^{2} liao^{2}liao tian^{1}.

Here, the single-syllable word 聊 can be understood as the short form of 聊天, and 天 could be seen as the object of 聊. For this reason, we can say—

请他过来聊聊天。qing^{3} ta^{1} guo^{4}lai^{2} liao^{2}liao tian^{1}.

I ask or invite you (plural) to please come up and have a look.

请你们过来看看。qing^{3} ni^{3}men guo^{4}lai^{2} kan^{4}kan.

I ask you, or invite you to come up and see this video for a while.

请你们过来看看这个视频。qing^{3} ni^{3}men guo^{4}lai^{2} kan^{4}kan zhe^{4} ge^{4} shi^{4}pin^{2}.

Ask them to come down and listen for a while.

请他们下来听听。qing^{3} ta^{1}men xia^{4}lai^{2} ting^{1}ting.

Ask them to come down and listen to this music for a while.

请他们下来听听这个音乐。qing^{3} ta^{1}men xia^{4}lai^{2} ting^{1}ting zhe^{4} ge^{4} yin^{1}yue^{4}.

All right. Now, after learning so many words and phrases, I would ask you to review this lesson for a while.

I ask you to review this lesson for a while.

我请你复习复习这一课。wo^{3} qing^{3} ni^{3} fu^{4}xi^{2} fu^{4}xi^{2} zhe^{4} yi^{1} ke^{4}.

Or

我请你复习一下这一课。wo^{3} qing^{3} ni^{3} fu^{4}xi^{2} yi^{1} xia^{4} zhe^{4} yi^{1} ke^{4}.

Or

我请你把这一课复习一下。wo^{3} qing^{3} ni^{3} ba^{3} zhe^{4} yi^{1} ke^{4} fu^{4}xi^{2} yi^{1} xia^{4}.

LESSON 11 第十一课

MEETING PEOPLE
会见 HUI^{4}JIAN^4

In introducing ourselves or our friends when meeting new people, we would use two interchangeable Chinese single-character words, which are as follows—

是 shi^4

And—

叫 jiao^4

Here the word 是 can be used as an equivalent to all forms of the English verb "to be", while 叫 literally corresponds to the English "to call" or "to name".

I am…

我是…… wo^3 shi^4...

I'm named or called, or my name is...

我叫…… wo^3 jiao^4...

Although the word for "my name" is not always necessary, you can use it if you want.

My name is...

我的名字是……wo^3 de^1 ming^{2}zi^4 shi^4...

Or

我的名字叫……wo^3 de^1 ming^{2}zi^4 jiao^4...

As we see, there are a few alternatives to use in this situation.

我是……wo^3 shi^4...

我叫……wo^3 jiao^4...

我的名字是……wo^3 de^1 ming^{2}zi^4 shi^4...

我名字叫……wo^3 ming^{2}zi^4 jiao^4...

Needless to say, the subject word can be changed to another person.

He is…

他是……ta^1 shi^4...

His name is… 他叫……ta^1 jiao^4...

他的名字是……ta^1 de^1 ming^{2}zi^4 shi^4...

他的名字叫……ta^{1} de^{1} ming^{2}zi^{4} jiao^{4}...

As a matter of fact, the word 叫 is not always exactly the same as the English "call", because in Chinese we need make clear if it is a call by telephone or not. Let's listen to the following:

Make a telephone call
打电话 da^{3} dian^{4}hua^{4}
Call by telephone for somebody to come
打电话叫 da^{3} dian^{4}hua^{4} jiao^{4}
Call him here by telephone
打电话叫他 da^{3} dian^{4}hua^{4} jiao^{4} ta^{1}
Or
打电话叫他来 da^{3} dian^{4}hua^{4} jiao^{4} ta^{1} lai^{2}
Call for the police by telephone
打电话叫警察 da^{3} dian^{4}hua^{4} jiao^{4} jing^{3}cha^{2}
Or
打电话叫警察来 da^{3} dian^{4}hua^{4} jiao^{4} jing^{3}cha^{2} lai^{2}

Furthermore, the word 叫 can mean either "ask" or "allow", depending on the context. In this case it is even more informal.

Ask him to start work.
叫他开始工作。jiao^{4} ta^{1} kai^{1}shi^{3} gong^{1}zuo^{4}.
Allow or let him sleep.
叫他睡。jiao^{4} ta^{1} shui^{4}.

OK! After explaining these important words, we can now continue with expressions used in meeting people.

Hello! I am …
您好！我是… nin^{2} hao^{3}! wo^{3} shi^{4}...
I'm Li Xiaoming.
我是李小明。wo^{3} shi^{4} li^{3}xiao^{3}ming^{2}.
This is my friend.
这是我的朋友。zhe^{4} shi^{4} wo^{3} de^{1} peng^{2}you^{3}.
His name is Zhang Tianming.
他的名字叫张天明。ta^{1} de^{1} ming^{2}zi^{1} jiao^{4} zhang^{1} tian^{1}ming^{2}.
He is my best friend.
他是我最好的朋友。ta^{1} shi^{4} wo^{3} zui^{4}hao^{3} de^{1} peng^{2}you^{3}.

After giving your own name, you may of course ask—

And you?
您呢？nin^{2} ne?
Or
您的名字呢？nin^{2} de^{1} ming^{2}zi^{1} ne?

As we see, the function of the word 呢 is to make the sentence short by omission. This is very much like the function of the English connective "and" or "and what about". However, 呢 can also add to the meaning of the sentence quite a few special nuances, such as expressing readiness and eagerness to carry on with the conversation, showing curiosity, and emphasizing what is said. Its particular meaning is highly dependent on the context. And question marks may apply in some cases. Let's look at some examples.

And later? And what happened later?
后来呢？ hou^{4}lai^{2} ne?
And then?
然后呢？ ran^{2}hou^{4} ne?
Go on speaking.
说呢。 shuo^{1} ne.
What do you say? Or, what is your opinion, then?
你说呢？ ni^{3} shuo^{1} ne?
What about the police? Or, where are the police?
警察呢？ jing^{3}cha^{2} ne?
How difficult to explain! Or, how embarrassing to explain!
怎么说呢！ zen^{3}me shuo^{1} ne!
What can we say about it? Or, it's a shame to mention it!
让人怎么说呢! rang^{4} ren^{2} zen^{3}me shuo^{1} ne!
Literally, he has not yet come, indeed, or for sure, he has not yet come.
他还没来呢！ ta^{1} hai^{2} mei^{2}lai^{2} ne!
But he is still on his way, for sure.
他还在路上呢！ ta^{1} hai^{2} zai^{4} lu^{4}shang^{4} ne!
Literally, what are you talking about, in the end?
你们在说什么呢？ ni^{3}men zai^{4} shuo^{1} shen^{2}me ne?
Literally, but it's not yet time, for sure!
还没到时间呢！ hai^{2} mei^{2} dao^{4} shi^{2}jian^{1} ne!
I haven't yet eaten, really!
我还没吃过呢！ wo^{3} hai^{2} mei^{2} chi^{1} guo^{4} ne!

OK! As we see, although 呢 is often used at the end of a question, it is nevertheless not always a question maker like the word 吗. And so, it is not always necessary.

But what is his name?
他叫什么名字呢？ ta^{1} jiao^{4} shen^{2}me ming^{2}zi^{1} ne?
What's his name?
他叫什么名字？ ta^{1} jiao^{4} shen^{2}me ming^{2}zi^{1}?

Literally, is he your friend, ultimately?
他是不是你的朋友呢？ ta^{1} shi^{4} bu^{4} shi^{4} ni^{3} de peng^{2}you^{3} ne?
Is he your friend?
他是不是你的朋友？ ta^{1} shi^{4} bu^{1} shi^{4} ni^{3} de peng^{2}you^{3}?

On the other hand, 吗 is a question maker and omitting it would change the interrogative sentence back into an indicative one. For example:

Is he your friend?
他是你的朋友吗？ ta^{1} shi^{4} ni^{3} de peng^{2}you^{3} ma^{1}?
He is your friend.
他是你的朋友。ta^{1} shi^{4} ni^{3} de peng^{2}you^{3}.

Let's compare more sentences:

Is it? Or, really? Or, is that right?
是吗？ shi^{4} ma^{1}?
Is it? Or, isn't it?
是不是？ shi^{4} bu^{1} shi^{4}?
是不是呢？ shi^{4} bu^{1} shi^{4} ne?
What's your name?
你叫什么名字？ ni^{3} jiao^{4} shen^{2}me ming^{2}zi^{1}?
And what's your name?
你叫什么名字呢？ ni^{3} jiao^{4} shen^{2}me ming^{2}zi^{1} ne?
Is this your name?
这是你的名字吗？ zhe^{4} shi^{4} ni^{3} de ming^{2}zi^{1} ma^{1}?
这是不是你的名字？ zhe^{4} shi^{4} bu^{1} shi^{4} ni^{3} de ming^{2}zi^{1}?
这是不是你的名字呢？ zhe^{4} shi^{4} bu^{1} shi^{4} ni^{3} de^{1} ming^{2}zi^{1} ne?

OK! Let's move on and learn another word for the interrogative "who".

Literally, who is this one? i.e. who is this person?
这是哪位？ zhe^{4} shi^{4} na^{3} wei^{4}?
This is…
这位是..... zhe^{4} wei^{4} shi^{4}...
Who are you? (informal)
您是哪位？ nin^{2} shi^{4} na^{3} wei^{4}?

Here, just as 您 is the formal and polite word for 你, the word 哪位 is the formal and polite way to ask "who" although it translates word-for-word as "which seat" or "which position". So, let's compare the following formal and informal expressions.

Or

And who are you? (formal and polite)
您是哪位呢？ nin^{2} shi^{4} na^{3} wei^{4} ne?

And who are you? (informal and casual)
你是谁呢？ ni^3 shi^4 $shui^2$ ne?

Being formal and polite, the word 哪位 is perhaps more often used with someone you are meeting for the first time. As well as this polite way to ask who a person is, there is a yet more formal way to ask the same question, which literally translates in English as—

Literally, dare I ask for your respected surname and great given name?
敢问尊姓大名？ gan^3 wen^4 zun^1xing^4 da^4ming^2?
Dare to ask 敢问 gan^3 wen^4
Respected surname 尊姓 zun^1xing^4
Great or big name 大名 da^4ming^2
Dare I ask your respected surname and great given name?
敢问尊姓大名？ gan^3 wen^4 zun^1xing^4 da^4ming^2?

Sometimes we may only ask for a person's surname. In this case, the formal way to show respect is—

May I ask your noble surname?
请问您贵姓？ $qing^3$ wen^4 nin^2 gui^4xing^4?
Or
May I ask your respected surname?
请问您尊姓？ $qing^3$ wen^4 nin^2 zun^1xing^4?

In the above, 贵姓 is a synonym of 尊姓. While 尊 literally means "respected", 贵 stands for "noble". So you can ask the same question using either word.

请问您尊姓？ $qing^3$ wen^4 nin^2 zun^1xing^4?
请问您贵姓？ $qing^3$ wen^4 nin^2 gui^4xing^4?

In fact, using both 尊 and 贵 is not simply a matter of being formal and serious, but is also understood as a way of showing modesty and courtesy. For this reason, the one who is asked is also expected to show modesty by saying something that literally means—

Don't mention "noble". My family name is Zhang.
免贵，我姓张。 $mian^3$ gui^4, wo^3 $xing^4$ $zhang^1$.

The word 免 means "exempt of" or "without". So the expression 免贵 literally translates as "without nobleness", and can be understood as "there is no need to stand on ceremony". So, let's listen.

There is no need to stand on ceremony. My surname is Zhang, and my given name Li.
免贵，我姓张，名力。 $mian^3$ gui^4, wo^3 $xing^4$ $zhang^1$, $ming^2$ li^4.

However, since 贵姓 and 尊姓大名 are very formal expressions that sound too serious, actually we often simply use the word 请, which can be understood as "may".

May I ask your name?

请问您的姓名？qing^{3} wen^{4} nin^{2} de xing^{4}ming^{2}?

Or, more literally—

Could you please tell me your name?

可以告诉我你的姓名吗？ke^{3}yi^{3} gao^{4}su^{4} wo^{3} ni^{3} de xing^{4}ming^{2} ma^{1}?

Or

可以告诉我你的名字吗？ke^{3}yi^{3} gao^{4}su^{4} wo^{3} ni^{3} de ming^{2}zi^{4} ma^{1}?

Here 可以 is equivalent to the English "may" or "could", and so can also be replaced by 能. The word 告诉 translates as "tell". The subject "you" can be omitted.

Could you tell me your name?

可以告诉我你的名字吗？ke^{3}yi^{3} gao^{4}su^{4} wo^{3} ni^{3} de ming^{2}zi^{4} ma^{1}?

Or

可以不可以告诉我你的名字？ke^{3}yi^{3} bu^{4} ke^{3}yi^{3} gao^{4}su^{4} wo^{3} ni^{3} de ming^{2}zi^{4}?

Or

能不能告诉我你的名字？neng^{2} bu^{4} neng^{2} gao^{4}su^{4} wo^{3} ni^{3} de ming^{2}zi^{4}?

If you have already heard the person's name and just want to make sure it is him or her you that are talking to, then you have several ways to ask the question. One is to use the Chinese tag question pattern of "verb not verb".

您是不是……？nin^{2} shi^{4} bu^{4} shi^{4}...?

Are you Mr. Wang?

您是不是王先生？nin^{2} shi^{4} bu^{4} shi^{4} wang^{2} xian^{1}sheng^{1}?

Another way is to use the question marker 吗 at the end of the sentence.

您是王先生吗？nin^{2} shi^{4} wang^{2} xian^{1}sheng^{1} ma^{1}?

And the third way is to finish the sentence with the word 吧, which functions as a marker of suggestion or guess.

您是王先生吧？nin^{2} shi^{4} wang^{2} xian^{1}sheng^{1} ba?

Or

您就是王先生吧？nin^{2} jiu^{4} shi^{4} wang^{2} xian^{1}sheng^{1} ba?

In the above, the word 就 is an adverb with the same function as the English adverb "just" or "right". And to answer the question, you also have a few choices, as the following:

It's just me.

就是我。jiu^{4} shi^{4} wo^{3}.

Or

Literally, I'm just the one, i.e. I'm exactly that person.

我就是。wo^{3} jiu^{4} shi^{4}.

Just as in English, we can also make the sentences as short as possible. For instance—

Exactly!

就是！ jiu4 shi4!

In fact, the adverb 就 is frequently used as a function word in Chinese. Let's listen to more of its uses.

I'm coming right away.

我就来。wo3 jiu4 lai2.

The train is just arriving.

火车就要到了。huo3che1 jiu4 yao4 dao4 le.

The bus station is right ahead.

公交车站就在前面。gong1jiao1 che1zhan4 jiu4 zai4 qian2mian4.

Our boss will be here right away.

我们的老板马上就到。wo3men de lao3ban3 ma3shang4 jiu4 dao4.

We will have dinner immediately.

我们马上就要吃饭了。wo3men ma3shang4 jiu4yao4 chi1 fan4 le.

The word 马上 literally translates as "on horseback", but it actually means "in no time" or "immediately".

老板马上就到。lao3ban3 ma3shang4 jiu4 dao4.

Or

老板马上到。lao3ban3 ma3shang4 dao4.

OK! Now we have learned so much about the use of the important word 就, let's review the expressions used when meeting people.

Excuse me. Are you Mr. Qian?

请问，您就是钱先生吧？qing3 wen4, nin2 jiu4shi4 qian2 xian1sheng1 ba?

Yes. I'm Mr. Qian.

是，我就是钱先生。shi4, wo3 jiu4shi4 qian2 xian1sheng1.

Or

Yes. I am.

是，我就是。shi4, wo3 jiu4shi4.

Since in Chinese the subject word can be omitted in the given context, you can simply answer—

就是 jiu4shi4

Or

正是 zheng4shi4

Here, 正是 is equivalent in function to 就是, but the word "正" literally means "straight", "right", or "upright" and is more formal in style. Therefore, 正是 can be understood as an equivalent of the English word "exactly".

Excuse me. Are you Mr. Qian?

请问，您就是钱先生吧？qing^{3} wen^{4}, nin^{2} jiu^{4}shi^{4} qian^{2} xian^{1}sheng^{1} ba?

Yes. Exactly.

正是。zheng^{4}shi^{4}.

OK! Let's go on.

Excuse me, which one of you is Mr. Sun?

请问，你们哪位是孙先生？qing^{3} wen^{4}, ni^{3}men na^{3} wei^{4} shi^{4} sun^{2} xian^{1}sheng^{1}?

Or

Which one is Mr. Sun?

孙先生是哪位？sun^{2} xian^{1}sheng^{1} shi^{4} na^{3} wei^{4}?

To this question, the answer is literally—

It's me.

就是我。jiu^{4}shi^{4} wo^{3}.

Or

I am.

我就是。wo^{3} jiu^{4}shi^{4}.

After the introduction, we would usually say the following:

I'm very glad to know you, or it's nice to meet you; or literally, very happy to know you!

很高兴认识您！hen^{3} gao^{1}xing^{4} ren^{4}shi nin^{2}!

Or

认识您很高兴。ren^{4}shi nin^{2} hen^{3} gao^{1}xing^{4}.

Or you can also use the word 能 which means "could" or "can".

很高兴能认识您。hen^{3} gao^{1}xing^{4} neng^{4} ren^{4}shi nin^{2}.

能认识您很高兴。neng^{4} ren^{4}shi nin^{2} hen^{3} gao^{1}xing^{4}.

In fact, there is yet another more formal expression to use in this situation, which literally means "honorable".

很荣幸！hen^{3} rong^{2}xing^{4}!

I feel very honored to know you.

能认识您很荣幸。neng^{4} ren^{4}shi nin^{2} hen^{3} rong^{2}xing^{4}.

Since it's the use in context that determines the part of speech in Chinese, the same word 荣幸 can also serve as a noun.

Knowing you is my honor, or it's my honor to know you.

认识你是我的荣幸。ren^{4}shi ni^{3} shi^{4} wo^{3} de^{4} rong^{2}xing^{4}.

Apart from the above, there is yet another very formal expression to say after the other person has introduced himself or herself, and this is—

久仰！jiu^{3}yang^{3}!

The word 久 means a long time, and 仰 indicates respect. And since repetition is normal in Chinese, you can also say—

久仰久仰！ jiu3yang3 jiu3yang3!

Remember, this is a very formal expression, and its English translation is not to be taken on the superficial meaning of the words. Generally, it indicates that you have heard of the person a lot, and have been looking forward to meeting him or her for a long time. Of course, the same meaning can be expressed in a much less formal way, as the following:

Literally, I have always been looking forward to seeing you, i.e. I have been hoping to meet you for a long time.

我一直希望能见到你。wo3 yi1zhi4 xi1wang4 neng4 jian4dao4 ni3.

Always, all along, all time

一直 yi1zhi4

Hope

希望 xi1wang4

Always hope

一直希望 yi1zhi4 xi1wang4

I have always hoped to be able to meet (lit. see) you.

我一直希望能见到你。wo3 yi1zhi4 xi1wang4 neng4 jian4dao4 ni3.

Sometimes a person may also add something else after the self-introduction, and the most common thing to add is—

请多关照。qing3 duo1 guan1zhao4.

This expression might be understood as "please give me your attention or patronage as a superior"; its meaning is usually not taken literally. In fact, it is a self-deprecatory expression used to show modesty.

请多关照。qing3 duo1 guan1zhao4.

In response to this, the other person is often expected to show modesty too, by saying something like "to each other", "likewise", or "the same to you", which in Chinese is—

彼此彼此。bi3ci3 bi3ci3.

The word 彼 means "the other side", and 此 means "this side", but again they are not to be interpreted literally.

彼此彼此。bi3ci3 bi3ci3.

There are yet two other possible responses to 请多关照. They may be simply understood as "not at all".

The first one is—

哪里哪里! na3li3 na3li3!

And the second is—

哪里的话! na3li3 de hua4!

In spite of the fact that 哪里 is an interrogative word with the basic meaning of "where" or "what place", you should never take its literal meaning in this context. Remember, it's just for the sake of modesty.

In the same context, however, you could also choose to be freer and less formal by using more casual expressions. If so, you might say the following:

Literally, don't be polite, i.e. don't stand on ceremony.

不客气。bu¹ ke⁴qi⁴.

Or

It's unnecessary to stand on ceremony.

不必客气。bu¹ bi⁴ ke⁴qi⁴.

All right! So far, we have learned many words and phrases to use when meeting new friends. Now we also need to learn more for greeting old friends whom we haven't seen for some time. Listen and repeat.

How is everything with you?

你一切好吗？yi¹qie⁴ hao³ ma¹?

As an alternative to this, we can omit the subject.

一切都好吗？yi¹qie⁴ dou¹ hao³ ma¹?

Since the this question in Chinese literally translates as "Is everything OK with you?", you can answer as if you were answering a Yes/No question.

Yes.

都好。dou¹ hao³.

All is not bad.

都不错。dou¹ bu⁴ cuo⁴.

Here the word 不错 doesn't translate literally as "not mistaken", but means "not bad".

不错。

Just so so.

马马虎虎 ma³ma³hu¹hu¹.

Literally "still well", i.e. quite good.

还可以 hai² ke³yi³.

In fact, there are quite a few alternatives to choose from for saying "it's quite good" or "it's not bad", which all have largely the same effect. Listen to the following:

Literally, "still good", or "relatively good".

还好。hai² hao³.

Fairly good.

蛮好。man² hao³.

Quite good.

挺好。ting3 hao3.

Literally, "still not wrong", i.e. not bad, relatively speaking.

还不错。hai2 bu4 cuo4.

Literally, "still can be counted as good", i.e. quite good.

还算不错。hai2 suan4 bu4 cuo4.

Literally, "still can pass", i.e. not so bad.

还过得去。hai2 guo4 de2 qu4.

Literally, "can make do", or "can make ends meet", i.e. not bad.

还凑合。hai2 cou4he.

Of course, with old friends, you often ask some particular questions to show your concern. For example:

How are your health conditions, or how is your health?

身体怎么样？shen1ti3 zen3meyang4?

How is your life there?

那里生活怎么样？na4li3 sheng1huo2 zen3meyang4?

Literally, "is work smooth"? Or, is work going smoothly?

工作顺利吧？gong1zuo4 shun4li4 ba?

Is your family all right?

家里都好吗？jia1 li3 dou1 hao3 ma1?

Or, to be more literal—

Are all your family members all right?

家里人都好吗？jia1 li3 ren2 dou1 hao3 ma1?

How is the weather there?

那里天气怎么样？na4li3 tian1qi4 zen3meyang4?

How is the climate there?

那里气候怎么样？na4li3 qi4hou4 zen3meyang4?

Can you get used to the climate there?

那里气候你能习惯吗？na4li3 qi4hou4 ni3 neng2 xi2guan4 ma1?

Yes. But I cannot adapt to the diet there.

习惯。但是不习惯那里的饮食。 xi2guan4, dan4shi4 bu4 xi2guan4 na4li3 de yin3shi2.

Can you adapt to the life here?

你能适应这里的生活吗？ni3 neng2 shi4ying4 zhe4li3 de sheng1huo2 ma1?

I can't adapt well to the climate here.

我不太适应这里的气候。wo3 bu4 tai4 shi4ying4 zhe4li3 de qi4hou4.

Or

我不大适应这里的气候。wo3 bu4 da4 shi4ying4 zhe4li3 de qi4hou4.

Here, although the primary meaning of 不太 and 不大 are literally corresponding to "not too much" and "not much", they are actually understood as "not quite". For example:

Recently I haven't been feeling quite well.
最近我感觉不太好。zui^{4}jin^{4} wo^{3} gan^{3}jue^{2} bu^{4} tai^{4} hao^{3}.
What's the matter? Or, what's wrong?
怎么啦？zen^{3}me la^{1}?
I've caught a cold.
我感冒了。wo^{3} gan^{3}mao^{4} le.
I've got a fever, or I have a temperature.
我发烧了。wo^{3} fa^{1}shao^{1} le.
I have a stomach ache.
我肚子痛。wo^{3} du^{4}zi tong^{4}.
I have lumbago.
我腰背痛。wo^{3} yao^{1}bei^{4} tong^{4}.
I have a headache.
我头痛。wo^{3} tou^{2} tong^{4}.
I have an ache in the leg.
我腿痛。wo^{3} tui^{3} tong^{4}.

All right! When an intimate friend confides to you such personal problems, you may show your concern by saying the following:

Is it severe?
严重吗？yan^{2}zhong^{4} ma^{1}?
Or
It's not severe?
不严重吧？bu^{4} yan^{2}zhong^{4} ba?
Or
Does it matter? Or, literally, doesn't it matter?
不要紧吧？bu^{4} yao^{4}jin^{3} ba?
Have you been to the hospital?
去医院了吗？qu^{4} yi^{1}yuan^{4} le ma^{1}?
Have you been to the hospital to have a check?
去医院看了吗？qu^{4} yi^{1}yuan^{4} kan^{4} le ma^{1}?

Here of course the word 看 is not to be interpreted as "look" or "see", but "to check". And so you can also say, literally—

Have you had the illness examined in the hospital?
去医院看病了吗？qu^{4} yi^{1}yuan^{4} kan^{4} bing^{4} le ma^{1}?
What does the doctor say?
医生说什么？yi^{1}sheng^{1} shuo^{1} shen^{2}me?
Or

医生怎么说？yi1sheng1 zen3me shuo1?

The doctor says it doesn't matter.

医生说不要紧。yi1sheng1 shuo1 bu4 yao4jin3.

Oh! I wish you an early recovery.

哦！祝你早日康复。o4! zhu4 ni1 zao3ri4 kang1fu1

Here 早日 literally means "early date", but as an adverb, it means "at the earliest date"; and 康复 literally translates as "health recovery". However, you can use the very simple word to instead of the formally used word 康复. That is 好了.

Have you recovered?

你好了吗？ni3 hao3 le ma3?

Or literally, has your physique turned for good?

你身体好了吗？ni3 shen1ti3 hao3 le ma3?

Besides, although it may seem strange, you can even say—

Literally, "has your illness become better?

你的病好了吗？ni3 de bing4 hao3 le ma3?

There may be various answers to this question:

Now it's much better.

现在好多了。xian4zai4 hao3 duo1 le.

It's a little better.

现在好点了。xian4zai4 hao3 dian3 le.

It is as it is.

还是老样子。hai2shi4 lao3 yang4zi.

What we least hope to say is—

It's even worse.

更不好了。geng4 bu4 hao3 le.

Or

It's more serious, or worse.

更严重了。geng4 yan2zhong4 le.

Or

更糟糕了。geng4 zao1gao1 le.

All right! Now let's round off this lesson by learning some good wishes.

Wish you all the best!

祝你一切好！zhu4 ni3 yi1qie4 hao3!

I hope everything is fine with you!

希望你一切好！xi1wang4 ni3 yi1qie4 hao3!

I wish you good health!

祝你健康！zhu4 ni3 jian4kang1!

I wish you early recovery.

祝你早日康复！zhu4 ni3 zao3ri4 kang1fu4!

Please remember me to all your family!
请代我向你全家问好！ qing^{3} dai^{4} wo^{3} xiang^{4} ni^{3} quan^{2} jia^{1} wen^{4} hao^{3}!

LESSON 12 第十二课

INTRODUCTION
介绍 JIE^{4}SHAO^4

In this lesson, we'll learn to introduce our friends or ourselves. For this purpose, we need to review one simple word that we have already learned. And this is—

Come 来 lai^2

However, this verb does not always literally mean "come". It can also serve an auxiliary function when used before another verb, such as offering to do something, showing willingness and readiness to do it. For instance—

I would like to give an introduction. Or, I would offer to introduce.

我来介绍一下。wo^3 lai^2 jie^3 shao^4 yi^1 xia^4.

Here the expression 我来 actually means "I would like to" or "I would offer to".

Let me introduce…

我来介绍一下。wo^3 lai^2 jie^3 shao^4 yi^1 xia^4.

让我来介绍一下…… rang^4 wo^3 lai^2 jie^3 shao^4 yi^1 xia^4...

One important thing to note is that the exact meaning of 来 may depend on the context. It can be very general and mean anything one is willing to do. For example:

Let me do it; let me deal with it; let me take it.

让我来。rang^4 wo^3 lai^2

Or, simply—

我来。wo^3 lai^2

Let him take care of it.

让他来。rang^4 ta^1 lai^2

Now, listen to the following:

Who will introduce us?

谁来介绍我们？shui^2 lai^2 jie^{4}shao^4 wo^{3}men?

Let me do it. Or, I would like to do it.

我来。wo^3 lai^2

Since the understanding of Chinese is highly context-dependent, we can choose to use both 让 and 来 or omit either one of them. So the following are all possible for expressing the meaning of "Let me introduce…" or "I would like to introduce…"

我介绍一下……wo^3 jie^{4}shao^4 yi^1 xia^4…

我来介绍一下……wo^3 lai^2 jie^{4}shao^4 yi^1 xia^4…

让我介绍一下……hao^{4}ma^3…rang^4 wo^3 jie^{4}shao^4 yi^1 xia^4…

让我来介绍一下……rang^4 wo^3 lai^2 jie^{4}shao^4 yi^1 xia^4…

In all the above, a preposition can be inserted before the one you introduce. It is originally a verb meaning "to give" but can function as the English preposition "for" or "to".

给 gei^3

Give me...

给我… gei^3 wo^3

Give me your email address.

给我你的电子邮箱。gei^3 wo^3 ni^3 de^1 dian^{4}zi^3 you^{2}xiang^1.

Give me your telephone number.

给我你的电话号码。gei^3 wo^3 ni^3 de^1 dian^{4}hua^4.

Telephone 电话 dian^{4}hua^4

Number 号码 hao^{4}ma^3

Can you give me your telephone number?

能不能给我你的电话号码？ neng^2 bu^4 neng^2 gei^3 wo^3 ni^3 de^1 dian^{4}hua^4 hao^{4}ma^3?

As we see, 给 as a preposition is normally used before an indirect object.

Let me introduce him to you.

让我给你介绍一下他。rang^4 wo^3 gei^3 ni^3 jie^{4}shao^4 yi^1 xia^4 ta^1.

Or

我来给你介绍一下他。wo^3 lai^2 gei^3 ni^3 jie^{4}shao^4 yi^1 xia^4 ta^1.

Please introduce your friend to me.

请给我介绍一下你的朋友。qing^3 gei^3 wo^3 jie^{4}shao^{4}yi^1 xia^4 ni^3 de^{1}peng^{2}you^3.

He has introduced his girlfriend to me.

他给我介绍了他的女朋友。ta^1 gei^3 wo^3 jie^{4}shao^4 le^1 ta^1 de^1 nv^3 peng^{2}you^3.

Let me introduce you to each other.

让我给你们介绍一下。rang^4 wo^3 gei^3 ni^{3}men jie^{4}shao^4 yi^1 xia^4.

Here, since the plural form of the second person 你们 is used, there is no need to use "each other", which in Chinese is—

互相 hu^{4}xiang^1

However, we cannot leave it out if the context does not make the meaning clear.

Let's introduce each other.

让我们互相介绍一下。rang^{4} wo^{3}men hu^{4} xiang^{1} jie^{4}shao^{4} yi^{1} xia^{4}.

They have introduced themselves to each other.

他们互相介绍了。ta^{1}men hu^{4}xiang^{1} jie^{4}shao^{4} le.

Of course, as in English, we can also introduce something instead of a person.

I would like to introduce this book to you.

我来给你介绍一下这本书。wo^{3} lai^{2} gei^{3} ni^{3} jie^{4}shao^{4} yi^{1} xia^{4} zhe^{4} ben^{3} shu^{1}.

Please note the frequent use of the measure word "一下". It may be interpreted as "once" or "one time", but this is no more important than its function to make the phrase or sentence feel completed. For the same function of completeness, we can also repeat the verb itself.

Let me give an introduction.

我来介绍介绍。wo^{3} lai^{2} jie^{4}shao^{4}jie^{4} shao^{4}.

Let him give an introduction.

让他来介绍介绍。rang^{4} ta^{1} lai^{2} jie^{4}shao^{4} jie^{4}shao^{4}.

Let me give an introduction. Or, simply, let me introduce.

我来介绍介绍。wo^{3} lai^{2} jie^{4}shao^{4} jie^{4}shao^{4}.

As we see, the word 来 precedes another verb or verbal phrase without any connectives. This is also the case with its antonym 去 and quite a few other verbs in Chinese. We simply call this category of verbs OPEN VERBS because they are open to take other verbs or verbal phrases as their objects. And the verbs they take can be open themselves. Therefore, we can form a verbal chain in the sentence. Here are some examples.

I want to go to see the movie.

我想去看电影。wo^{3} xiang^{3} qu^{4} kan^{4} dian^{4}ying^{3}.

I hope to be able to go traveling.

我希望能去旅游。wo^{3} xi^{1}wang^{4} neng^{2} qu^{4} lv^{3}you^{2}.

You go and invite him here to have dinner.

你去请他来吃饭。ni^{3} qu^{4} qing^{3} ta^{1} lai^{2} chi^{1} fan^{4}.

I want to go and ask him to come and help me.

我要去请他来帮我。wo^{3} xiang^{3} qu^{4} qing^{3} ta^{1} lai^{2} bang^{1} wo^{3}.

He plans to come to China to study.

他计划来中国学习。ta^{1} ji^{4}hua^{4} lai^{2} zhong^{1}guo^{2} xue^{2}xi^{2}.

All right! Now we'll come to self-introduction. There are two words for "self" in Chinese. One is—

自己 zi^{4}ji^{3}

And the other is—

自我 zi4 wo3

A major difference between these two words is that the word 自己 can be a suffix like the English "self" for making a reflexive pronoun, while 自我 can never be used in this way. So let's listen to the reflexive pronouns first.

Myself

我自己 wo3 zi4ji3

Yourself

你自己 ni3 zi4ji3

Himself

他自己 ta1 zi4ji3

Themselves

他们自己 ta1men zi4ji3

Another difference between 自己 and 自我 is that 自己 can function as an adverbial but 自我 cannot. Therefore, 自己 is often used to mean "by oneself" or "on one's own", and 自我 is understood as a modifier of a nominal construct. Let's listen to the following:

Self-introduction

自我介绍 zi4wo3 jie4shao4

To make a self-introduction

做自我介绍 zuo4 zi4wo3 jie4shao4

To introduce oneself

介绍自己 jie4shao4 zi4ji3

To make a self-introduction is to introduce yourself.

做自我介绍就是介绍自己。zuo4 zi4wo3 jie4shao4 jiu4 shi4jie4shao4 zi4ji3.

Learn by oneself

自己学 zi4ji3 xue2

I learn Chinese by myself.

我自己学中文。wo3 zi4ji3 xue2 zhong1wen2.

I cook by myself.

我自己做饭。wo3 zi4ji3 zuo4 fan4.

She drives by herself. Or, she drives herself.

她自己开车。ta1 zi4ji3 kai1 che1.

Let me introduce myself.

让我介绍一下自己。rang4 wo3 jie4shao4 yi1 xia4 zi4ji3.

Let me make a self-introduction.

让我做一个自我介绍。rang4 wo3 zuo4 yi1 ge4 zi4wo3 jie4shao4.

OK! Let's go on and listen to the following.

You still don't know him, I guess.
你还不认识他吧？ ni^{3} hai^{2} bu^{4} ren^{4}shi ta^{1} ba?
Then, let me introduce.
那么，我来介绍一下吧。na^{4}me wo^{3} lai^{2} jie^{2} shao^{4} yi^{1} xia^{4} ba.
You may not know each other yet.
你们还不认识吧？ ni^{3}men hai^{2} bu^{4} ren^{4}shi ba?
Then, let me introduce.
那么我来介绍一下。na^{4}me wo^{3} lai^{2} jie^{4}shao^{4} yi^{1} xia^{4}.
There are a few words to emphasize. Let's listen to them one by one.
The first is—
Still or yet 还 hai^{2}
This 还 is often followed by a negative word like 不, 没有 to form a collocation.
Still not, not yet
还不 hai^{2} bu^{4}
Or
还没有 hai^{2} mei^{2} you^{3}
Or
还没 hai^{2} mei^{2}
You still don't know him, I guess.
你还不认识他吧？ ni^{3} hai^{2} bu^{4} ren^{4}shi ta^{1} ba?
Not yet.
还不认识。hai^{2} bu^{4} ren^{4}shi.
I think you don't know each other yet.
我想你们还不认识吧。wo^{3} xiang^{3} ni^{3}men hai^{2} bu^{4} ren^{4}shi ba.
I haven't introduced myself yet.
我还没有介绍我自己。wo^{3} hai^{2} mei^{2} you^{3} jie^{4}shao^{4} wo^{3} zi^{4}ji^{3}.
The second word to emphasize is—
Then 那么 na^{4}me
Then, please introduce.
那么，介绍介绍吧。na^{4}me, jie^{4}shao^{4} jie^{4}shao^{4} ba.
Or
那么，就介绍一下吧。na^{4}me, jiu^{4} jie^{4}shao^{4} yi^{1} xia^{4} ba.
Or
那就介绍一下吧。na^{4} jiu^{4} jie^{4}shao^{4} yi^{1} xia^{4} ba.
The word 就 is the third word to emphasize. It serves the same function as the English adverb "just", and 那么 can be shortened to 那. So, we can simply say—
Then, just introduce.
那就介绍一下吧。na^{4} jiu^{4} jie^{4}shao^{4} yi^{1} xia^{4} ba.

Or

那就介绍介绍吧。na^4 jiu^4 jie shao^4 jie^{2}shao^4 ba.

The fourth word to emphasize is 吧, which we call a sentence final. Frequently appearing at the end of the sentence, it indicates that what is said is a guess, or a suggestion, or a proposal, often with the intention to ask for the other person's confirmation or approval. Therefore, we may choose to use either a question mark or a full stop when it ends the sentence. So, let's listen again.

You don't know each other, I suppose.

你们还不认识吧？ni^{3}men hai^2 bu^4 ren^{4}shi ba?

No. We don't.

不。不认识。bu^4, bu^4 ren^{4}shi.

Then, just make an introduction.

那就介绍介绍吧。na^4 jiu^4 jie^{4}shao^4 jie^2 shao^4 ba.

Remember, since the Chinese sentence final only appears at the end of the sentence, we should not confuse this 吧 with another word that has the same pronunciation but is usually used before a noun. Let's listen and compare the following pairs of sentences that basically mean the same.

Introduce yourself.

介绍一下你自己吧。jie^{4}shao^4 yi^1 xia^4 ni^3 zi^{4}ji^3 ba.

把你自己介绍一下吧。ba^{3}ni^3 zi^{4}ji^3 jie^{4}shao^4 yi^1 xia^{4}ba.

Please introduce him.

请介绍一下他吧。qing^3 jie^{4}shao^4 yi^1 xia^4 ta^1 ba.

请把他介绍一下吧。qing^3 ba^3 ta^1 jie^{4}shao^4 yi^1 xia^4 ba.

Learn Chinese well, please.

请学好中文吧。qing^3 xue^2 hao^3 zhong^{1}wen^2 ba.

请把中文学好吧。qing^3 ba^3 zhong^{1}wen^{2}xue^2 hao^3 ba.

You have read that book, I suppose. Or, you have read that book, haven't you?

你读了那本书吧？ni^3 du^2 le na^4 ben^3 shu^1 ba?

你把那本书读了吧？ni^3 ba^3 na^4 ben^3 shu^{1}du^2 le ba?

In fact, the word 把 is a verb by origin, meaning "to take hold", "to handle" or "to deal with". It is written differently and has the grammatical function of "taking hold of" the object and foregrounding it before the verb.

Let's compare more sentences using 把 and those which don't use it.

Let me introduce him.

我来介绍他。wo^3 lai^2 jie^{4}shao^4 ta^1.

我来把他介绍一下。wo^3 lai^2 ba^3 ta^1 jie^{4}shao^4 yi^1 xia^4.

Please introduce him.

请介绍一下他。qing^3 jie^{4}shao^4 yi^1 xia^4 ta^1.

请把他介绍一下。qing^3 ba^3 ta^1 jie^{4}shao^4 yi^1 xia^4.

Let me introduce you.

我来介绍一下你。wo^3 lai^2 jie^{4}shao^4 yi^1 xia^4 ni^3.

我来把你介绍一下。wo^3 lai^2 ba^3 ni^3 jie^{4}shao^4 yi^1 xia^4.

I want to introduce you to my friend.

我想介绍你给我的朋友。wo^3 xiang^3 jie^{4}shao^4 ni^3 gei^3 wo^3 de^1 peng^{2}you^3.

我想把你介绍给我的朋友。wo^3 xiang^3 ba^3 ni^{3}jie^{4}shao^4 gei^3 wo^3 de^1 peng^{2}you^3.

All right! Now, after learning these important words, let's go on with our practice in starting an introduction.

You probably don't know each other yet. Do you?

你们还不认识吧？ni^{3}men hai^2 bu^4 ren^{4}shi ba?

No.

不认识。bu^4 ren^{4}shi.

Then, let me introduce.

那我来介绍介绍。na^4 wo^3 lai^2 jie^{4}shao^4 jie^{4}shao^4.

You haven't introduced yourself to each other. Right?

你们还没有互相介绍吧？ni^{3}men hai^2 mei^2 you^3 hu^{4}xiang^1 jie^{4}shao^4 ba?

Not yet.

还没有。hai^2 mei^2 you^3

Then, just introduce.

那就介绍介绍吧。na^4 jiu^4 jie^{4}shao^4 jie^{4}shao^4 ba.

Who will introduce?

谁来介绍？shui^2 lai^2 jie^{4}shao^4?

Let me do it. Or, I will.

我来吧。wo^3 lai^2 ba.

Of course, some people may know each other but have not met yet. In this case, we'll say—

They know each other, but haven't met yet.

他们认识，但还没有见过面。ta^{1}men ren^{4}shi, dan^4 hai^2 mei^2 you^3 jian^4 guo^4 mian^4.

The expression 见过面 comes from the word 见面, which literally translates as "to see the face", but here it is an equivalent to the English verb "to meet". The word 过 means "to pass" or "to cross" when used as a verb, but when following another verb, it serves as a function word to mark the past tense or perfect tense, similar to the sentence final 了. So, there are different ways to express the same meaning. Let's listen to the following:

They have met each other.

他们见面了。ta^{1}men jian^{4} guo^{4} mian^{4} le.

他们见过面。ta^{1}men jian^{4} guo^{4} mian^{4}.

They have met each other already.

他们已经见过面了。ta^{1}men yi^{3}jing^{1} jian^{4} guo^{4} mian^{4} le.

OK! Let's have a review of what we have learned so far.

Let me introduce for to (plural "you").

我来给你们介绍一下。wo^{3} lai^{2} gei^{3} ni^{3}men jie^{2} shao^{4} yi^{1} xia^{4}.

Let me make an introduction for you.

我来给你们做个介绍吧。wo^{3} lai^{2} gei^{3} ni^{3}men zuo^{4} ge^{4} jie^{4}shao^{4} ba.

Let me introduce her to you.

我给你介绍一下她吧。wo^{3} lai^{2} gei^{3} ni^{3} jie^{4}shao^{4} yi^{1} xia^{4} ta^{1} ba.

Or

我把她介绍给你吧。wo^{3} ba^{3} ta^{1} jie^{4}shao^{4} gei^{3} ni^{3} ba.

Let me introduce you to her.

我给她介绍一下你吧。wo^{3} gei^{3} ta^{1} jie^{4}shao^{4} yi^{1} xia^{4} ni^{3} ba.

Or

我把你介绍给她吧。wo^{3} ba^{3} ni^{3} jie^{4}shao^{4} gei^{3} ta^{1} ba.

Let me introduce myself.

我来介绍一下我自己吧。wo^{3} lai^{2} jie^{4}shao^{4} yi^{1} xia^{4} wo^{3}zi^{4}ji^{3} ba.

Or

我来做个自我介绍吧。wo^{3} lai^{2} zuo^{4} ge^{4} zi^{4} wo^{3} jie^{4}shao^{4} ba.

Have you introduced yourselves to each other?

你们互相介绍了吗？ni^{3}men^{2} hu^{4}xiang^{1} jie^{4}shao^{4} le ma^{1}?

Not yet.

还没有。hai^{2} mei^{2} you^{3}.

Then, just introduce to each other.

那么，就互相介绍介绍吧。na^{4}me, jiu^{4} hu^{4}xiang^{1} jie^{4}shao^{4} jie^{4}shao^{4} ba.

They know each other, but haven't met yet.

他们认识，但是还没有见过面。ta^{1}men ren^{4}shi, dan^{4}shi^{4} hai^{2} mei^{2} you^{3} jian^{4} guo^{4} mian^{4}.

Now we know each other.

现在我们认识了。xian^{4}zai^{4} wo^{3}men ren^{4}shi le.

Now they have met.

现在他们见面了。xian^{4}zai^{4} ta^{1}men jian^{4}mian^{4} le.

We have met, or met at last.

我们终于见面了。wo^{3}men zhong^{1}yu^{2} jian^{4}mian^{4} le.

At last, finally 终于 zhong^{1}yu^2

We have met, or met at last.

我们终于见面了。wo^{3}men zhong^{1}yu^2 jian^{4}mian^4 le.

Could you give me your email?

可以给我你的电子邮箱吗？ke^{3}yi^3 gei^3 wo^3 ni^3 de^1 dian^{4}zi^{3}you^{2}xiang^1 ma^1?

Let's leave each other a business card.

我们互相留个名片吧。wo^{3}men hu^{4}xiang^1 liu^2 ge^4 ming^2 pian^4 ba.

Here the word 留 literally means "leave", and it can also take the verbal complement 下. For example:

Please leave your email to us.

请给我们留下你的电子邮箱。qing^3 gei^3 wo^3 liu^2 xia^4 ni^3 de^1 dian^{4}zi^3 you^{2}xiang^1.

Please leave your luggage here.

请把行李留在这里。qing^3 ba^3 xing^{2}li^3 liu^2 zai^4 zhe^4 li^3.

Please leave your umbrella outside.

请把你的雨伞留在外面。qing^3 ba^3 ni^3 de^1 yu^3 san^3 liu^2 zai^4 wai^4 mian^4.

However, the meaning of 留 may sometimes be different from the English "leave". Here is an example:

Keep the change.

留下找头吧。liu^2 xia^4 zhao^3 tou^4 ba.

This example shows that 留 can also loosely mean "to have" or "to keep".

Let's have each other's telephone number.

我们互相留个电话吧。wo^{3}men hu^{4}xiang^1 liu^2 ge^4 dian^{4}hua^4 ba.

Of course, to leave to each other means to exchange, which in Chinese is—

交换 jiao^1 huan^4

Let's exchange our business cards.

我们交换一下名片吧。wo^{3}men jiao^1 huan^4 yi^1 xia^4 ming^{2}pian^4 ba.

Could we exchange our telephone numbers?

我们互相留个电话好吗？wo^{3}men hu^{4}xiang^1 liu^2 ge^4 dian^{4}hua^4 hao^3 ma?

Could you leave me your WeChat?

可以留下你的微信吗？ke^{3}yi^3 liu^2 xia^4 ni^3 de^1 wei^{1}xin^4 ma?

Can you give me your website?

能不能给我你的网址？neng^2 bu^4 neng^2 gei^3 wo^3 ni^3 de^1 wang^3 zhi^3?

Website 网址 wang^3 zhi^3

Of course.

当然可以。dang^{1} ran^{2} ke^{3}yi^{3}.
OK! Let's keep in contact.
好了。我们保持联系吧。hao^{3} le, wo^{3}men bao^{3} chi^{2} lian^{2} xi^{4} ba.
Keep 保持 bao^{3} chi^{2}
Keep in contact!
保持联系！ bao^{3} chi^{2} lian^{2} xi^{4}!

LESSON 13 第十三课

WHEN?
什么时间？SHEN^{2}ME SHI^{2}JIAN^{1}

In this lesson, we'll learn to use words relating to time. Let's start with the very basic ones.

When? Or what time?

什么时间？shen^{2}me shi^{2}jian^{1}?

What hour? Or literally, what o'clock?

几点？ji^{3} dian^{3}?

Or

几点钟？ji^{3} dian^{3} zhong^{1}?

Or, to be more formal—

何时？he^{2} shi^{2}?

Or, to be exact, what hour and what minute?

几点几分？ji^{3} dian^{3} ji^{3} fen^{1}?

From these, we can see the words corresponding to each other in Chinese and English.

Time

时间 shi^{2}jian^{1}

Point

点 dian^{3}

O'clock; or literally, point of the clock

点钟 dian^{3} zhong^{1}

The single-syllable word 何 (he^{2}) and the two-syllable word 什么 (shen^{2}me) are the same in meaning, and 时 (shi^{2}) is the short form of 时间 (shi^{2}jian^{1}).

When? Or what time?

何时？he^{2} shi^{2}?

Or

什么时间？shen^{2}me shi^{2}jian^{1}?

In more casual situations, the Chinese may also use another less formal word for 时间. That is—

Time 时候 shi2hou4

When will he come?

他什么时候来？ ta1 shen2me shi2hou4 lai2?

When do you go?

Or

When are you going?

你什么时候去？ ni3 shen2me shi2hou4 qu4?

When shall we meet?

我们什么时候见面？ wo3men shen2me shi2hou4 jian4mian4?

When shall we meet next time?

我们下一次什么时候见面？ wo3men xia4 yi1 ci4 shen2me shi2hou4 jian4mian4?

Of course, we can also literally translate the English "at what time" into Chinese.

在什么时间？ zai4 shen2me shi2jian1?

The preposition 在 is like the English "at", "in", or "on", but it may also serve as a verb to mean "exist", "be present", or "be located in". When used as a preposition, it can often be omitted.

在什么时间？ zai4 shen2me shi2jian1?

什么时间？ shen2me shi2jian1?

Next, let's look at the uses of 在 when it can be considered as a Chinese verb.

When are you in? Or, when are you available? Or, are you there?

你什么时候在？ ni3 shen2me shi2hou4 zai4?

Are you in? Are you there? Or, are you here?

你在不在？ ni3 zai4 bu4 zai4?

Yes, I'm.

我在。wo3 zai4.

Are you at home?

你在家吗？ ni3 zai4 jia1 ma?

Yes.

在。zai4.

When is he in the office?

他什么时候在办公室？ ta1 shen2me shi2hou4 zai4 ban4gong1 shi4?

When are you at home?

你什么时候在家？ ni3 shen2me shi2hou4 zai4 jia1?

All right! Now it's time for us to learn more words giving a particular time of the clock.

Hour 小时 xiao3shi2

One hour 一小时 yi1 xiao3shi2

Or

一个小时 yi^1 ge^4 xiao^{3}shi^2

O'clock 点 dian^3

Or

点钟 dian^3 zhong^1

Minute 分 fen^1

1 o'clock 一点 yi^1 dian^3

Or

一点钟 yi^1 dian^3 zhong^1

2 o'clock 两点 liang^3 dian^3

Or

两点钟 liang^3 dian^3 zhong^1

3 o'clock 三点 san^1 dian^3

Or

三点钟 san^1 dian^3 zhong^1

4 o'clock 四点 si^4 dian^3

Or

四点钟 si^4 dian^3 zhong^1

Five past four, or literally, 4 o'clock and 5 minutes 四点五分 si^4 dian^3 wu^3 fen^1

Or

四点零五分 si^4 dian^3 ling^2 wu^3 fen^1

So we see that the word for "zero"—零 can be omitted, and that the o'clock would normally precede the minute in Chinese. So, let's see the following by using English explanations that literally correspond to the Chinese word order.

5 o'clock and 6 minutes 五点零六分 wu^3 dian^3 ling^2 liu^4 fen^1

7 o'clock and 10 minutes 七点十分 qi^1 dian^3 shi^2 fen^1

8 o'clock and 10 minutes 八点十分 ba^1 dian^3 shi^2 fen^1

8 o'clock and 15 minutes 八点十五分 ba^1 dian^3 shi^2 wu^3 fen^1

Or

8 o'clock and 15 八点一刻 ba^1 dian^3 yi^2 ke^4

Here, we see that the "quarter" translates directly to "刻".

8 o'clock and 15 minutes 八点一刻 ba^1 dian^3 yi^2 ke^4

Of course, the word for the minute can be omitted, as in English.

9 o'clock and 40 minutes 九点四十 jiu^3 dian^3 si^4 shi^2

9 o'clock and 45 minutes 九点四十五 jiu^3 dian^3 si^4 shi^2 wu^3

Or

9 o'clock and three-quarters (i.e. nine forty-five) 九点三刻 jiu^3 dian^3 san^1 ke^4

Next, we should learn the Chinese for "half".

Half 半 ban^{4}

Half past ten 十点半 shi^{2} dian^{3} ban^{4}

Of course, we can also use the number 30:

Thirty minutes past eleven 十一点三十分 shi^{2} yi^{1} dian^{3} san^{1} shi^{2} fen^{1}

Or, omitting the word for "minute":

Eleven thirty 十一点三十 shi^{2} yi^{1} dian^{3} san^{1} shi^{2}

12 o'clock 十二点 shi^{2} er^{4} dian^{3}

Or

12 o'clock sharp 十二点整 shi^{2} er^{4} dian^{3} zheng^{3}

The word 整 means "neat" or an integral number, but here it means "sharp". Let's use this word in a 24-hour system.

Literally, 13 hours sharp 十三点整 shi^{2} san^{1} dian^{3} zheng^{3}

Literally, 14 o'clock sharp 十四点整 shi^{2} si^{4} dian^{3} zheng^{3}

As we have learned, to ask questions about the time, we would say—

What time is it?

什么时间？ shen^{2}me shi^{2}jian^{1}?

Or

什么时候？ shen^{2}me shi^{2}hou^{4}?

Or

Literally, what o'clock, i.e. what time?

几点？ ji^{3} dian^{3}?

Or

几点钟？ ji^{3} dian^{3} zhong^{1}?

And if we want to be exact we can also ask, literally—

Which hour and which minute?

几点几分？ ji^{3} dian^{3} ji^{3} fen^{1}?

What time do you go to work?

你几点上班？ ni^{3} ji^{3} dian^{3} shang^{4}ban^{1}?

I start work at 8:30.

我八点三十上班。wo^{3} ba^{1} dian^{3} san^{1} shi^{2} shang^{4}ban^{1}.

Or

I start work at half past eight.

我八点半上班。wo^{3} ba^{1} dian^{3} ban^{4} shang^{4}ban^{1}.

Then, what time do you go off work?

那么，几点下班？ na^{4}me, ji^{3} dian^{3} xia^{4}ban^{1}?

5 o'clock sharp.

五点整。wu^{3} dian^{3} zheng^{3}.

We work 8 hours. 我们上班 8 小时。wo^{3}men shang^{4}ban^{1}ba^{1} xiao^{3}shi^{2}.

Or

我们上 8 个小时的班。wo3men shang4 ba1 ge4 xiao3shi2 de1 ban1.

To ask about a time span with a beginning and end, we would use an expression equivalent to the English—

From 从 cong2

To 到 dao4

From when to when?

从几点到几点？cong2 ji3 dian3 dao4 ji3 dian3?

Or

从什么时间到什么时间？cong2 shen2me shi2jian1 dao4 shen2me shi2jian1?

From when to when are you at work?

你从几点到几点上班？ni3 cong2 ji3 dian3 dao4 ji3 dian3 shang4ban1?

From 9 to 6.

从九点到六点。cong2 jiu3 dian3 dao4 liu4 dian3.

When are you free? Or literally, when do you have a vacancy or an opening?

你什么时候有空？ni3 shen2me shi2hou4 you3 kong4?

I will be free from 11:30 to 1:30.

我从 11 点班到 1 点半有空。wo3 cong2 shi2 yi1 dian3 dao4 yi1 dian3 ban4 you3 kong4.

For different parts of the day, we have the following:

Morning, usually early morning 早上 zao3 shang4

Morning, the whole morning before noon 上午 shang4wu3

Afternoon 下午 xia4wu3

Noon 中午 zhong1 wu3

Evening 晚上 wan3shang4

Early in the evening or at the dusk 傍晚 bang4wan3

Night 夜晚 ye4 wan3

Midnight 半夜 ban4 ye4

Daytime, or literally, "white day" 白天 bai2tian1

All right! Now let's use these words in sentences.

When is he here? Or, when is he there or available?

他什么时候在？ta1 shen2me shi2hou4 zai4?

He is available in the morning.

他上午在。ta1 shang4wu3 zai4.

When are you, or will you, be in the office?

你什么时候在办公室？ni3 shen2me shi2hou4 zai4 ban4gong1shi4?

I'm in the office in the afternoon.

我上午在办公室。wo3 shang4wu3 zai4 ban4gong1shi4.

Or, to be short—

我上午在。wo^{3} shang^{4}wu^{3} zai^{4}.

From when to when are you in the office?

你从几点到几点在办公室？ni^{3} cong^{2} ji^{3} dian^{3} dao^{4} ji^{3} dian^{3} zai^{4} ban^{4}gong^{1}shi^{4}?

When are you at home?

你什么时候在家？ni^{3} shen^{2}me shi^{2}hou^{4} zai^{4} jia^{1}?

I'm at home in the evening.

我晚上在家。wo^{3} wan^{3}shang^{4} zai^{4} jia^{1}.

Or, to be short—

晚上 wan^{3}shang^{4}

From when to when are you at work?

你从几点到几点上班？ni^{3} cong^{2} ji^{3} dian^{3} dao^{4} ji^{3} dian^{3} shang^{4}ban^{1}?

From 8 to 5 o'clock.

从八点到五点。cong^{2} ba^{1} dian^{3} dao^{4} wu^{3} dian^{3}.

Or

From 8 in the morning to 5 in the afternoon.

从上午八点到下午五点。cong^{2} shang^{4}wu^{3} ba^{1} dian^{3} dao^{4} xia^{4}wu^{3} wu^{3} dian^{3}.

How about the lunch break?

午饭休息呢？wu^{3}fan^{4} xiu^{1}xi ne?

Or

午饭休息时间呢？wu^{3}fan^{4} xiu^{1}xi shi^{2}jian^{1} ne?

It's from 12 noon to 1 o'clock in the afternoon.

从中午十二点到下午一点。cong^{2} zhong^{1} wu^{3} shi^{2} er^{4} dian^{3} dao^{4} xia^{4}wu^{3} yi^{1} dian^{3}.

When are you free? Or, when will you be free?

你什么时候有空？ni^{3} shen^{2}me shi^{2}hou^{4} you^{3} kong^{4}?

I'm free after work.

我下班后有空。wo^{3} xia^{4}ban^{1} hou^{4} you^{3} kong^{4}.

I'm free, or I'll be free after dinner.

我晚饭后有空。wo^{3} wan^{3}fan^{4} hou^{4} you^{3} kong^{4}.

In Chinese, 上班 can mean both "at work" and "go to work" although it literally translates as "go on the shift". The word "work" in its general sense translates as 工作 but may be interchangeable with 上班 if it is the regular daily work one does on his job.

When do you go to work?

你几点上班？ni^{3} ji^{3} dian^{3} shang^{4}ban^{1}?

Or

Literally, when do you start work?

你几点开始工作？ni^{3} ji^{3} dian^{3} kai^{1}shi^{3} gong^{1}zuo^{4}?

From when to when are you at work?

你从几点到几点工作？ ni^{3} cong^{2} ji^{3} dian^{3} dao^{4} ji^{3} dian^{3} gong^{1}zuo^{4}?

However, the opposite expression 下班 is taken to mean a one-time act.

I get off work at 5 in the afternoon.

我下午五点下班。wo^{3} xia^{4}wu^{3} wu^{3} dian^{3} xia^{4}ban^{1}.

Literally, I have come off work.

我下班了。wo^{3} xia^{4}ban^{1} le.

Or, I have already come off work.

我已经下班了。wo^{3} yi^{3}jing^{1} xia^{4}ban^{1} le.

Already 已经 yi^{3}jing^{1}

我已经下班了。wo^{3} yi^{3}jing^{1} xia^{4}ban^{1} le.

I'll take a rest now.

我现在要休息了。wo^{3} xian^{4}zai^{4} yao^{4} xiu^{1}xi le.

The word 休息 actually corresponds to "rest", but if it is being used to refer to a break from work, we need to add a word to modify this rest. This is:

Middle, or in the middle 中间 zhong^{1}jian^{1}

The middle, or in the middle 中间 zhong^{1}jian^{1}

A break 中间休息 zhong^{1}jian^{1} xiu^{1}xi

Rest 休息 xiu^{1}xi

When do you take a break?

几点中间休息？ ji^{3} dian^{3} zhong^{1}jian^{1} xiu^{1}xi?

From 12 to 1 o'clock.

从十二点到一点。cong^{2} shi^{1} er^{4} dian^{3} dao^{4} yi^{1} dian^{3}.

OK! Now we can learn more words and phrases to put to use. The first to learn is—

Today 今天 jin^{1}tian^{1}

Tomorrow 明天 ming^{2}tian^{1}

Yesterday 昨天 zuo^{2}tian^{1}

The day after tomorrow 后天 hou^{4}tian^{1}

I work today, or literally, I go on shift or I'm on shift today.

我今天上班。wo^{3} jin^{1}tian^{1} shang^{4}ban^{1}.

Tomorrow I will work too.

我明天也上班。wo^{3} ming^{2}tian^{1} ye^{3} shang^{4}ban^{1}.

How about the day after tomorrow?

后天呢？ hou^{4}tian^{1} ne^{1}?

The day after tomorrow I will still work.

后天还上班。hou^{4}tian^{1} hai^{2} shang^{4}ban^{1}.

I will work all days: today, tomorrow and the day after tomorrow.

我今天、明天和后天都上班。wo^{3} jin^{1}tian^{1} ming^{2}tian^{1} hou^{4}tian^{1} dou^{1}

shang^{4}ban^1.

As we can see, the English adverbs "too", "still" and "all" translate into Chinese respectively as 也, 还, and 都. Let's listen once more.

Tomorrow I will work too.

我明天也上班。wo^3 ming^{2}tian^1 ye^3 shang^{4}ban^1.

How about the day after tomorrow?

后天呢？hou^{4}tian^1 ne^1?

The day after tomorrow I will still work or still be working.

后天还上班。hou^{4}tian^1 hai^2 shang^{4}ban^1.

I will work all today, tomorrow and the day after tomorrow.

我今天、明天和后天都上班。wo^3 jin^{1}tian^1 ming^{2}tian^1 hou^{4}tian^1 dou^1 shang^{4}ban^1.

To talk about the past, we may use the perfect tense marker 了, which also functions as a sentence final. However, we can choose to leave it out if the tense is understandable in the context.

I also worked yesterday. Or, I worked yesterday too.

我昨天也上班了。wo^3 zuo^{2}tian^1 ye^3 shang^{4}ban^1 le.

我昨天也上班。wo^3 zuo^{2}tian^1 ye^3 shang^{4}ban^1.

I took a rest the day before yesterday.

我前天休息了。wo^3 qian^{2}tian^1 xiu^{1}xi le.

我前天也休息。wo^3 qian^{2}tian^1 ye^3 xiu^{1}xi.

How about the kids?

孩子们呢？hai^{2}zimen ne?

The kids go to school every day.

孩子们天天上学。hai^{2}zimen tian^{1}tian^1 shang^4 xue^2.

Except, or apart from, the weekends.

除了周末。chu^{2}le^1 zhou^{1}mo^4.

They go to school every day except the weekends.

他们除了周末天天上学。ta^{1}men chu^2 le^1 zhou^{1}mo^4 tian^{1}tian^1 shang^4 xue^2.

When do you usually finish school?

他们一般几点下学？ta^{1}men yi^{1}ban^1 ji^3 dian^3 xia^4 xue^2?

Or

他们一般几点放学？ta^{1}men yi^{1}ban^1 ji^3 dian^3 fang^4 xue^2?

Their class is over at half past three, and then they finish school.

他们三点半下课，然后放学。ta^{1}men san^1 dian^3 ban^4 xia^4 ke^4, ran^{2}hou^{4}fang^4 xue^2.

Interestingly, there is one special word to use for expressing the day before the day before yesterday and the day after the day after tomorrow. It is the word that literally means "big"—

大 da^{4}.

The day before the day before yesterday.

大前天 da^{4} qian^{2}tian^{1}

The day after the day after tomorrow.

大后天 da^{4} hou^{4}tian^{1}

I was at home the day before the day before yesterday.

我大前天在家。wo^{3} da^{4} qian^{2}tian^{1} zai^{4} jia^{1}.

I will be in the office the day after the day after tomorrow.

我大后天在办公室。wo^{3} da^{4} hou^{4}tian^{1} zai^{4} ban^{4}gong^{1}shi^{4}.

Now let's learn the days of the week, along with the connective 和.

Monday and Tuesday 星期一和星期二 xing^{1}qi^{1}yi^{1} he^{2} xing^{1}qi^{1}er^{4}

Wednesday and Thursday 星期三和星期四 xing^{1}qi^{1}san^{1} he^{2} xing^{1}qi^{1}si^{4}

Friday and Saturday 星期五和星期六 xing^{1}qi^{1}wu^{3} he^{2} xing^{1}qi^{1}liu^{4}

Saturday and Sunday 星期六和星期天 xing^{1}qi^{1}liu^{4} he^{2} xing^{1}qi^{1}tian^{1}

As we see, for the English "Sunday", the word 天, is used instead of the number 7. And for "week", there is yet another single-character word apart from 星期. This is 周. So we can choose either of them.

星期一和星期二 xing^{1}qi^{1}yi^{1} he^{2} xing^{1}qi^{1}er^{4}

Or

周一和周二 zhou^{1} yi^{1} he^{2} zhou^{1} er^{4}

星期三和星期四 xing^{1}qi^{1}san^{1} he^{2} xing^{1}qi^{1}si^{4}

Or

周三和周四 zhou^{1} san^{1} he^{2} zhou^{1} si^{4}

星期五和星期六 xing^{1}qi^{1}wu^{3} he^{2} xing^{1}qi^{1}liu^{4}

Or

周五和周六 zhou^{1} wu^{3} he^{2} zhou^{1} liu^{4}

Remember, for "Sunday", we can choose to use 星期天, 星期日, or 周日, but never the number 7. Besides, while 日 can follow both 星期 and 周, its synonym in this context 天 is only used after 星期.

星期天 xing^{1}qi^{1}tian^{1}

Or

星期日 xing^{1}qi^{1}ri^{4}

Or, to be formal—

周日 zhou^{1}ri^{4}

For "the weekend", the Chinese has a strict literal correspondence. It is—

周末 zhou^{1}mo^{4}

Now let's listen to the following short sentences.

Today is Sunday.

今天是星期天。jintian^{1} shi^{4} xing^{1}qi^{1}tian^{1}.

Or

今天是周日 jin^{1}tian^{1} shi^{4} zhou^{1} ri^{4}.

Tomorrow is Monday.

明天是星期一。ming^{2}tian^{1} shi^{4} xing^{1}qi^{1}yi^{1}.

Or

明天是周一。ming^{2}tian^{1} shi^{4} zhou^{1} yi^{1}.

The day after tomorrow is Tuesday.

后天是星期二。hou^{4}tian^{1} shi^{4} xing^{1}qi^{1}er^{4}.

Or

后天是周二。hou^{4}tian^{1} shi^{4} zhou^{1}er^{4}.

The day after the day after tomorrow is Wednesday.

大后天是星期三。da^{4} hou^{4}tian^{1} shi^{4} xing^{1}qi^{1}san^{1}.

Or

大后天是周三。da^{4} hou^{4}tian^{1} shi^{4} zhou^{1}san^{1}.

Yesterday was Saturday.

昨天是星期六。zuo^{2}tian^{1} shi^{4} xing^{1}qi^{1}liu^{4}.

Or

昨天是周六。zuo^{2}tian^{1} shi^{4} zhou^{1} liu^{4}.

The day before yesterday was Friday.

前天是星期五。qian^{2}tian^{1} shi^{4} xing^{1}qi^{1}wu^{3}.

Or

前天是周五。qian^{2}tian^{1} shi^{4} zhou^{1} wu^{3}.

The day before the day before yesterday was Thursday.

大前天是星期四。da^{4} qian^{2}tian^{1} shi^{4} xing^{1}qi^{1}si^{4}.

Or

大前天是周四。da^{4} qian^{2}tian^{1} shi^{4} zhou^{1}si^{4}.

When we refer to a week or a day of the week before or after the present, we use two important words, 上 and 下. Although they literally mean "go up" and "go down", they are nevertheless used together with the week or weekdays to mean "last" and "next".

Last week

上星期 shang^{4} xing^{1}qi^{1}

上个星期 shang^{4} ge^{4} xing^{1}qi^{1}

Next week

下星期 xia^{4} xing^{1}qi^{1}

下个星期 xia^{4} ge^{4} xing^{1}qi^{1}

Since the measure word 个 and the number "one" can be omitted in context, we actually have a few alternatives to the same week. They are—

Last week

上一个星期 shang^{4} yi^{1} ge^{4} xing^{1}qi^{1}

上个星期 shang4 ge4 xing1qi1
上星期 shang4 xing1qi1
Next week
下一个星期 xia4 yi1 ge4 xing1qi1
下个星期 xia4 ge4 xing1qi1
下星期 xia4 xing1qi1
Last Monday 上一个星期一 shang4 yi1 ge4 xing1qi1yi1
上个星期一 shang4 ge4 xing1qi1yi1
上星期一 shang4 xing1qi1yi1
Next Tuesday
下一个星期二 xia4 yi1 ge4 xing1qi1er4
Last Saturday
上一个星期六 shang4 yi1 ge4 xing1qi1liu4
Last weekend
上一个周末 shang4 yi1 ge4 zhou1mo4
上个周末 shang4 ge4 zhou1mo4
Next weekend
下周末 xia4 ge4 zhou1mo4
下一个周末 xia4 yi1 ge4 zhou1mo4

To say a week still earlier or later, we can simply repeat the word 上 or 下.

The week before last week
上上一个星期 shang4 shang4 yi1 ge4 xing1qi1
The week after next week
下下一个星期 xia4 xia4 yi1 ge4 xing1qi1
This use of 上 and 下 also applies to "month" which is—
月 yue4
Last month
上个月 shang4 ge4 yue4
The month before the last
上上一个月 shang4 shang4 yi1 ge4 yue4
Next month
下个月 xia4 ge4 yue4
The month after the next
下下个月 xia4 xia4 ge4 yue4
All right! Now let's come to the Chinese word for "year".
年 nian2

With the word for "year", the Chinese will use the same modifiers for "day".

This year

今年 jin^{1}nian^2
Next year
明年 ming^{2}nian^2
The year after the next
后年 hou^{4}nian^2
The year after the year after the next
大后年 da^4 hou^{4}nian^2
The year before last year
前年 qian^{2}nian^2
The year before the year before last year
大前年 da^4 qian^{2}nian^2

So let's have a quick review of the modifiers for different time words again.

Today 今天 jin^{1}tian^1
This week 这个星期 zhe^4 ge^4 xing^{1}qi^1
This month 这个月 zhe^4 ge^4 yue^4
This year 今年 jin^{1}tian^1

Let's put them together in the Chinese sequence, which is just contrary to the English.

今年，这个月，这个星期，今天 jin^{1}tian^1, zhe^4 ge^4 yue^4, zhe^4 ge^4 xing^{1}qi^1, jin^{1}tian^1

OK! We have learned so much already. Let's now put these words to use in sentences as we learn some more new words.

Shop, or store 商店 shang^{1}dian^4
In business, or to run business 营业 ying^{2}ye^4
When is the shop in business, i.e. what are the shop's business hours?
商店什么时候营业？shang^{1}dian^4 shen^{2}me shi^{2}hou^4 ying^{2}ye^4?
It is in business, i.e. open for business, 24 hours.
二十四小时营业。er^4 shi^2 si^4 xiao^{3}shi^2 ying^{2}ye^4?
Every day?
每天吗？mei^3 tian^1 ma^1?
No, it's not in business on Wednesday, i.e. it's not open on Wednesday.
不，星期三不营业。bu^4, xing^{1}qi^{1}san^1 bu^4 ying^{2}ye^4.
Or
No, it's closed on Wednesday.
不，星期三关门。bu^4, xing^{1}qi^{1}san^1 guan^1 men^2.
Is it open on weekends?
周末开门吗？zhou^{1}mo^4 kai^1 men^2 ma?
Yes, it's open. 是，开门。shi^4, kai^1 men^2.

As we see, the Chinese for "open" and "closed" is 开门 and 关门

respectively, which literally translate as "open the door" and "close the door" but are understood as "in business" and "not in business".

The shop is in business, i.e. open for business, on weekends.

商店周末营业。shang^{1}dian^{4} zhou^{1}mo^{4} ying^{2}ye^{4}.

Or, to be more informal

The shops is open on weekends.

商店周末开门。shang^{1}dian^{4} zhou^{1}mo^{4} kai^{1} men^{2}.

It doesn't open on Monday.

周一不开门。zhou^{1}yi^{1} bu^{4} kai^{1} men^{2}.

It isn't open for business on Monday.

周一不营业。zhou^{1}yi^{1} bu^{4} ying^{2}ye^{4}.

It opens from Sunday to Saturday.

从星期天到星期六都开门。cong^{2} xing^{1}qi^{1}tian^{1} dao^{4} xing^{1}qi^{1}tian^{1} dou^{1} kai^{1} men^{2}.

From when to when?

Or, literally—

From what hour to what hour?

从几点到几点？cong^{2} ji^{3} dian^{3} dao^{4} ji^{3} dian^{3}?

From 8:30 in the morning to 5:30 in the afternoon.

从早上八点半到下午五点半。cong^{2} zao^{3} shang^{4} ba^{1}dian^{3} ban^{4} dao^{4} xia^{4}wu^{3} wu^{3}dian^{3} ban^{4}.

All right! Now let's learn to tell the date of the month in a year. And the first thing to know is that for date the Chinese has two words.

Date

日 ri^{4}

Or, to be less formal—

号 hao^{4}

While 日 can be used for both "day" of the week and "date" of the month, 号 can only be used for the day of the month. It actually means the word "number". As for months, numbers are used directly because in Chinese they don't have specific names as in English. Let's listen.

January 一月 yi^{1} yue^{4}

February 二月 er^{4} yue^{4}

March 三月 san^{1} yue^{4}

April 5 四月五日 si^{4} yue^{4} wu^{3} ri^{4}

Or

四月五号 si^{4} yue^{4} wu^{3} hao^{4}

May 6 五月六日 wu^{3} yue^{4} liu^{4} ri^{4}

Or

五月 6 号 wu^{3} yue^{4} liu^{4} hao^{4}

June 7 七月七日 qi^{1} yue^{4} qi^{1} ri^{4}
August 10 八月十号 ba^{1} yue^{4} shi^{2} hao^{4}
September 11 九月十一号 jiu^{3} yue^{4} shi^{2} yi^{1} hao^{4}
October 12 十月十二号 shi^{2} yue^{4} shi^{2} er^{4} hao^{4}
November 19 十一月十九号 shi^{2} yi^{1} yue^{4} shi^{2} jiu^{3} hao^{4}
December 21 十二月二十一号 shi^{2} er^{4} yue^{4} er^{4} shi^{2} yi^{1} hao^{4}

As we have learned, the word 日 used for date is formal, and thus is often used in writing, while 号 is more informal and mainly used in speech. Let's take an example.

When, or literally, on what date do the holidays begin?
几号开始放假？ji^{3} hao^{4} kai^{1}shi^{3} fang^{4}jia^{4}?
You see, it's written on the calendar: June 5.
你看，写在日历上：七月五日。ni^{3} kan^{4}, xie^{3} zai^{4} ri^{4}li^{4} shang^{4}, qi^{1} yue^{4} wu^{3} ri^{4}.
Calendar 日历 ri^{4}li^{4}
It's written on the calendar.
写在日历上 xie^{3} zai^{4} ri^{4}li^{4} shang^{4}.

OK! Now let's listen to some short sentences using what we have learned.

Are you going to China this year?
你今年去中国吗？ni^{3} jin^{1}nian^{2} qu^{4} zhong^{1}guo^{2} ma?
No. I'm not going.
不。我不去。bu^{4}, wo^{3} bu^{4} qu^{4}.
Going the next year?
明年去吗？ming^{2}nian^{2} qu^{4} ma?
Nor the next year.
明年也不去。ming^{2}nian^{2} ye^{3} bu^{4} qu^{4}.
Then, how about the year after the next?
那后年呢？na^{4} hou^{4}nian^{2} ne?
I'll see if I will go then.
后年再看吧。na^{4}hou^{4} zai^{4} kan^{4} ba.
Why?
为什么？wei^{4} shen^{2}me?
Because I went to China last year.
因为去年去过了。yin^{1}wei^{4} qu^{4}nian^{2} qu^{4} guo^{4} le.
When does he plan to go to Beijing?
他计划什么时候去北京？ta^{1} ji^{4}hua^{4} shen^{2}me shi^{2}hou^{4} qu^{4} bei^{3} jing^{1}?
Plan
计划 ji^{4}hua^{4}
When does he plan to go to Beijing?

他计划什么时候去北京？ta1 ji4hua4 shen2me shi2hou4 qu4 bei3 jing1?

His plan is to go in spring or autumn.

他打算明年春天或秋天去。ta1 da3suan4 ming2nian2 chun1tian1 huo4 qiu1tian1 qu4.

Why spring or autumn?

为什么春天或秋天？wei4 shen2me chun1tian1 huo4 qiu1tian1?

Because it is too hot in summer and too cold in winter.

因为夏天太冷，冬天太热。yin1wei4 xia4tian1 tai4 re4 dong1 tian1 tai4 leng3.

As we see, the four seasons are respectively 春 (chun1), 夏 (xia1), 秋 (qiu1) and 冬 (dong1). Since Chinese has the tendency to use two-syllable words, each of them takes up the additional single syllable word 天 (tian1). Of course, you don't have to use it all time. For instance—

There are four seasons in a year: spring, summer, autumn, and winter.

一年有四季：春，夏，秋，冬。yi1 nian2 you3 si4 ji4 chun1 xia4 qiu1 dong1.

Or, for more rhythmic expression and quick tempo, we can say—

一年四季，春夏秋冬。yi1 nian2 si4 ji4, chun1 xia4 qiu1 dong1.

Remember, the Chinese for "why" and "because" are "为什么" and "因为" respectively.

你为什么不去？ni3 wei4 shen2me bu4 qu4?

Because I have been there.

因为去过了。yin1wei4 qu4 guo4le.

Because I have been there already.

因为已经见过面了。yin1 wei4 yi3jing1 jian4 guo4 mian4 le.

Why do you, or will you go in spring or autumn?

为什么春天或秋天去？wei4 shen2me chun1tian1 huo4 qiu1tian1 qu4.

Because it is too hot in summer and too cold in winter.

因为夏天太热，冬天太冷。yin1wei4 xia4tian1 tai4 re4 dong1tian1 tai4 leng3.

All right! Let's carry on with the dialogues.

Did you go to work yesterday?

昨天你上班了吗？zuo2tian1 ni3 shang4ban1 le1 ma?

No.

没有。mei2 you3.

Or

没有上班。mei2 you3 shang4ban1.

How about the day before yesterday? Did you work?

前天呢？上班了吗？qian2tian1 ne? shang4ban1 le1 ma?

Not then either.

也没有。ye3 mei2 you3.

Then did you work the day before the before yesterday?

那么大前天是不是上班了？na4me da4 qian2tian1 shi4 bu4 shi4 shang4ban1 le?

—Yes. I did.

——是，大前天上班了。shi4, da4 qian2tian1 shang4ban1 le.

Or

是的，大前天上了。shi4 de, da4 qian2tian1 shang4 le.

As we see, in giving a positive answer we can use 是的 as well as 是. The difference is that 是的 carries a more emphatic tone than 是 for clearing up any doubt.

Is it? Is it so? Or, is it really?

是吗？shi4 ma?

Yes. Or, yes indeed.

是的。shi4 de.

In fact, 是 plus 的 can form a structure for emphasizing something inserted between them. In this case, it is usually stressed in pronunciation. For example—

Literally, it is indeed what I have said.

是我说的。shi4 wo3 shuo1 de.

The shop is indeed open today.

商店今天是开门的。shang1dian4 jin1tian1 shi4 kai1 men2 de.

It is he who worked on shift yesterday.

昨天是他上班的。zuo2tian1 shi4 ta1 shang4ban1 de.

It is the day before yesterday that I took a rest.

我是前天休息的。wo3 shi4 qian2tian1 xiu1xi de.

Rest 休息 xiu1xi

The pattern 是 + 的 can also be used to indicate some past action as a fact. Therefore, it sometimes serves as a past tense marker. For example:

When did you begin to learn Chinese?

你是什么时候开始学中文的？ni3 shi4 shen2me shi2hou4 kai1shi3 xue2 zhong1wen2 de?

It was last summer when I began.

是去年夏天开始的。shi4 qu4nian2 xia4tian1 kai1shi3 de.

When did they come?

他们是什么时候来的？ta1men shi4 shen2me shi2hou4 lai2 de?

When did they come to China?

他是什么时候来中国的？ta1 shi4 shen2me shi2hou4 lai2 zhong1guo2 de?

When was the contract signed?

合同是什么时候签订的？he2tong2 shi4 shen2me shi2hou4 qian1 ding4

de?

When did the negotiation begin?

谈判是什么时候开始的？tan^{2}pan^4 shi^4 shen^{2}me shi^{2}hou^4 kai^{1}shi^3 de?

When did it end?

什么时候结束的？shen^{2}me shi^{2}hou^4 jie^{2}shu^4 de?

When was the meeting held?

会议是什么时候召开的？hui^{4}yi^4 shi^4 shen^{2}me shi^{2}hou^4 zhao^{4}kai^1 de?

When did that happen?

那是什么时候发生的？na^4 shi^4 shen^{2}me shi^{2}hou^4 fa^1 sheng^1 de?

When was the email sent out?

邮件是什么时候发出的？you^{2}jian^4 shi^4 shen^{2}me shi^{2}hou^4 fa^1 chu^1 de?

When was this email received?

这个邮件是什么时候收到的？zhe^4 ge^4 you^{2}jian^4 shi^4 shen^{2}me shi^{2}hou^4 shou^1 dao^4 de?

OK! Now, let's learn the two words that directly correspond to "begin" and "finish"—

Begin or start 开始 kai^{1}shi^3

Finish or end 结束 jie^{2}shu^4

When does the Spring Festival begin?

春节什么时间开始？chun^{1}jie^2 shen^{2}me shi^{2}jian^1 kai^{1}shi^3?

February 15.

二月十五号。er^4 yue^4 shi^2 wu^3 hao^4.

When does it end?

什么时间结束？shen^{2}me shi^{2}jian^1 jie^{2}shu^4?

February 29.

二月二十九号。er^4 yue^4 er^4 shi^2 jiu^3 hao^4.

When do you begin work?

你什么时候开始工作？ni^3 shen^{2}me shi^{2}hou^4 kai^{1}shi^3 gong^{1}zuo^4?

Half past 8.

八点半。ba^1 dian^3 ban^4.

When does the meeting begin?

会议几点开始？hui^{4}yi^4 ji^3 dian^3 kai^{1}shi^3?

9 o'clock or 9 o'clock sharp.

九点整。jiu^3 dian^3 zheng^3.

The meeting will begin immediately, or in no time.

会议马上开始。hui^{4}yi^4 ma^3 shang^4 kai^{1}shi^3.

It will soon finish.

马上结束。ma^3 shang^4 jie^{2}shu^4.

OK! Let's finish this lesson here.

好了。我们在这里结束这一课。hao^3 le, wo^{3}men zai^4 zhe^{4}li^3 jie^{2}shu^4

zhe^4 yi^2 ke^4.

Or, more naturally—

好了。这一课就在这里结束。hao^3 le, zhe^4 yi^2 ke^4 jiu^4 zai^4 zhe^{4}li^3 jie^{2}shu^4.

Just here. Or, right here.

就在这里。jiu^4 zai^4 zhe^{4}li^3.

LESSON 14 第十四课

FROM HERE TO THERE 从这里到那里 CONG2 ZHE4LI3 DAO4 NA4LI3

In asking for and giving directions, there are two basic words to use.

From… to…

从……到……cong2...dao4...

From where to where?

从哪里到哪里？cong2 na3li3 dao4 na3li3?

From where and to where are you going?

你要从哪里到哪里？ni3 yao4 cong2 na3li3 dao4 na3li3?

From here to there.

从这里到那里。cong2 zhe4li3 dao4 na4li3.

How can I get there from here? Or literally, how to go there from here?

从这里到那里怎么走？cong2 zhe4li3 dao4 na4li3 zen3me zou3?

How can I get to the city center from here?

从这里到市中心怎么走？cong2 zhe4li3 dao4 shi4zhong1xin1 zen3me zou3?

To the nearest Bank of China

到最近的中国银行 dao4 zui4 jin4 de zhong1guo2 yin2hang2

How can I get to the nearest Bank of China?

到最近的中国银行怎么走？dao4 zui4 jin4 de zhong1guo2 yin2hang2 zen3me zou3?

Is this one nearer than that one?

这个比那个更近吗？zhe4 ge4 bi3 na4 ge4 geng4 jin4 ma1?

No. This one is relatively distant.

不。这个比较远。bu4. zhe4 ge4 bi3jiao4 yuan3.

But this one is bigger, bigger than that one.

但是这个更大，比那个更大。dan4shi4, zhe4 ge4 geng4 da4, bi3 na4 ge4 geng4 da4.

Which restaurant is better?

哪一家餐馆更好？na3 yi1 jia1 can1guan3 geng4 hao3?

Or

哪一家餐馆更好一点？na3 yi1 jia1 can1guan3 geng4 hao3 yi1dian3?

Is it this one here or that one there?

是这里这一家还是那里那一家？shi4 zhe4 yi1 jia4 hai2shi4 na4 yi1 jia1?

Of course, it's this one.

当然是这一家。dang1ran2 shi4 zhe4 yi1 jia1.

However, that one is cheaper somewhat.

不过，那一家更便宜一些。bu4guo4, na4 yi1 jia1 geng4 pian2yi4.

Or

但是，那一家更便宜一些。dan4shi4, na4 yi1 jia1 geng4 pian2yi4.

But, that one is too far.

但是，那一家太远。dan4shi4, na4 yi1 jia1 tai4 yuan4.

However, that one is cheaper.

不过，那一家更便宜。bu4guo4, na4 yi1 jia1 geng4 pian2yi4.

How can I get to the Great Wall?

到长城怎么走？dao4 chang2cheng2 zen3me zou3?

Which line bus gets there?

几路公交车可以到？ji3lu4 gong1jiao1 ke3yi3 dao4?

The word 可以 is equivalent to the English "may" or "can". So, we can replace it with 能.

几路公交车能到那里？ji3lu4 gong1jiao1ke3yi3 dao4 na4li3?

Which bus should I take?

我该乘几路车？wo3 gai1 cheng2 ji3 lu4 che1?

Here the single-character word 该 is a more colloquial way of saying 应该, which corresponds to "should" in English. And 乘 is also interchangeable with 乘坐 or simply 坐, although 坐 literally translates as "sit".

我该坐几路公交车？wo3 gai1zuo4 ji3 lu4 gong1jiao1che1?

Or

我该乘坐几路公交车？wo3 gai1 cheng2zuo4 ji3 lu4 gong1jiao1che1?

What means of transportation are there apart from the bus?

除了公交车还有什么交通工具？chu2le gong1jiao1che1 hai2you shen2me jiao1tong1 gong1ju4?

Means of transportation, or literally, tools of transportation

交通工具 jiao1tong1 gong1ju4

What else?

还有什么？hai2you3 shen2me?

What other means of transportation are available to get there?

到那里还有什么交通工具？dao4 na4li3 hai2you3 shen2me jiao1tong1 gong1ju4?

Or

还有什么交通工具到那里？hai2you3 shen2me jiao1tong1 gong1ju4 dao4 na4li3?

You can also use the train.

你还可以乘坐火车。ni3 hai2 ke3yi3 cheng2zuo4 huo3che1.

Are bus and metro both available?

公交和地铁都有吗？gong1jiao1 he2 di4tie3 dou1 you3 ma1?

There is only the bus, but not the metro.

只有公交，没有地铁。zhi3you3 gong1jiao1, mei2you3 di4tie3.

Is there a plane?

有没有飞机？you3 mei2 you3 fei1ji1?

Is there a flight?

有没有航班？you3 mei2 you3 hang2ban1?

Are both plane and passenger ship available?

飞机和邮轮都有吗？fei1ji1 he2 you2lun2 dou1 you3 ma1?

Yes. Both plane and passenger ship are available.

有的。飞机和邮轮都有。you3 de, fei1ji1 he2 you2lun2 dou1 you3.

All right! Now we may need to know another word for the passenger ship.

客船 ke4chuan2

Is there a passenger ship?

有客船吗？you3 ke4chuan2 ma1?

Both the flight and the passenger ship are available.

航班和客船都有。hang2ban1 he2 ke4chuan2 dou1 you3.

Are they direct?

是直达吗？shi4 zhi2da2 ma1?

Some are direct, and some are not.

有的是直达，有的不是。you3 de shi4 zhi2da2, you3 de bu4 shi4?

Can I get there by metro?

OK! Now let's learn another important word that is used in big cities.

The metro or the underground

地铁 di4tie3

乘坐地铁能到吗？cheng2zuo4 di4tie3 neng2 dao4 ma1?

Yes. You can get there by metro too.

能。乘坐地铁也能到。neng2. cheng2zuo4 di4tie3 ye3 neng2 dao4.

Both bus and metro go there.

公交和地铁都能到。gong1jiao1 he2 di4tie3 dou1 neng2 dao4.

How many kilometers is it?

有多少公里？you3 duo1shao3 gong1li3?

How many miles?

有多少英里？you3 duo1shao3 ying1li3?

Is it very far?
很远吗？hen3 yuan3 ma1?
It's not very far, but nor is it very near.
不远，但是也不很近。bu4 yuan3, dan4shi4 ye3 bu4 hen3 jin4.
How far is it?
有多远？you3 duo1 yuan3?
About 7 or 8 kilometers.
大约七八公里。da4yue1 qi1 ba1 gong1li3.
Or
大概七八公里。da4gai4 qi1 ba1 gong1li3.
Or
七八公里左右。qi1 ba1 gong1li3 zuo3you4.
What is the distance?
距离是多少？ju4li2 shi4 duo1shao3?
Is it a long distance? Or, is it far?
距离远吗？ju4li2 yuan3 ma1?
Or
距离长吗？ju4li2 chang2 ma1?
No. It's very near, or literally, it's very short.
不长，很短。bu4 chang2, hen3 duan3.
Is there a metro from the railway station to the airport?
从火车站到机场有地铁吗？cong2 huo3che1zhan4 dao4 ji1chang3 you3 di4tie3 ma1?
There is no metro. There is only the airport shuttle bus.
没有地铁，只有机场大巴。mei2 you3 di4tie3, zhi3you3 ji1chang3 da4ba1.
Do I need to change lines to get to the city center?
到市中心要换乘吗？dao4 shi4 zhong1xin1 yao4 huan4 cheng2 ma1?
Literally, change the ride. Or simply, change lines
换乘 huan4 cheng2
Is there a high-speed train?
有没有高铁？you3 mei2 you3 gao1tie3?
Is there a high-speed train from Nanjing to Beijing?
从南京到北京有高铁吗？cong2 nan2jing1 dao4 bei3jing1 you3 gao1tie3 ma1?
Of course there is.
当然有。dang1ran2 you3.
How long does it take to get there?
到那里需要多长时间？dao4 na3li3 xu1yao4 duo1 chang2 shi2jian1?
It takes about 25 minutes.

需要二十五分钟左右。xu1yao2 er4shi2wu3 fen1zhong1 zuo3you4.

How long does it take by train?

乘火车需要多长时间？cheng2 huo3che1 xu1yao4 duo1 chang2 shi2jian1?

How long does it take to get there by bus? Or, then how long by bus?

那么乘公交需要多长时间呢？na4me cheng2 gong1jiao1 xu1yao4 duo1 chang2 shi2jian1 ne?

To give directions to a particular place within a city, you need to learn some more words and phrases, which can be used as sentences in context. For instance—

Go straight ahead. 向前走。xiang4 qian2 zou3

Or

往前走。wang4 qian2 zou3.

Go directly ahead. 向前直走。xiang4 qian2 zhi2 zou3.

Go straight ahead all the way.

一直往前走。yi1 zhi2 wang4 qian2 zou3.

All the way

一直 yi1zhi2

Go straight ahead all the way.

一直往前走。yi1 zhi2 wang4 qian2 zou3.

Or

一直向前走。yi1 zhi2 xiang4 qian2 zou3.

Then, turn left.

然后向左拐。ran2hou4, xiang4 zuo3 guai3.

When you reach the intersection, turn right.

走到路口向右拐。zou3 dao4 lu4kou3 xiang4 you4 guai3.

Then turn left again.

然后冉往左拐。ran2hou4 zai4 wang4 zuo3 guai3.

Go straight along this road, and turn right when you reach the crossroads.

沿着这条路直走。yan2zhe zhe4 tiao2 lu4 zhi2 zou3.

到路口向右拐。dao4 lu4 kou3 xiang4 you4 guai3.

In the above, 往 and 向 are interchangeable, and 沿着 means "along".

Along the main road

沿着大路 yan2zhe da4lu4

Another word for 沿着 is—

顺着 shun4zhe

Along this road

顺着这条路 shun4zhe zhe4 tiao2 lu4

Go along or go down the main road.

沿着大路走。yan2zhe da4lu4 zou3.

Go straight ahead down this road.

沿着这条路往前直走。yan2zhe zhe4 tiao2 lu4 wang4 qian2 zou3.

Or

顺着这条路一直往前走。shun4zhe zhe4 tiao2 lu4 yi1zhi2 wang4 qian2 zou3.

All along, all the way

一直 yi1zhi2

All the way to the end

一直到底 yi1zhi2 dao4di3

Go straight down this road until you come to the end.

顺着这条路一直走到底。shun4zhe zhe4 tiao2 lu4 yi1zhi2 zou3 dao4di3.

All right! Now we should know that both 一直 and 到底 are also frequently used adverbs. Let's listen.

For the last two years, I have been learning Chinese all the time.

这两年我一直在学中文。zhe4 liang3 nian2 wo3 yi1zhi2 zai4 xue2 zhong1wen2.

Today he has been playing the piano the whole time.

他今天一直在弹钢琴。ta1 jin1tian1 yi1zhi2 zai4 tan2 gang1qin2.

I can never write this Chinese character well, or literally, I have not been able to write it well all the time.

我一直写不好这个汉字。wo3 yi1zhi2 xie3 bu4hao3 zhe4 ge4 han4zi4.

This child never listens to his mother, or literally, he has not been listening to his mother all the time.

这个孩子一直不听他妈妈的话。zhe4 ge4 hai2zi yi1zhi2 bu4 ting1 ta1 ma1ma de hua4.

As we see, 一直 is similar in meaning to "always", which in Chinese can also be expressed with another word:

总是 zong3shi4

He is always studying.

他总是在学习。ta1 zong3shi4 zai4 xue2xi2.

It's always raining these days.

这些天总是下雨。zhe4xie1 tian1 zong4shi4 xia4yu3.

Don't be late all the time, or stop being late all the time.

不要总是迟到。bu4 yao4 zong3shi4 chi2dao4.

Now we should know that in the case of the negative, 总是不 and 一直不 can be simply understood as "never".

He never listens to what I say.

他总是不听我的话。ta1 zong3shi4 bu4 ting1 wo3 de hua4.

He always listens to what I say.

他总是听我的话。ta1 zong3shi4 ting1 wo3 de hua4.

He never listens to what I say.
他一直不听我的话。ta1 yi1zhi2 bu4 ting1 wo3 de hua4.
He always listens to what I say.
他一直都听我的话。ta1 yi1zhi2 dou1 ting1 wo3 de hua4.
OK! Now let's look at 到底 as it is used in different contexts.
Go straight down this road until you come to the end.
顺着这条路一直走到底。shun4zhe zhe4 tiao2 lu4 yi1zhi2 zou3 dao4di3.
Where do you want to go, ultimately? Or where is it you actually want to go?
你到底要去哪里？ni3 dao4di3 yao4 qu4 na3li3?
What do you want, actually?
你到底想要什么？ni1 dao4di3 xiang3yao4 shen2me?
What does he want to say, actually?
他到底想说什么？ta1 dao4di3 xiang3 shuo1 shen2me?
In fact, 到底 is often used for showing strong emotion, like the English "what the devil" or "what the hell".
What the hell is he doing?
他到底在干什么？ta1 dao4di3 zai4 gan4 shen2me?
There is another adverb using 到, but it means "everywhere". This is—
到处 dao4chu4
Everywhere in China there are many people.
中国到处有很多人。zhong1guo2 dao4chu4 you3 hen3 duo1 ren2.
Or
中国到处都是人。zhong1guo2 dao4chu4 dou1 shi4 ren2.
Such things happen everywhere.
这种事情到处都会发生。zhe4 zhong4 shi4qing4 dao4chu4 dou1 hui4 fa1sheng1.
However, the concept of "never" can also be expressed in another way:
从来不 cong2lai2 bu4
Or
从来没有 cong2lai2 mei2you3
I have never known him.
我从来不认识他。wo3 cong2lai2 bu4 ren4shi ta1.
We have never met.
我们从来没有见过面。wo3men cong2lai2 mei2you3 jian4 guo4 mian4.
We have never met before.
我们以前从来没有见过面。wo3men yi3qian2 cong2lai2 mei2you3 jian4 guo4 mian4.
I have never heard there is such a thing.

我从来没有听说过有这种事。wo^3 cong^{2}lai^2 mei^{2}you^3 ting^{1}shuo^1 guo^4 you^3 zhe^4 zhong^3 shi^4.

I never read lying down.

我从来都不躺着看书。wo^3 cong^{2}lai^2 dou^1 bu^4 tang^{3}zhe kan^4 shu^1.

In the two-character word "躺着", the second character 着 is actually an important Chinese function word indicating the present state of being while something is going on. For example—

Let me read it while you listen.

我来读，你听着。wo^3 lai^2 du^2, ni^3 ting^{1}zhe.

The library is still open.

图书馆还开着。tu^{2}shu^{1}guan^3 hai^2 kai^{1}zhe.

He went out riding a bike.

他骑着自行车出去了。ta^1 qi^{2}zhe zi^{4}xing^{2}che^1 chu^{1}qu^4 le.

Don't let the kid read lying down.

不要让孩子躺着看书。bu^{4}yao^4 rang^4 hai^{2}zi tang^{3}zhe kan^{4}shu^1.

As they walked on, they found themselves there.

他们走着走着就走到了。ta^{1}men zou^{3}zhe zou^{3}zhe jiu^4 dao^4 le.

They stand there talking.

他们站在那里谈话。Ta^{1}men zhan^{4}zai^4 na^{4}li^3 tan^{2}hua^4.

What are you doing inside with the door closed?

你关着门在里面干什么？ni^3 guan^{1}zhe men^2 zai^4 li^{3}mian^4 gan^4 shen^{2}me?

We often go traveling, taking the child along with us.

我们经常带着孩子旅游。wo^{3}men jing^{1}chang^2 dai^{4}zhe hai^{2}zi lv^{3}you^2.

I often fall asleep while listening to music.

我经常听着音乐就睡着了。wo^3 jing^{1}chang^2 ting^{1}zhe yin^{1}yue^4 jiu^4 shui^{4}zhao^2 le.

OK! Let's now come back to giving directions.

Go straight, cross two streets, and then there you are.

直走，过两条街，然后就到了。zhi^2 zou^3, guo^4 liang^3 tiao^2 jie^1, ran^{2}hou^4 jiu^4 dao^4 le.

And then there you are.

然后就到了。ran^{2}hou^4 jiu^4 dao^4 le.

You will be there after 10 minutes.

十分钟后就到了。shi^1 fen^{1}zhong^2 jiu^4 dao^4 le.

The word 就 is a very frequently used adverb that can be understood as "just" or "just right", or simply as "and then". However, it often suggests a mood which is hard to translate into English. Let's listen.

Walk 10 minutes and then you'll be there.

走十分钟就到了。zou^3 shi^1 fen^{1}zhong^2 jiu^4 dao^4 le.

I'll be right there.
我就到。wo3 jiu4 dao4.
The train is arriving in no time.
火车就要到了。huo3che1 jiu4yao4 dao4 le.
The bus station is right ahead.
公交车站就在前面。gong1jiao1che1 jiu4 zai4 qian2mian4.
I just want to see the Great Wall. Or, I insist on visiting the Great Wall.
我就是要去看长城。wo3 jiu4shi4 yao4 qu4 kan4 chang2cheng2.

If someone is going in the same direction or to the same place as you, he may say the following:

I'm also going there. Just follow me.
我也去那里，就跟着我走吧。wo3 ye3 qu4 na4li3, jiu4 gen1zhe wo3 zou3 ba.

Or simply—

跟我走！ gen1 wo3 zou3!

Or

跟我来！ gen1 wo3 lai2!

I'm also going there. Just follow me.
我也去那里。就跟我走。wo3 ye3 qu4 na4li3. jiu4 gen1 wo3 zou3.

Or

我也去那里。跟我来。wo3 ye3 qu4 na4li3. gen1 wo3 lai2.
Lead to; connect to
通
Where does this road go? Or, where does it lead to?
这条路通到哪里？ zhe4 tiao2 lu4 tong1 dao4 na3li3?

There is a two-character noun that uses the word 通 too, and this is—

Path 通道 tong1dao4

Please note that this two-character word is a noun and should not be confused with the verbal phrase that consists of a verb meaning "to connect" and the preposition 到. In fact, they have two different second characters in writing. Let's listen to the following sentence which uses both the noun 通道 and the verbal phrase 通到.

Does this path connect to the exit? Or, literally can this path lead to the exit?

这条通道能通到出口吗？ zhe4 tiao2 tong1dao4 neng2 tong1 dao2 chu1kou3 ma1?

Of course, we can make it simpler by saying the following—
这条路能通到出口吗？ zhe4 tiao2 lu4 neng2 tong1 dao2 chu1kou3 ma1?

In fact, we can also drop the preposition and say—

这条通道通不通出口？ zhe4 tiao2 tong1dao4 tong1 bu4 tong1 chu1kou3?

The word 出口 literally translates as "out mouth" but simply means "exit".

Excuse me. Where is the exit?

请问，出口在哪里？qing3 wen4, chu1kou3 zai4 na3li3?

Although, as we know, the antonym of 出 is 进, the more commonly used word for entrance is not 进口 but 入口, in which 入 is a more formal word and another antonym of 出.

Where is the entrance?

哪里是入口？na3li3 shi4 ru4kou3?

Or

哪里有入口？na3li3 you3 ru4kou3?

Here it is important to know that in Chinese we use the word 进口 in a different situation, where it mainly means "to import". Then the single-character 口 means the port instead of "mouth" or "opening". Let's listen to the following and learn the differences.

Do you import or export?

你们进口还是出口？ni3men jin4kou3 hai2shi4 chu1kou3?

We do both, import and export.

我们都做，进口和出口。wo3men dou1zuo4, jin4kou3 he2 chu1kou3.

Or

我们都做，做进出口。wo3men dou1 zuo4, zuo4 jin4chu1kou3.

Or

我们进出口都做。wo3men jin4chu1kou3dou1 zuo4.

Some commodities are imported, and some are exported.

有些商品是进口的，有些是出口的。you3xie1 shang1pin3 shi4 jin4kou3 de, you3xie1 shi4 chu1kou3 de.

Is this imported?

这是进口的吗？zhe4 shi4 jin4kou3 de ma1?

Yes. It is imported.

是的，是进口的。shi4 de, shi1 jin1kou1 de.

From which country is it imported?

是从哪个国家进口的？shi4 cong2 na3 ge4 guo2jia1 jin4kou3 de?

It is imported from China.

是从中国进口的。shi4 cong2 zhong1guo2 jin4kou3 de.

Are those also imported from China?

那些也是从中国进口的吗？na4xie1 ye3 shi4 cong2 zhong1guo2 jin4kou3 de ma1?

No, not all. Some are to be exported to the US.

不是。有些是要出口到美国的。bu4 shi4. you3xie1 shi4 yao4 chu1kou3 dao4 mei3guo2 de.

To be exported to the US
要出口到美国 yao^{4} chu^{1}kou^{3} dao^{4} mei^{3}guo^{2}
OK! Now let's come back to directions.
Is this the entrance to the metro?
这是地铁的入口吗？ zhe^{4} shi^{4} di^{4}tie^{3} ru^{4}kou^{3} ma^{1}?
No. This is the exit.
不是。这是出口。bu^{4}shi^{4}。zhe^{4} shi^{4} chu^{1}kou^{3}.
OK! Now, what do you say if you want to ask for the bus number? For example—
Which line of bus should I take?
乘几路公交车？ cheng^{2} ji^{3}lu^{4} gong^{1}jiao^{1}che^{1}?
Take bus no. 11.
乘 11 路公交。cheng^{2} shi^{2}yi^{1} lu^{4} gong^{1}jiao^{1}che^{1}.
Here 几路 means "which line", and 公交车 can be shortened to 公交.
乘几路公交车？
乘 11 路公交。
And then?
然后呢？ ran^{2}hou^{4} ne?
Then change to no. 22.
然后换乘 22 路。ran^{2}hou^{4} huan^{4}cheng^{2} er^{4}shi^{2}er^{4} lu^{4}.
Then
然后 ran^{2}hou^{4}
Change lines, or literally, "change the ride"
换乘 huan^{4}cheng^{2}
Then change to no. 22
然后换乘 22 路。ran^{2}hou^{4} huan^{4}cheng^{2} er^{4}shi^{2}er^{4} lu^{4}.
Very regrettably, there is no direct bus.
很遗憾，没有直达公交。hen^{3} yi^{2}han^{4}, mei^{2}you^{3} zhi^{2}da^{2} gong^{1}jiao^{1}.
Very regrettably 很遗憾。hen^{3} yi^{2}han^{4}.
Direct bus 直达公交。zhi^{2}da^{2} gong^{1}jiao^{1}
Very regrettably, there is no direct bus.
很遗憾，没有直达公交。hen^{3} yi^{2}han^{4}, mei^{2}you^{3} zhi^{2}da^{2} gong^{1}jiao^{1}.
But there is a metro station nearby.
但是，附近有地铁站。dan^{4}shi^{4}, fu^{4}jin^{4} you^{3} di^{4}tie^{3} zhan^{4}.
Nearby 附近 fu^{4}jin^{4}
But there is a metro station nearby.
但是，附近有地铁站。dan^{4}shi^{4}, fu^{4}jin^{4} you^{3} di^{4}tie^{3} zhan^{4}.
You need to change from bus to metro.
你要从公交换乘地铁。ni^{3} yao^{4} cong^{2} gong^{1}jiao^{1} huan^{4}cheng^{2} di^{4}tie^{3}.

Now, we should remember that the measure word for the number of the bus line is different from that of the metro.

Change to which metro line?

换乘地铁几号线？huan^{4}cheng^2 di^{4}tie^3 ji^3 hao^4 xian^4?

Change to line 3.

换乘三号线地铁。huan^{4}cheng^2 san^1 hao^4 xian^4 di^{4}tie^3.

Which bus line should I take?

要乘几路公交？yao^4 cheng^2 ji^3 lu^4 gong^{1}jiao^1?

Which metro line?

几号线地铁？ji^{3}lu^4 di^{4}tie^3 xian^4?

Which bus should I take to get there?

到那里乘几路公交？dao^4 na^{4}li^3 cheng^2 ji^3 lu^4 gong^{1}jiao^1?

Is it no. 11 or no. 22?

是 11 路还是 22 路？shi^4 shi^{2}yi^1 lu^4 hai^{2}shi^4 er^{4}shi^{2}er^4 lu^4?

Neither. You need to take no. 33.

都不是。要乘 33 路 dou^1 bu^{4}shi^4。yao^4 cheng^2 san^{1}shi^{2}san^1 lu^4.

Where to get off the bus?

在哪里下车？zai^1 na^{3}li^3 xia^4 che^1?

Get off at the fourth stop.

在第四站下。zai^4 di^{4}si^{4}zhan^4 xia^4.

It's not the fourth stop. It's the fifth.

不是第四站，是第五站。bu^{4}shi^4 di^{4}si^{4}zhan^4, shi^4 di^{4}wu^{3}zhan^4.

Then turn back and walk. Or, then walk back.

然后回头走。ran^{2}hou^4 hui^{2}tou^2 zou^3.

Turn back and walk 5 minutes.

回头走 5 分钟。hui^{2}tou^2 zou^3 wu^3 fen^{1}zhong^1.

Turn back and cross an intersection.

回头过一个路口。hui^{2}tou^2 guo^4 yi^1 ge^4 lu^{4}kou^3.

After crossing the next intersection, you will see it.

过了下一个路口你就看见了。guo^{4}le xia^4 yi^1 ge^4 lu^{4}kou^3 ni^3 jiu^4 kan^{4}jian^4 le.

Pass a supermarket, and then there you are.

经过一家超市就到了。jing^{1}guo^4 yi^1 jia^1 chao^{1}shi^4 jiu^4 dao^4 le.

Now, we should know there is a subtle difference between 过 and 经过: while 过 has a wider meaning that covers not only "pass" and "pass by" but also "cross" and "get over", 经过 is mostly used to mean "pass by" or "go through". Let's listen to the following:

Cross the bridge

过桥 guo^4 qiao^2

Cross the flyover or overpass; literally "cross the sky bridge"

过天桥 guo^4 tian^{1}qiao^2

Cross the road

过马路 guo^4 ma^{3}lu^4

After crossing the road, turn left.

过了马路向左拐。guo^4 le ma^{3}lu^4 xiang^4 zuo^3 guai^3.

After crossing the flyover or overpass, turn right.

过了天桥向右拐。guo^4 le tian^{1}qiao^2 xiang^4 you^4 guai^4.

Cross two intersections and then turn west.

过两个路口后向西拐。guo^4 liang^{3}ge^4 lu^{4}kou^3 hou^4 xiang^4 xi^1 guai^3.

Please note that the verb 拐 which means "to turn" is mainly used as an informal one. The more formal word is—

转 zhuan^4

Literally, turn a curve, or turn a corner

转一个弯 zhuan^4 yi^1 ge^4 wan^1

Or

拐一个弯 guai^3 yi^1 ge^4 wan^1

To get to the bank, you need to pass the post office.

到银行要经过邮局。dao^4 yin^{2}hang^2 yao^4 jing^{1}guo^4 you^{2}ju^2.

After passing the post office, you will see the bank.

过了邮局后，你会看到银行。guo^4 le you^{2}ju^2 hou^4, ni^3 hui^4 kan^{4}dao^4 yin^{2}hang^2.

Then there is another word that also uses 过, and this is 通过, which often translates as "pass through" or simply "pass". You would use this word for going through a channel or passing an exam.

The train is passing through the tunnel.

火车正在通过隧道。huo^{3}che^1 zheng^{4}zai^4 tong^{1}guo^4 sui^{4}dao^4.

Have you passed the exam?

你通过考试了吗？ni^3 tong^{1}guo^4 kao^{3}shi^4 le ma^1?

OK! Let's continue with our words and phrases for directions.

Go straight east. 向东直走。xiang^4 dong^1 zhi^2 zou^3.

Go straight west. 向西直走 xiang^4 xi^1 zhi^2 zou^3

Go south. 向南走。xiang^4 nan^2 zou^3

Go straight south.向南直走。xiang^4 nan^2 zhi^2 zou^3

To the north; towards the north 往北 wang^4 bei^3

Go north or towards the north. 往北走。wang^4 bei^3 zou^3

Turn to the southeast. 向东南拐。xiang^4 dong^{1}nan^2 guai^3

Turn to the northwest. 向西北拐。xiang^4 xi^{1}bei^3 guai^3

As we see, although in English north and south come before east and west in compound forms such as southeast and northwest, in Chinese they are always put at the end.

Northeast 东北 dong^{1}bei^3
Northwest 西北 xi^{1}bei^3
Southeast 东南 dong^{1}nan^2
Southwest 西南 xi^{1}nan^2
From southwest to northeast
从西南到东北 cong^2 xi^{1}nan^2 dao^4 dong^{1}bei3
From southeast to northwest
从东南到西北 cong^2 dong^{1}nan^2 dao^4 xi^{1}bei^3

OK! Now, we need to learn two single-syllable words that are frequently used as suffixes of a direction word. They literally mean "surface" and "side" respectively.

面 mian^4
And
边 bian^1
The front or ahead
前面 qian^{2}mian^4
Or
前边 qian^{2}bian^1
In front of the bookstore is a restaurant.
书店前面是一家餐厅。shu^{1}dian^4 qian^{2}mian^4 shi^4 yi^1 jia^1 can^{1}ting^1.
The rear or back
后面 hou^{4}mian^4
Or
后边 hou^{4}bian^1
The restroom is in the back of the bookstore.
洗手间在书店后面。xi^{3}shou^{3}jian^1 zai^4 shu^{1}dian^4 hou^{4}mian^4.
The left side
左面 zuo^{3}mian^4
Or
左边 zuo^{3}bian^1
The right side
右面 you^{4}mian^4
Or
右边 you^{4}bian^1
The telephone is on the left of the bed.
电话在床的左面。dian^{4}hua^4 zai^4 chuang^2 de zuo^{3}mian^4.
On; above; the top; the upper side
上面 shang^{4}mian^4.
Or
上边 shang^{4}bian^1

The mobile phone is on the desk.
手机在桌子上面。shou3ji1 zai4 zhuo1zi shang4mian4.
Under; below; the lower side
下面 xia4mian4
Or
下边 xia4bian1
The telephone directory is under the telephone.
电话本在电话下面。dian4hua4ben3 zai4 dian4hua4 xia4mian4.
Inside, or the inside
里面 li3mian4
Or
里边 li3bian1
The bedroom is inside.
卧室在里面。wo4shi4 zai4 li3mian4.
Outside
外面 wai4mian4
Or
外边 wai4bian1
The dining room is outside the lobby.
餐厅在大厅外面。can1ting1 zai4 da4ting1 wai4mian4.
The east side
东面 dong1mian4
Or
东边 dong1bian2
On the east side is a bank.
东边有一家银行。dong1bian1 you3 yi1 jia1 yin2hang2.
The west side
西面 xi1mian4
Or
西边 xi1bian1

On the west of the hotel is the express service, or literally, express company.

酒店西边是快递公司。jiu3dian4 xi1bian1 shi4 kuai4di4 gong1si1.
The south or south side
南面 nan2mian4
Or
南边 nan2bian1
There is a parking area on the south side.
南边有一个停车场。nan2bian1 you3 yi1 ge4 ting2che1chang3.
The north or north side

北面 bei^{3}mian^4

Or

北边 bei^{3}bian^1

The railway station is to the north of the city center.

火车站在市中心北面。huo^{3}che^{1}zhan^4 zai^4 shi^{4}zhong^{1}xin^1 bei^{3}mian^4.

However, these two words, 面 and 边, are not considered as suffixes in the following:

The opposite or the opposite side

对面 dui^{4}mian^4

On the opposite side of the supermarket is a coffee bar.

超市对面是咖啡吧。chao^{1}shi^4 dui^{4}mian^4 shi^4 ka^{1}fei^{1}ba^1.

The edge, the opposite side

对边 dui^{4}bian^1

There are two other words that can be useful for giving the location of a place. Let's listen.

Next door

隔壁 ge^{2}bi^4

There is a bookstore next to the coffee bar.

咖啡吧隔壁有一家书店。ka^{1}fei^{1}ba^1 ge^{2}bi^4.

The bank is next door to the supermarket.

银行就在超市隔壁。yin^{2}hang^2 jiu^4 zai^4 chao^{1}shi^4 ge^{2}bi^4.

Literally, next door on the other side of the street, i.e. across the street and one door down.

斜对面 xie^2 dui^{4}mian^4

Literally, the store is just next door across the street, i.e. across the street and one door down.

那家商店就在斜对面。na^4 jia^1 shang^{1}dian^4 jiu^4 zai^4 xie^2 dui^{4}mian^4.

LESSON 15 第十五课

LEARN CHINESE WELL 把汉语学好 BA^3 HAN^{4}YU^3 XUE^2 HAO^3

The word 把 (ba^3) is a function word for forming a structure, rather than denoting something substantial. It is used to put the object of the verb in the beginning as the topic of the sentence and emphasize the result of the action or how the action is done. Therefore, the ba-structure usually calls for a verbal complement at the end. Let's listen to the following:

Learn well 学好 xue^2 hao^3

Learn Chinese well 学好汉语 xue^2 hao^3 han^{4}yu^3

In the above, the basic word of 好 hao^3 serves as the complement of the verb 学 xue^2, meaning the result of learning is good. We can use the word 把 to introduce the object 汉语 as the topic and emphasize the result by saying—

把汉语学好 ba^3 han^{4}yu^3 xue^2 hao^3

Since the word 把 also means "to take" or "to take hold of" when used as a verb, learners might expediently understand it as such.

I want to take Chinese and learn it well.

我要把汉语学好。wo^3 yao^4 ba^3 han^{4}yu^3 xue^2 hao^3.

Let's listen to more verbs with a complement and then use 把 to emphasize the result.

Learn to master; learn and master as a result

学会 xue^2 hui^4

Learn Chinese characters and as a result master them.

学会汉字 xue^2 hui^4 han^{4}zi^4

把汉字学会 ba^3 han^{4}zi^4 xue^2 hui^4

Write well

写好 xie^3 hao^3

Write Chinese characters well

写好汉字 xie^3 hao^{3}han^{4}zi^4

把汉字写好 ba^3 han^{4}zi^4 xie^3 hao^3

Damage or ruin, or literally, "make bad"

搞坏 gao^3 huai^4

Have or has damaged

搞坏了 gao^3 huai^4 le

He damaged or has damaged the mobile phone.

他搞坏了手机。gao^3 huai^4 le shou^{3}ji^1.

他把手机搞坏了。ta^1 ba^3 shou^{3}ji^1 gao^3 huai^4 le.

The word 搞 (gao^3) has a synonym, 弄 (nong^4). Both 搞 (gao^3) and 弄 (nong^4) are more casual or colloquial than 做 (zuo^4) in style.

He has damaged the mobile phone.

他搞坏了手机。ta^1 gao^3 huai^4 le shou^{3}ji^1.

他弄坏了手机。ta^1 nong^4 huai^4 le shou^{3}ji^1.

他把手机弄坏了。ta^1 ba^3 shou^{3}ji^1 nong^4 huai^4 le.

If we want to take "the mobile phone" as the subject and change the sentence into the passive voice in Chinese, we can use another word. And this is—

被 bei^4

Let's compare the following:

He has damaged the mobile phone.

他把手机搞坏了。ta^1 ba^3 shou^{3}ji^1 gao^3 huai^4 le.

他把手机弄坏了。ta^1 ba^3 shou^{3}ji^1 nong^4 huai^4 le.

The mobile phone is damaged or has been damaged by him.

手机被他搞坏了。shou^{3}ji^1 bei^4 ta^1 gao^3 huai^4 le.

手机被他弄坏了。shou^{3}ji^1 bei^4 ta^1 nong^4 huai^4 le.

Let's listen to more sentences using the word 被 and compare them with the active expressions.

The thief is caught by the police.

小偷被警察抓住了。xiao^{3}tou^1 bei^4 jing^{3}cha^2 zhua^1 zhu^4 le.

The police have caught the thief.

警察抓住了小偷。jing^{3}cha^2 zhua^1 zhu^4 le xiao^{3}tou^1.

警察把小偷抓住了。jing^{3}cha^2 ba^3 xiao^{3}tou^1 zhua^1 zhu^4 le.

Literally, the key has been lost by me.

钥匙被我丢了。yao^{4}shi bei^4 wo^3 diu^1 le.

I have lost the key.

我丢了钥匙。wo^3 diu^1 le yao^{4}shi.

Or

我把钥匙丢了。wo^3 ba^3 yao^{4}shi diu^1 le.

Now, please note one important thing: the word 被 is not an equivalent to the English preposition "by" in sentences using the passive voice, because it cannot be omitted even if the agent of the action is missing.

The thief is caught.

小偷被抓住了。xiao^{3}tou^1 bei^4 zhua^1 zhu^4 le.
钥匙被丢了。yao^{4}shi bei^4 diu^1 le.
手机被搞坏了。shou^{3}ji^1 bei^4 gao^3 huai^4 le.

Another point to note is that the word 被 as a passive voice marker can often be dropped in Chinese. For example—

小偷抓住了。xiao^{3}tou^1 zhua^1 zhu^4 le.
钥匙丢了。yao^{4}shi diu^1 le.
手机搞坏了。shou^{3}ji^1 gao^3 huai^4 le.

One thing to note is that the word 被 (bei^4) is also interchangeable with the word 给 (gei^3), especially in colloquial northern Mandarin.

The car is driven away by my friend.
汽车给我朋友开走了。qi^{4}che^1 gei^3 wo^3 peng^{2}you kai^1 zou^3 le.
The car is driven away.
汽车给开走了。qi^{4}che^1 gei^3 kai^1 zou^3 le.
The computer is damaged by him.
电脑给他搞坏了。dian^{4}nao^3 gei^3 ta^1 gao^3 huai^4 le.
The computer is damaged.
电脑给搞坏了。dian^{4}nao^3 gei^3 gao^3 huai^4 le.

Then again we have another alternative for expressing the passive voice. This involves using the word 让, the original meaning of which is "to let" or "to allow". However, when using 让, we cannot omit the agent of the action.

The car is driven away by my friend.
汽车给我朋友开走了。qi^{4}che^1 gei^3 wo^3 peng^{2}you kai^1 zou^3 le.
The computer is damaged by him.
电脑给他搞坏了。dian^{4}nao^3 gei^3 ta^1 gao^3 huai^4 le.

As we see, the complement words in the above structure need not only be adjectives such as 好 and 坏, but also verbs, such as 走 in 开走 and 住 in 抓住. Let's listen to some more two-syllable words in which the second was originally a verb. Then we'll apply them to the sentence structure using 把.

Listen and understand as a result.
听懂。ting^{1}dong^3
Listen to me and understand what I say, or simply, comprehend my words
听懂我的话。ting^{1}dong^{3}wo^3 de hua^4
Have you understood what I said?
你听懂我的话了吗？ting^{1}dong^{3}wo^3 de hua^{4}le ma^1?
你把我的话听懂了吗？ni^3 ba^3 wo^3 de hua^4 ting^1 dong^3 le ma^1?
Try to memorize, or remember as a result.

记住。ji4 zhu4.
Memorize this word.
记住这个单词。ji4 zhu4 zhe3 ge4 dan1ci2.
把这个单词记住 ba3 zhe3 ge4 dan1ci2 ji4 zhu4.
I need to memorize this word.
我要记住这个单词。wo3 yao4 ji4 zhu4 zhe3 ge4 dan1ci2.
我要把这个单词记住。wo3 yao4 ba3 zhe3 ge4 dan1ci2 ji4 zhu4.
Note down
记下 ji4 xia4
Note down the teacher's words.
记下老师的话。ji4 xia4 lao3shi1 de hua4.
把老师的话记下。ba3 lao3shi1 de hua4 ji4 xia4.
I have noted down what the teacher said, or the teacher's words.
我把老师的话记下了。wo3 ba3 lao3shi1 de hua4 ji4 xia4 le.
Shut, or literally, close up, when referring to a window or door
关上 guan1 shang4
Or
闭上 bi4 shang4
Please shut the window, or close the window.
请关上窗户。qing3 guan1 shang4 chuang1hu.
请把窗户关上。qing3 ba3 chuang1hu guan1 shang4.
Shut up! Or, shut your mouth!
闭上你的嘴！ bi4 shang4 ni3 de zui3!
把你的嘴闭上！ ba3 ni3 de zui3 bi4 shang4!
I put on my clothes.
我穿上衣服。wo3 chuan1 shang4 yi1fu.
我把衣服穿上。wo3 ba3 yi1fu chuan1 shang4.

In the above, the word 上 corresponds to the English "up" or "on" and is also a verb. Here it simply serves as the complement of the first verb characters "关" or "穿", which respectively mean "close" or "wear". So, let's listen again.

Please shut the window, or close the window.
请关上窗户。qing3 guan1 shang4 chuang1hu.
请把窗户关上。qing3 ba3 chuang1hu guan1 shang4.
I put on my clothes.
我穿上衣服。wo3 chuan1 shang4 yi1fu.
我把衣服穿上。wo3 ba3 yi1fu chuan1 shang4.

Of course, we should know the antonym of the word 关上:

Open
打开 da3 kai1

Open the window, please.
请打开窗户。qing^{3} da^{3} kai^{1} chuang^{1}hu.
请把窗户打开。qing^{3} ba^{3} chuang^{1}hu da^{3} kai^{1}.
Open the door
打开门 da^{3} kai^{1} men^{2}
Please open the door.
请把门打开。qing^{3} ba^{3} men^{2} da^{3} kai^{1}.
For the opposite expression of 穿上, we say—
Take off
脱下 tuo^{1} xia^{4}
Take off your coat.
脱下你的外套。tuo^{1} xia^{4} ni^{3} de wai^{4}tao^{4}.
把你的外套脱下。ba^{3} ni^{3} de wai^{4}tao^{4} tuo^{1} xia^{4}.

Here we see the word 开 is used as the complement of the verb 打, which is also a basic word. Although the original meaning of 打 is "to strike", "to beat", "to hit", or even "to fight", it is often used more generally as the English "make", "do" and "get". So it should be understood according to the context. For the time being, let's just remember that 开 is the result of 打. And for this reason, we can say—

Please open the door.
请把门打开。qing^{3} ba^{3} men^{2} da^{3} kai^{1}.
Please open the book.
请把书打开。qing^{3} ba^{3} shu^{1} da^{3} kai^{1}.
Literally, please open the computer, i.e. start the computer.
请把电脑打开。qing^{3} ba^{3} dian^{4}nao^{3} da^{3} kai^{1}.
Please shut the computer, i.e. please shut the computer down.
请把电脑关上。qing^{3} ba^{3} dian^{4}nao^{3} guan^{1} shang^{4}.

Without using the introducing word 把, the sentence will be in its normal order.

Please start the computer, or literally, please open the computer.
请打开电脑。qing^{3} da^{3} kai^{1} dian^{4}nao^{3}.
Please shut the computer, or please close the computer down.
请关上电脑。qing^{3} guan^{1} shang^{4} dian^{4}nao^{3}.
Please shut the door.
请关上门。qing^{3} guan^{1} shang^{4} men^{2}.
请把门关上。qing^{3} ba^{3} men^{2}guan^{1} shang^{4}.

If you know the Chinese verb for "to end", "to finish", or "to complete" is 完 (wan^{2}), you can now understand the following:

Read to the end, read through, or read to the end.
读完 du^{2} wan^{2}

Finish reading that book
读完那本书 du^2 wan^2 na^4 ben^3 shu^1.
把那本书读完 ba^3 na^4 ben^3 shu^1 du^2 wan^2.
Have you finished reading that book?
你读完那本书了吗？ ni^3 du^2 wan^2 na^4 ben^3 shu^1 le ma^1?
你把那本书读完了吗？ ni^3 ba^3 na^4 ben^3 shu^1 du^2 wan^2 le ma^1?
Finish one's word, or finish speaking
说完 shuo^1 wan^2
Let me finish what I'm saying.
让我说完话。rang^4 wo^3 shuo^1 wan^2 hua^4.
Or
让我说完。rang^4 wo^3 shuo^1 wan^2.
Or
让我把话说完。rang^4 wo^3 ba^3 hua^4 shuo^1 wan^2.

Here we should note: although the original function of 完 (wan^2) is that of a verb, it can also serve a complementary function, but 了 (le) is only a function word to be used at the end of a sentence or verbal construct. So the following expressions are all correct.

I have finished reading that book.
我读完了那本书。wo^3 du^2 wan^2 le na^4 ben^3 shu^1.
我读了那本书。wo^3 du^2 le na^4 ben^3 shu^1.
我把那本书读完了。wo^3 ba^3 na^4 ben^3 shu^1 du^2 wan^2 le.
我把那本书读了。wo^3 ba^3 na^4 ben^3 shu^1 du^2 le.
I have said already.
我说了。wo^3 shuo^1 le.
Literally, I have finished my words, i.e., I have finished speaking.
我说完了。wo^3 shuo^1 wan^2 le.
I have done, or in context, I have done it, I'm done.
我做了。wo^3 zuo^4 le.
I have finished.
我做完了。wo^3 zuo^4 wan^2 le.

Since the word 把 (ba^3) is used to introduce the object of the verb, we have to add 话 (hua^4), which means "words" or "speech" and serves as the object of the verb 说 (shuo^1).

Literally, I have finished saying my words.
我把话说完了。wo^3 ba^3 hua^4 shuo^1 wan^2 le.

OK! Now we should know that as well as adjectives and verbs, the so-called Chinese measure words can be used as complements too. For example—

Please read the sentence once.

请把那句话读一遍。qing3 ba3 na4 ju4 hua4 du2 yi1 bian4.

Please repeat it once more.

请把它再重复一遍。qing3 ba3 ta1 zai4 chong2fu4 yi1 bian4.

Or

请把它再重复一次。qing3 ba3 ta1 zai4 chong2fu4 yi1 ci4.

Please explain it in English, or literally, explain it in English once.

请把这个词用英语解释一下。qing3 ba3 zhe4 ge4 ci2 yong4 ying1yu3 jieshi4 yi1 xia4.

Please translate it. Or, literally please translate it once.

请把它翻译一下。qing3 ba3 ta1 fan1yi4 yi1 xia4.

OK! Now let's go on to some more useful verbal phrases and change the order in which the word 把 appears.

Write an email

写邮件 xie3 you2jian4

He has finished writing the email.

他写完了邮件。ta1 xie3 wan2 le you2jian4.

他把邮件写完了。ta1 ba3 you2jian4 xie3 wan2 le.

Send a text, or literally, send a short message

发短信 fa1 duan3xin4

I have sent the email.

我发了短信 wo3 fa1 le duan3xin4

我把短信发了 wo3 ba3 duan3xin4 fa1 le

Of course you can add the Chinese word for "out", so that it literally corresponds to the English "send out".

Send out

发出去 fa1 chu1qu4

Or simply–

发出 fa1 chu1

I have sent out the text. Or, literally, I've sent out the short message.

我把短信发出去了。wo3 ba3 duan3xin4 fa1 chu1qu4 le.

Have you sent out the email?

你把邮件发出去了吗？ni3 ba3 you2jian4 fa1 chu1qu4 le ma1?

Here the two-syllable word 出去 (chu1qu4) is used as a verbal complement but not a verb in its original function which, as we have learned in Lesson 1, literally translates as "out go", meaning "go out". There are quite a few cases in which this two-character verb is used as the complement of the preceding verb. Let's listen to the following examples.

Literally, sell out

卖出去 mai4 chu1qu4

I have sold my used computer, or literally, I have sold out my old computer.

我把旧电脑卖出去了。wo3 ba3 jiu4 dian4nao3 mai4 chu1qu4 le.

Literally send out

送出去 song4 chu1qu4

Have you sent the gift? Or literally, have you sent out the gift?

你把礼物送出去了吗？ ni3 ba3 li3wu4 song4 chu1qu4 le ma1?

Take out or carry out

带出去 dai4 chu1qu4

Would you please take out your dog?

你把你的狗带出去好吗？ ni3 ba3 ni3 de gou3 dai4 chu1qu4 hao3 ma?

In the same pattern, we can use the opposite word 进来 (jin4lai2) as a complement.

Take or bring somebody or something in

带进来 dai4 jin4lai2

Please bring the guest in.

请把客人带进来。qing3 ba3 ke4ren2 dai4 jin4lai2.

Or

Literally, invite the guest in, or ask the guest to come in.

把客人请进来。ba3 ke4ren2 qing3 jin4lai2.

Please bring the breakfast in.

请把早饭带进来。qing3 ba3 zao3fan4 dai4 jin4lai2.

Move the desk in.

把桌子搬进来。ba3 zhuo1zi ban1 jin4lai2.

In the last sentence of these examples, the word 搬 literally means lift up and carry. And now for practice, let's listen to more phrases or sentences using 进来 (jin4lai2), 进去 (jin4qu4) and 出来 (chu1lai2), 出去 (chu1qu4).

Put the money in.

把钱放进去。ba3 qian2 fang4 jin4qu4.

Take the ticket out.

把票拿出来。ba3 piao4 na1 chu1lai2.

Take out, or literally, take out by hand

拿出来 na1 chu1lai2

Please take out your passport.

请把你的护照拿出来。qing3 ba3 ni3 de hu4zhao4 na1 chu1lai2.

Take the coffee in, or literally, send the coffee in.

把咖啡送进去。ba3 ka1fei1 song1 jin1qu4.

Key in this message, or input this message.

把这个消息输入进去。ba3 zhe4 ge4 xiao1xi1 shu1ru1 jin4qu4.

Key in, or input

输入进去 shu^{1}ru^1 jin^{4}qu^4

把这个消息输入进去。ba^3 zhe^4 ge^4 xiao^{1}xi^1 shu^{1}ru^1 jin^{4}qu^4.

Print out

打印出来 da^{3}yin^4 chu^{1}lai^2

Print out the picture.

把照片打印出来。ba^3 zhao^{4}pian^4 da^{3}yin^4 chu^{1}lai^2.

After learning these, we can now understand the following:

Literally, please call your manager out, or please ask the manager to come out.

请把经理叫出来。qing^3 ba^3 jing^{1}li^3 jiao^4 chu^{1}lai^2.

Of course, 进 (jin^4) and 出 (chu^1) could be replaced by 上 (shang^4) and 下 (xia^4) if the movement involves the direction of "up" and "down". For example—

Carry my luggage up.

把行李带上来。ba^3 xing^{2}li^3 dai^4 shang^{4}lai^2.

Luggage 行李 xing^{2}li^3

把行李带上来。ba^3 xing^{2}li^3 dai^4 shang^{4}lai^2.

Carry my luggage down.

把行李带下去。ba^3 xing^{2}li^3 dai^4 xia^{4}qu^4.

All right! Let's look at more examples of the verb-complement structure as we learn more phrases.

Literally, send there

送去 song^{4}qu^4

Have you sent the gift? Or literally, have you sent the gift there?

你把礼物送去了吗？ni^3 ba^3 li^{3}wu^4 song^4 chu^{1}qu^4 le ma^1?

Take there, or literally, carry there

带去 dai^{4}qu^4

Would you please take your dog there?

你把你的狗带去好吗？ni^3 ba^3 ni^3 de gou^3 dai^{4}qu^4 hao^3 ma?

Bring somebody or something here

带来 dai^{4}lai^2

Please bring the guest here.

请把客人带来。qing^3 ba^3 ke^{4}ren^2 dai^{4}lai^2.

Or

Literally, invite the guest here.

把客人请来。ba^3 ke^{4}ren^2 qing^{3}lai^2.

Please bring the breakfast here.

请把早饭带来。qing^3 ba^3 zao^3 fan^4 dai^{4}lai^2.

Move the desk in.

把桌子搬来。ba^3 zhuo^{1}zi ban^{1}lai^2.

Bring here, or literally, bring here by hand

拿来 na^{2}lai^2

Please bring your passport here.

请把你的护照拿来。qing^3 ba^3 ni^3 de hu^4 zhao^4 na^{2}lai^2.

Please take out your passport.

请把你的护照拿出来。qing^3 ba^3 ni^3 de hu^4 zhao^4 na^2 chu^{1}lai^2.

All right! Now let's reverse the direction by using 去 (qu^4) to replace the word 来 (lai^2). Remember that 去 (qu^4) may be replaced by 走 (zou^3), the original meaning of which is "to walk" or "to go".

Literally, I sent away my friend, i.e. I went to see my friend off.

我把朋友送走了。wo^3 ba^3 peng^{2}you song^4 zou^3 le.

Or

我送走了朋友。wo^3 song^4 zou^3 le peng^{2}you^3.

He has sent the gift.

他把礼物送去了。ta^1 ba^3 li^{3}wu^4 song^4 qu^4 le.

他送去了礼物。ta^1 song^4 qu^4 le li^{3}wu^4.

Please remember: 去 (qu^4) and 走 (zou^3) don't always have exactly the same meaning. For instance, while 去 (qu^4) can mean "go there" or to some place or in some destination, 走 (zou^3) as a complement is understood as "away". Let's listen to the following:

I want to take my son there.

我想把我的儿子带去。wo^3 xiang^3 ba^3 wo^3 de er^{2}zi dai^{4}qu^4.

Or

我想带儿子去。wo^3 xiang^3 dai^4 er^{2}zi qu^4.

I want to take my son away, or take my son there.

我想把儿子带走。wo^3 xiang^3 ba^3 er^{2}zi dai^4 zou^3.

Or

我想带儿子走。wo^3 xiang^3 dai^4 er^{2}zi zou^3.

Send a text, or literally, send a short message

发短信 fa^1 duan^3 xin^4

Have you sent the phone text? Or literally, have you sent out the short message?

你把短信发出去了吗？ni^3 ba^3 duan^3 xin^4 fa^1 chu^{1}qu^4 le ma^1?

Sign a contract

签合同 qian^1 he^{2}tong

Have you signed the contract?

你把合同签了吗？ni^3 ba^3 he^{2}tong qian^1 le ma^1?

Have you sent out the contract?

你把合同寄出去了吗？ni^3 ba^3 he^{2}tong ji^4 chu^{1}qu^4 le ma^1?

Make or prepare a meal, dinner

做饭 zuo^4 fan^4

Has Mom prepared the meal?

妈妈把饭做了吗？ ma^{1}ma ba^3 fan^4 zuo^4 le ma^1?

Or

妈妈把饭做好了吗？ ma^{1}ma ba^3 fan^4 zuo^4 hao^3 le ma^1?

Of course, the verb can also be of two characters. For instance, the verb 做 (zuo^4) in the above sentence can be replaced by 准备 (zhun^3 bei^4), which literally means "prepare".

妈妈把饭准备好了吗？ ma^{1}ma ba^3 fan^4 zhun^3 bei^4 hao^3 le ma^1?

So, let's learn more verbs with two characters.

Fix the computer

修理电脑 xiu^1 li^3 dian^4 nao^3

Have they fixed or repaired the computer?

他们把电脑修理好了吗？ ta^{1}men ba^3 dian^4 nao^3 xiu^1 li^3 hao^3 le ma^1?

Or simply—

修电脑 xiu^1 dian^4 nao^3

他们把电脑修好了吗？ ta^{1}men ba^3 dian^4 nao^3 xiu^1 hao^3 le ma^1?

Clean the room

打扫房间 da^3 sao^3 fang^2 jian^1

Have you cleaned the room?

你把房间打扫了吗？ ni^3 ba^3 fang^2 jian^1 da^3 sao^3 le ma^1?

Do the homework or assignment

做作业 zuo^4 zuo^{4}ye^4

I have done the homework or assignment.

我把作业做了。wo^3 ba^3 zuo^4 ye^4 zuo^4 le.

Answer the question

回答问题 hui^2 da^2 wen^4 ti^2

I have answered the question.

我把问题回答了。wo^3 ba^3 wen^4 ti^2 hui^2 da^2 le.

Solve the problem

解决问题 jie^3 jue^2 wen^4 ti^2

He has solved the problem.

他把问题解决了。ta^1 ba^3 wen^4 ti^2 jie^3 jue^2 le.

OK! Let's take a review of what we have learned. Or, let's review what is learned.

好了！让我们把学过的复习一下吧。hao^3 le, rang^4 wo^{3}men ba^3 xue^2 guo^4 de fu^4 xi^{2}yi^1 xia^4 ba.

Let's take a review of this lesson.

让我们把这一课复习一下吧。rang^{4} wo^{3}men ba^{3} zhe^{4} yi^{1} ke^{4} fu^{4} xi^{2}yi^{1} xia^{4} ba.

LESSON 16 第十六课

USEFUL INDIRECT COLLOCATIONS
常用间接搭配
CHANG²YONG⁴ JIAN⁴JIE¹ DA¹PEI⁴

In Chinese, as in other languages, some words frequently appear together in collocation with one another to form structural patterns. Such words can not only directly follow one another, but can also be separated by other words. Since direct collocations are obvious and easy to learn, we will focus on the indirect ones in this lesson.

1. First... then... 先 (xian¹)……后 (hou²)……

First go straight, and then turn right.

先直走，后向右拐。xian¹ zhi² zou³, hou⁴ xiang⁴ you⁴ guai³.

Please get aboard the bus, then buy the ticket.

请先上车，后买票。qing³ xian¹ shang⁴ che¹, hou⁴ mai³ piao⁴.

Please note that this indirect collocation pattern can be extended with an additional word—

再 zai⁴

First go straight, then turn right, then again turn left.

先直走，后向右拐，再向左拐。xian¹ zhi² zou³, hou⁴ xiang⁴ you⁴ guai³, zai⁴ xiang⁴ zuo³ guai³.

Please get aboard the bus and buy the ticket. And then, find your own seat.

请先上车，后买票。再找自己的座位。qing³ xian¹ shang⁴ che¹, hou⁴ mai³ piao⁴。zai⁴ zhao³ zi⁴ji³ de zuo⁴wei⁴.

In these sentences, the word 后 is also interchangeable with a two-syllable word that is a little more formal but still means "then".

然后 ran²hou⁴

First, go straight, then, turn right.

先直走，然后向右拐。xian¹ zhi² zou³, ran²hou⁴ xiang⁴ you⁴ guai³.

First, get in the vehicle, then buy the ticket.

请先上车，然后再买票。qing^3 xian^1 shang^4 che^1, ran^{2}hou^4 zai^4 mai^3 piao^4.

As we see, the word 再, which literally means "again", can also be used in direct collocation with "然后", especially in the last part of the sequence.

Please get aboard bus first, then buy the ticket, and then find your seat.

请先上车后买票，然后再找自己的座位。xian^1 shang^4 che^1 hou^4 mai^3 piao^4, ran^{2}hou^4 zai^4 zhao^3 zi^{4}ji^3 de zuo^{4}wei^4.

I need to take a rest first, and then eat.

我需要先休息，然后再吃饭。wo^3 xu^{1}yao^4 xian^1 xiu^{1}xi, ran^{2}hou^4 zai^4 chi^1 fan^4.

Now, let's listen to a longer sentence with more phrases in sequence.

To learn a language well, we need to read and listen first, then speak, and finally write.

要学好一种语言，我们要先读先听，然后说，最后再写。yao^4 xue^3 hao^3 yi^1 zhong^3 yu^{3}yan^2, wo^{3}men yao^4 xian^1 du^2 xian^1 ting^1, ran^{1}hou^4 shuo^1, zui^{4}hou^4 zai^4 xie^3.

To be more formal, we can replace the words used in this pattern with the following:

首先……其次……最后……

Firstly, I'm a teacher; secondly, a researcher; and lastly, a poet.

我首先是老师，其次是研究者，最后才是诗人。wo^3 shou^{3}xian^1 shi^4 lao^{3}shi^1, qi^{2}ci^4 shi^4 yan^{2}jiu^{1}zhe^3, zui^{4}hou^4 cai^{2}shi^4 shi^{1}ren^2.

Firstly, I will explain the topic…

首先，我要解释一下题目。shou^{3}xian^1, wo^3 yao^4 jie^{3}shi^4 yi^1 xia^4 ti^{2}mu^4.

Secondly, I will discuss the keywords.

其次，我要讨论关键词。qi^{2}ci^4, wo^3 yao^4 tao^{3}lun^4 guan^{1}jian^{4}ci^2.

And lastly, I will tell (you) my idea.

最后，我说说我的想法。zui^{4}hou^4, wo^3 shuo^{1}shuo^1 wo^3 de xiang^{3}fa^3.

2. Before...; after... 在 (zai^4)……之前 (zhi^{1}qian); 在 (zai^4) ……之后 (zhi^{1}hou^4)

Before coming to China, I couldn't speak any Chinese.

在来中国之前，我一点儿都不会说中文。zai^4 lai^2 zhong^{1}guo^2 zhi^{1}qian^2, wo^3 yi^1 dian'r^3 dou^1 bu^4 hui^4 shuo^1 zhong^{1}wen^2.

Only after arriving in China did my level of Chinese begin to rise, i.e. improve.

在来到中国之后，我的中文水平才开始提高。zai^4 lai^2 dao^4 zhong^{1}guo^2 zhi^{1}hou^4, wo^3 de zhong^{1}wen^2 shui^3 ping^2 cai^2 kai^{1}shi^3 ti^2 gao^1.

Here we should note that the opening preposition can be omitted.

Before coming to China, I couldn't speak any Chinese.

来中国之前，我一点儿都不会说中文。lai^{2} zhong^{1}guo^{2} zhi^{1}qian^{2}, wo^{3} yi^{1} dian'r^{3} dou^{1} bu^{4} hui^{4} shuo^{1} zhong^{1}wen^{1}.

Only after arriving in China did my level of Chinese begin to improve.

来到中国之后，我的中文水平才开始提高。lai^{2} dao^{4} zhong^{1}guo^{2} zhi^{1}hou^{4}, wo^{3} de zhong^{1}wen^{2} shui^{3} ping^{2} cai^{2} kai^{1}shi^{3} ti^{2} gao^{1}.

However, there are also two other words that can be used to replace 之前 and 之后. They are—

以前 yi^{3}qian^{2}

and

以后 yi^{3}hou^{4}

Before coming to China

在来中国以前 zai^{4} lai^{2} zhong^{1}guo^{2} yi^{3}qian^{2}

After arriving in China

在来到中国以后 zai^{4} lai^{2} dao^{4} zhong^{1}guo^{2} yi^{3} hou^{4}

Or, omit the preposition 在

来中国以前 lai^{2} dao^{4} zhong^{1}guo^{2} yi^{3}qian^{2}

来到中国以后 lai^{2} dao^{4} zhong^{1}guo^{2}yi^{3}hou^{4}

Let's see their uses in sentences.

I hadn't learned any Chinese before coming to China.

我来中国以前没有学过任何中文 wo^{3} lai^{2} dao^{4} zhong^{1}guo^{2} yi^{3}qian^{2} mei^{2} you^{3} xue^{2} guo^{4} ren^{4} he^{2} zhong^{1}wen^{2}.

I began learning Chinese only after I came to China.

我来到中国以后才开始学中文。wo^{3} lai^{2} dao^{4} zhong^{1}guo^{2} yi^{3}hou^{4} cai^{2} kai^{1}shi^{3} xue^{2} zhong^{1}wen^{2}.

There are no differences between the two pairs of words in this context, except that using 之前 and 之后 may sound a little more formal. So it's mostly a matter of personal choice. However, there is also the case where 以前 and 以后 are used independently as adverbs, which is not the case with 之前 and 之后.

Before, or in the past, I was a student. Now, I'm a teacher.

以前，我是学生。现在，我是老师。yi^{3}qian^{2}, wo^{3} shi^{4} xue^{1}sheng^{1}。xian^{4}zai^{4}, wo^{3} shi^{4} lao^{3}shi^{1}.

From now on, you can just call me Jimmy.

以后，你们就可以叫我吉米。yi^{3}hou^{4}, ni^{3}men jiu^{4} ke^{3}yi^{3} jiao^{4} wo^{3} ji^{2} mi^{3}.

Or

从此以后，你们就可以叫我吉米。cong^{2} ci^{3} yi^{3}hou^{4}, ni^{3}men jiu^{4} ke^{3}yi^{3} jiao^{4} wo^{3} ji^{2}mi^{3}.

As for this matter, we'll come to it later. Or literally, we'll talk about it later.

关于这件事，我们以后再说吧。guan1yu2 zhe4 jian4 shi4, wo3men yi3hou4 zai4 shuo1 ba.

3. As soon as... 一(yi1)……就(jiu4)……

As soon as I arrived, he left.

我一来他就走了。wo3 yi1 lai2 ta1 jiu4 zou3 le.

As soon as you explained, I understood.

你一解释我就懂了。ni3 yi1 jie3shi4 wo3 jiu4 dong3 le.

This child can learn immediately, or literally, as soon as this child begins to learn, he becomes good at it.

这孩子一学就会。zhe4 hai2zi yi1 xue2 jiu4 hui4.

In this pattern of collocation, the word 一 can be replaced with 刚

As soon as the day broke, he got up.

天一亮他就起床了。tian1 yi2 liang4 ta1 jiu4 qi3chuang2 le.

天刚亮他就起床了。tian1 gang1 liang4 ta1 jiu4 qi3chuang2 le.

Here the word 亮 literally corresponds to "light up" or "bright", and 天亮 translates to "the day breaks" or "daybreak".

Let's listen to more examples using the collocation of 刚 plus 就.

He is able to speak after he has learned it only for two months.

他刚学了两个月就会说了。ta1 gang1 xue2 le liang3 ge4 yue4 jiu4 hui4 shuo1 le.

They became close friends as soon as they got to know each other.

他们刚认识就成好朋友了。ta1men gang1 ren4shi4 jiu4 cheng2 hao3 peng2you3 le.

He got up as early as it was only 6 o'clock.

刚 6 点钟他就起床了。gang1 liu4 dian3 zhong1 ta1 jiu4 qi3chuang2 le.

I have forgotten it, although I learned it just now.

我刚学过就忘了。wo3 gang1 xue2 guo4 jiu4 wang4 le.

The bell rang as soon as the teacher entered the classroom.

老师刚进教室就打铃了。lao3shi1 gang1 jin4 jiao4shi4 jiu4 da3 ling2 le.

Apart from 一 plus 就 and 刚 plus 就, there is yet another frequently used collocation that is similar in effect. This literally translates as—

Speaking of … and then it…

说…… 就……shuo1...jiu4...

Speaking of rain, it is now raining.

说下雨就下雨。Shuo1 xia4 yu3 jiu4 xia4 yu3.

I say it and I will do it, or simply, I mean what I say.

我说到就做到。wo3 shuo1 dao4 jiu4 zuo4 dao4.

I say I will come, and here I am.
我说来就来。wo3 shuo1 lai2 jiu4 lai2.

In fact, the word 说 in this pattern is often simply understood as a mood, and may not mean that someone really says something, because its function is simply to indicate the immediacy of the action. For example:

How can you leave in such haste?
你怎么说走就走？ni3 zen3me shuo1 zou3 jiu4 zou3?

He came all of a sudden, or he appeared so quickly.
他说来就来。ta1 shuo1 lai2 jiu4 lai1.

It is raining all of a sudden.
雨说下就下。yu3 shuo1 xia4 jiu4 xia4.

I mean I will get up right now.
我说起床就起床。wo3 shuo1 qi3chuang2 jiu4 qi3chuang2.

The boss has arrived immediately.
老板说到就到。lao3 ban3 shuo1 dao4 jiu4 dao4.

The police have come immediately.
警察说来就来。jin3 cha2 shuo1 lai2 jiu4 lai2.

There is one thing to remember: since Chinese often doesn't have to use tense markers, the understanding of the same sentences above may depend on the context. For instance, they may also be in the past or future tense.

The boss came quite unexpectedly. Or, the boss may come anytime.
老板说到就到。lao3 ban3 shuo1 dao4 jiu4 dao4.

The police came immediately. Or, they will come immediately.
警察说来就来。jin3 cha2 shuo1 lai2 jiu4 lai2.

OK! Let's continue.

You have just arrived. How can you leave so suddenly?
你刚到，怎么说走就走？ni3 gang1 dao4, zen3me shuo1 zou3 jiu4 zou3?

I decide to learn Chinese and I mean it.
我说学中文就学中文。wo3 shuo1 xue2 zhong1wen2 jiu4 xue2 zhong1wen2.

Of course, the word 说 can also be factual when the context is a contrast between speaking and acting.

Whatever he says he means it, or simply, he always lives up to his word.
他说到就能做到。ta1 shuo1 dao4 jiu4 neng2 zuo4 dao4.

This same sentence can be changed into a compact sentence like the following:

他说到做到。Ta1 shuo1 dao4 zuo4 dao4

4. The more..., the more... 越 (yue^4)……越 (yue^4)……

The more I read, the more I want to read.

我越读书越想读书。wo^3 yue^4 du^2 shu^1 yue^4 xiang^3 du^2 shu^1.

The more I learn Chinese, the more interested I am in it.

我越学中文越对它感兴趣。wo^3 yue^4 xue^2 zhong^{1}wen^2 yue^4 dui^4 ta^1 gan^3 xing^{4}qu^4.

This girl is becoming more beautiful as she grows up.

这女孩越长越漂亮。zhe^4 nv^{3}hai^2 yue^4 zhang^3 yue^4 piao^{4}liang^4.

The rain is becoming heavier.

雨越下越大。yu^3 yue^4 xia^4 yue^4 da^4.

As we see, the word 越 is always followed by a verbal phrase. However, the word that most frequently follows it is 来. So, 越来越 is usually regarded as a set phrase that means "more and more" or simply "increasingly".

I read more and more books.

我读书越来越多了。wo^3 du^2 shu^1 yue^4 lai^2 yue^4 duo^1 le.

More and more I want to read.

我越来越想读书。wo^3 yue^4 lai^2 yue^4 xiang^3 du^2 shu^1.

This girl has become more and more beautiful.

这女孩越来越漂亮了。zhe^4 nv^{3}hai^2 yue^4 lai^2 yue^4 piao^4 liang^4 le.

The rain has become heavier and heavier.

雨下得越来越大了。yu^3 xia^4 de yue^4 lai^2 yue^4 da^4 le.

5. Not only..., but also... 不但 (bu^{4}dan^4)……而且 (er^{3}qie^3)……

He can not only speak Chinese, but also speak German.

他不但会说汉语，而且会说德语。ta^1 bu^{4}dan^4 hui^4 shuo^1 han^{4}yu^3, er^{3}qie^3 hui^4 shuo^1 de^{2}yu^3.

We not only work well, but are also healthy.

我们不但工作好，而且身体好。wo^{3}men bu^{4}dan^4 gong^{1}zuo^4 hao^3, er^{3}qie^3 shen^{1}ti^3 hao^3.

She is not only pretty, but also intelligent.

她不但漂亮，而且聪明。ta^1 bu^{4}dan^4 piao^{4}liang^4, er^{3}qie^3 cong^{1}ming.

Please note that the word 不但 is interchangeable with two other words.

The first is—

不仅 bu^{4}jin^3

You need not only to learn the pronunciation, but also the tones.

你不仅需要学习语音，而且要学习声调。ni^3 bu^{4}jin^3 xu^{1}yao^4 xue^{2}xi^2 yu^{3}yin^1, er^{3}qie^3 yao^4 xue^{2}xi^2 sheng^{1}diao^4.

The second expression that can be used in place of 不但 is—

不只是 bu4 zhi3shi4

We come to China not only to travel, but also to make friends.

我们来中国不只是要旅游，而且要交朋友。wo3men lai2 zhong1guo2 bu4 zhi3shi4 yao4 lv3you2, er3qie3 yao4 jiao1 peng2you3.

Make friends 交朋友。jiao1 peng2you3.

6. And... too; both... and...; or...; in addition 又 (you4)……又 (you4)……

I have to work and have to study too.

我又要工作，又要学习。wo3 you4 yao4 gong1zuo4, you4 yao4 xue2xi2.

He studies both English and Chinese, and he learns both well.

他又学英文又学中文，都学得很好。ta1 you4 xue2 ying1 wen2 you4 xue2 zhong1wen2, dou1 xue2 de4 hen3 hao3.

They are good friends, and are always happy when together. Literally, they are good friends, and will always talk and laugh when together.

他们是好朋友，在一起总是又说又笑。ta1men shi4 hao3 peng2you, zai4 yi1 qi3 zong3 shi4 you4 shuo1 you4 xiao4.

This man is very lazy. He neither works nor studies.

这个人很懒，又不工作，又不学习。zhe4 ge4 ren2 hen3 lan3, you4 bu4 gong1zuo4, you4 bu4 xue2xi2.

It's raining and windy. The weather is too bad.

又是下雨，又是刮风，天气太糟糕了。you4 shi4 xia4 yu3, you4 shi4 gua1 feng1, tian1qi4 tai4 zao1 gao1 le.

Here we need to know that there is another expression to replace this structure with the repeated 又. It is—

既……又……ji4... you4...

I have to work and have to study too.

我既要工作，又要学习。wo3 ji4 yao4 gong1zuo4, you4 yao4 xue2xi2.

He studies both English and Chinese. And he learns both well.

他既学英文又学中文，都学得很好。ta1 ji4 xue2 ying1 wen2 you4 xue2 zhong1wen2, dou1 xue2 de4 hen3 hao3.

This man neither works nor studies. He is very lazy.

这个人既不工作，又不学习。他很懒。zhe4 ge4 ren2 ji4 bu4 gong1zuo4, you4 bu4 xue2xi2。ta1 hen3 lan3.

7. While...; in the meantime... 一边 (yi1bian1)…… 一边 (yi1bian1)……

This child often plays while eating.

这孩子经常一边吃饭一边 玩。zhe4 hai2zi jing1chang2 yi1bian1 chi1 fan4 yi1bian1 wan2.

She likes to sing while doing manual work.

她喜欢一边唱歌一边做手工工作。ta1 xi3huan1 yi1bian1 chang4 ge1 yi1bian1 zuo4 shou3 gong1 gong1zuo4.

Many young people like to listen to music while walking.

很多年轻人都喜欢一边走路一边听音乐。hen3 duo1 nian1qing1 ren2 dou1 xi3huan1 yi1bian1 zou3lu4 yi1bian1 ting1 yin1yue4.

We always have a chat while drinking tea.

我们总是一边喝茶一边聊天。wo3men zong3 shi4 yi1bian1 he1 cha2 yi1bian1 liao2 tian1.

Don't use the telephone while driving.

不要一边开车一边打电话。bu4 yao4 yi1bian1 kai1 che1 yi1bian1 da3 dian4hua4.

One thing to note is that this pattern can have the word 一 dropped sometimes.

They entered the room together, talking and laughing.

他们边说边笑地走进了房间。ta1men bian1 shuo1 bian1 xiao4 de zou3 jin4 le fang2 jian1.

This child will always play the game while eating.

这孩子总是要边吃边玩。zhe4 hai2zi zong3 shi4 yao4 bian1 chi1 bian1 wan2.

I just like listening to music while taking a walk.

我就是喜欢边散步边听音乐。wo3 jiu4 shi4 xi3huan1 bian1 san4 bu4 bian1 ting1 yin1yue4.

They often sing songs while working.

他们经常边工作边唱歌。ta1men jing1chang2 bian1 gong1zuo4 bian1 chang4 ge1.

8. Whatever...; however... 怎么 (zen3me)…… 也 (ye3)……

However I say, or however I explain, he doesn't understand.

我怎么说他也不懂。wo3 zen3me shuo1 ta1 ye3 bu4 dong3.

He can never write Chinese characters well however he tries.

汉字他怎么写也写不好。han4zi4 ta1 zen3me xie3 ye3 xie3 bu4 hao3.

This is something that you cannot explain clearly whatever you say.

这件事情怎么说也说不清。zhe4jian4 shi4 zen3me shuo1 ye3 shuo1bu4qing1.

Cantonese is something I can never speak well no matter how I try.

广东话我怎么说也说不好。guang3dong1hua4 wo3 zen3me shuo1 ye shuo1 bu4 hao3.

Basketball is something I can never play well however I try.

篮球我怎么打也打不好。lan2qiu2 wo3 zen3me da4 ye da3 bu4 hao3.

Now, we should know that 怎么 and 也 can be in direct collocation to each other.

He doesn't understand after all.
他怎么也不懂。ta1 zen3me ye3 bu4 dong3.
He can't write Chinese characters well anyhow.
他怎么也写不好汉字。ta1 zen3me ye3 xie3 bu4 hao3 han4zi4.
This matter cannot be explained clearly anyway.
这件事怎么也说不清。zhe4 jian4 shi4 zen3me ye3 shuo1 bu4 qing1.
Cantonese is something I can never speak well.
广东话我怎么也说不好。guang3dong1 hua4 wo3 zen3me ye3 shuo1 bu4 hao3.
I can't play basketball well anyway.
篮球我怎么也打不好。lan2qiu2 wo3 zen3me ye3 da3 bu4 hao3.

9. In whatever condition... 无论(wu2lun4)……都(dou1)……

Whether it rains or not, we will go to the Great Wall.
无论下不下雨，我们都要去长城。wu2 lun4 xia4 bu4 xia4 yu3, wo3men dou1 yao4 qu4 chang2cheng2.
Or
无论下雨不下雨，我们都要去长城。wu2 lun4 xia4 yu3 bu4 xia4 yu3, wo3men dou1 yao4 qu4 chang2cheng2.
No matter how heavy the rain is, we will go to the Great Wall.
无论雨下得多么大，我们都要去长城。wu2 lun4 yu3 xia4 de4 duo1 me da4, wo3men dou1 yao4 qu4 chang2cheng2.
No matter how long the road is, I will go and find him.
无论路远还是不远，我都要去找他。wu2 lun4 lu4 yuan3 hai2shi4 bu4 yuan3, wo3 dou1 yao4 qu4 zhao3 ta1.
Or
无论路远不远，我都要去找他。wu2 lun4 lu4 yuan3 bu4 yuan3, wo3 dou1 yao4 qu4 zhao3 ta1.
However distant it is, I will go and find him.
无论路有多么远，我都要去找他。wu2 lun4 lu4 you3 duo1 me yuan3, wo3 dou1 yao4 qu4 zhao3 ta1.
No matter if Chinese is difficult or not, I will learn it.
无论汉语难不难，我都要学。wu2 lun4 han4yu3 nan2 bu4 nan2, wo3 dou1 yao4 xue2.
However hard Chinese is, I will learn it.
无论汉语有多么难我都要学。wu2 lun4 han4yu3 you3 duo1 me nan2, wo3 dou1 yao4 xue2.

Here 无论 is a relatively formal word. It can be replaced by the informal word—

不管

Whether it rains or not, we will go to the Great Wall.

不管下不下雨，我们都要去长城。bu^4 guan^3 xia^4 bu^4 xia^4 yu^3, wo^{3}men dou^1 yao^4 qu^4 chang^{2}cheng^2.

Regardless of how distant it is, I will go and find him.

不管路有多远，我都要去找他。bu^4 guan^3 lu^4 you^3 duo^1 yuan^3, wo^3 dou^1 yao^4 qu^4 zhao^3 ta^1.

Regardless of how difficult Chinese is, I will learn it.

不管汉语有多难，我都要学。bu^4 guan^3 han^{4}yu^3 you^3 duo^1 nan^2, wo^3 dou^1 yao^4 xue^2.

As we see, the single-syllable word 多 is the short form of 多么 in this context.

10. Unless... 非 (fei^1)…… 不可 (bu^4 ke^3)……

I won't give up unless I learn Chinese well, or I absolutely must learn Chinese well.

我非学好中文不可。wo^3 fei^1 xue^3 hao^3 zhong^{1}wen^2 bu^4 ke^3.

This matter is what I must talk about.

这件事我非说不可。zhe^4 jian^4 shi^4 wo^3 fei^1 shuo^1 bu^4 ke^3.

To hear you telling a joke absolutely makes me laugh to death.

听你讲笑话我非笑死不可。ting^1 ni^3 jiang^3 xiao^4 hua^4 wo^3 fei^1 xiao^4 si^3 bu^4 ke^3.

Whenever he drinks, he always gets drunk.

他一喝酒就非喝醉不可。ta^1 yi^1 he^1 jiu^3 jiu^4 fei^1 he^1 zui^4 bu^4 ke^3.

The child is determined to follow me anyway.

孩子非跟我走不可。hai^{2}zi fei^1 gen^1 wo^3 zou^3 bu^4 ke^3.

I will marry you anyway.

我非和你结婚不可。wo^3 fei^1 he^2 ni^3 jie^{2}hun^1 bu^4 ke^3.

This book is what you must read for sure.

这本书你非读不可。zhe^3 ben^3 shu^1 ni^3 fei^1 du^2 bu^4 ke^3.

It's so cheap and such a good book; I must buy it anyway.

这么好又这么便宜的书，我非买不可。zhe^4 me^4 hao^3 you^4 pian^{2}yi^4 de shu^1, wo^3 fei^1 mai^3 bu^4 ke^3.

11. If only... then... 只要 (zhi^{3}yao^4)……就 (jiu^4)……

If only you'd persist, or persevere, then you would succeed.

只要你坚持就会成功。zhi^3 yao^4 ni^3 jian^{1}chi^2 jiu^{4}hui^4 cheng^{2}gong^1.

You can, if only you will.

只要你愿意就能。zhi^3 yao^4 ni^3 yuan^{4}yi^4 jiu^4 neng^2.

If you'd just work hard, then you will learn it anyway.

只要你努力学，怎么也能学会。zhi^3 yao^4 ni^3 nu^3 li^4 xue^2, zen^{3}me ye^3 neng^2 xue^2 hui^4.

If only I had the money, then I'd buy it.

我只要有钱就买。wo^3 zhi^{3}yao^4 you^3 qian^2 jiu^4 mai^3.

Or

只要有钱我就买。zhi^{3}yao^4 you^3 qian^2 wo^3 jiu^4 mai^3.

If you just persist, you will succeed.

只要你坚持，你就会成功。zhi^{3}yao^4 ni^3 jian^1 chi^2, ni^3 jiu^4 hui^4 cheng^{2}gong^1.

If the weather were good, we'd go out.

只要天气好，我们就出去。zhi^{3}yao^4 tian^{1}qi^4 hao^3, wo^{3}men jiu^4 chu^1 qu^4.

OK! Remember that we can put 只要 after the subject of the sentence.

If you would like it, I will give it to you.

你只要喜欢我就给你。ni^3 zhi^{3}yao^4 xi^{3}huan^1 wo^3 jiu^4 gei^3 ni^3.

We will make it, if you'd sign the contract.

你们只要签合同我们就做。ni^{3}men zhi^3 yao^4 qian^1 he^{2}tong^2 wo^{3}men^2 jiu^4 zuo^4.

If you just stick to it, or persevere, you will succeed.

你只要努力就会成功。ni^3 zhi^{3}yao^4 nu^{3}li^4 jiu^4 hui^4 cheng^{2}gong^1.

12. Only... 只有 (zhi^{3}you^3)……才 (cai^2)……

Only he knows the answer.

只有他才知道答案。zhi^{3}you^3 ta^1 cai^2 zhi^1 dao^4 da^2 an^4.

Only by making an effort can we succeed.

我们只有努力才会成功。wo^{3}men zhi^{2}you^3 nu^3 li^4 cai^2 hui^4 cheng^{2}gong^1.

You will believe it only after you see it. Or, you won't believe until you see it.

你只有看见才会相信。ni^3 zhi^{3}you^3 kan^4 jian^4 cai^2 hui^4 xiang^{1}xin^4.

Only by taking a plane can one arrive there.

只有乘飞机才能到那里。zhi^{3}you^3 cheng^2 fei^{1}ji^1 cai^2 neng^2 dao^4 na^{4}li^3.

It can be done well only in this way.

只有这样才能做好。zhi^{3}you^3 zhe^4 yang^4 cai^2 neng^2 zuo^4 hao^3.

You can only master it by consistent practice.

你只有不断练习才能掌握。ni^3 zhi^{3}you^3 bu^4 duan^4 lian^{4}xi^2 cai^2 neng^2 zhang^{3}wo^4.

We can only get off work at weekends. Or, we can only rest at the weekend.

我们只有周末才能休息。wo3men zhi3you3 zhou1mo4 cai2 neng2 xiu1xi.

13. If..., then... 如果 (ru2guo3)……那么就 (na4me jiu4)……

If you want to learn Chinese, then learn follow me.

如果你想学中文，那么就跟我学吧。ru2 guo3 ni3 xiang3 xue2 zhong1wen2, na4me jiu4 gen1 wo3 xue2 ba.

The second part 那么就 can also be shortened to 那就, or simply 就. All three mean "then", or "and then". Let's listen to some examples.

If you are hungry, then go and eat.

如果你饿了，那就去吃吧。ru2 ni3 e4 le, na4 jiu4 qu4 chi1 ba.

If you are tired, then go take a rest.

如果你累了，那就去休息吧。ru2 guo3 ni3 lei4 le, na4 jiu4 qu4 xiu1xi ba.

In fact, there are also two alternatives to the word 如果 which we can use for expressing a supposed condition.

The first one is—

要是 yao4shi4

If you want to learn Chinese, then follow me.

你要是想学中文，那就跟我学吧。ni3 yao4shi4 xiang3 xue2 zhong1wen2, na4 jiu4 gen1 wo3 xue2 ba.

If you are hungry, then go and eat.

你要是饿了那就去吃吧。ni3 yao4shi4 e4 le na4 jiu4 qu4 chi1 ba.

If you are tired, then go take a rest.

你要是累了那就去休息吧。ni3 yao4shi4 lei4 le na4 jiu4 qu4 xiu1xi ba.

Sometimes, the word 要是 itself can also be followed by another complementing construct to form a correlation structure. This is:

要是……的话 yao4shi4……de hua4

So, what we have just learned can also be expressed as the following:

If you want to learn Chinese, then learn after me.

你要是想学中文的话，那就跟我学吧。ni3 yao4shi4 xiang3 xue2 zhong1wen2 de hua4, na4 jiu4 gen1 wo3 xue2 ba.

If you are hungry, then go and eat.

你要是饿了的话，那就去吃吧。ni3 yao4shi4 e4 le de hua4, na4 jiu4 qu4 chi1 ba.

If you are tired, then go to take a rest.

你要是累了的话那就去休息吧。ni3 yao4shi4 lei4 le de hua4 na4 jiu4 qu4 xiu1xi ba.

The second one that may be used interchangeably with 如果 is—

假如 jia^{3}ru^2

It may be noted that this word is more appropriately used for conditions that are unlikely to be true.

If I were you, I would do it.

假如我是你，我就愿意做。jia^{3}ru^2 wo^3 shi^4 ni^3, wo^3 jiu^4 yuan^{4}yi^4 zuo^4.

If there is a war, we will leave this place.

假如发生战争，那么我们就离开这里。jia^{3}ru^2 fa^{1}sheng^1 zhan^4 zheng^1, na^{4}me wo^{3}men jiu^4 li^{2}kai^1 zhe^{4}li^3.

If human beings can live on Mars, I would like to go.

假如人类能在火星上生活，我就愿意去。jia^{3}ru^2 ren^2 lei^4 neng^4 zai^4 huo^{3}xing^1 shang^4 sheng^{1}huo^2, wo^3 jiu^4 yuan^{4}yi^4 qu^4.

If there is a war, what can we do?

假如发生战争，那么我们怎么办？jia^{3}ru^2 fa^{1}sheng^1 zhan^{4}zheng^1, na^{4}me wo^{3}men zen^{3}me ban^4?

If human beings can live on Mars, would you like to go?

假如人类能在火星上生活，那么你愿意不愿意去？jia^{3}ru^2 ren^2 lei^4 neng^4 zai^4 huo^{3}xing^1 shang^4 sheng^{1}huo^2, na^{1}me ni^3 yuan^{4}yi^4 bu^4 yuan^{4}yi^4 qu^4?

As we see, the word 就 is used only for indicative sentences, but not used in questions. Let's listen again and compare.

If there is a war, what can we do?

假如发生战争，那么我们怎么办？jia^{3}ru^2 fa^{1}sheng^1 zhan^{4}zheng^4, na^{1}me wo^{3}men zen^{3}me ban^4?

If there is a war, we will leave here.

如果发生战争，那我们就离开。ru^2 guo^3 fa^{1}sheng^1 zhan^{4}zheng^1, na^1 wo^{3}men jiu^4 li^{2}kai^1?

14. Even if... 即使 (ji^{4}shi^3)…… 也 (ye^3)……

即使……也…… ji^{4}shi^3... ye^3...

Even if it rains, we will go to the Great Wall.

即使下雨，我们也要去长城。ji^{4}shi^3 xia^4 yu^3, wo^{3}men ye^3 yao^4 qu^4 chang^{2}cheng^2.

Even if the road is long, I will go and look for him.

即使路远，我也要去找他。ji^{4}shi^3 lu^4 yuan^3, wo^3 ye^3 yao^4 qu^4 zhao^3 ta^1.

Even if Mandarin Chinese is very difficult, I will learn it.

汉语即使很难，我也要学。han^{4}yu^3 ji^{4}shi^3 hen^3 nan^2, wo^3 ye^3 yao^4 xue^2.

Here we may need to know that the word 即使 is somewhat formal. There are two informal words to use in its place—

就算 jiu4suan4

And

哪怕 na3pa4

Even if it were a ghost, I would not be afraid.

就算是鬼，我也不怕。jiu4suan4 shi4 gui3, wo3 ye3 bu4 pa4.

Or

哪怕是鬼，我也不怕。na3pa4 shi4 gui3, wo3 ye3 bu4 pa4.

Even if you are poor, I will still marry you.

就算你穷，我也要和你结婚。jiu4suan4 ni3 qiong2, wo3 ye3 yao4 he2 ni3 jie2hun1.

Or

哪怕你穷，我也要和你结婚。na3pa4 ni3 qiong2, wo3 ye3 yao4 he2 ni3 jie2hun1.

Please note that the English word "marry" has three Chinese equivalents, but they are used differently. When referring to marriage in general, the word to use is an intransitive verb—

结婚 jie2hun1

And so, "to marry you" would be "to marry with you" in Chinese—

和你结婚 he2 ni3 jie2hun1

Even if you are poor, I will marry you.

就算你穷，我也要和你结婚。jiu4suan4 ni3 qiong2, wo3 ye3 yao4 he2 ni3 jie2hun1.

If it is a man who marries a woman, the Chinese would say—

娶 qu3

Even if you are poor, I will marry you.

就算你穷，我也要娶你。jiu4suan4 ni3 qiong2, wo3 ye3 yao4 qu3 ni3.

If it is a girl who marries a man, the Chinese would say—

嫁 jia4

就算你穷，我也要嫁给你。jiu4suan4 ni3 qiong2, wo3 ye3 yao4 jia4 gei3 ni3.

All right! Now we probably need to mention that among the three words—即使, 就算, and 哪怕—the first one is more frequently used in formal speech, while the other two are a little casual in style.

15. Although... nevertheless... 虽然 (sui1ran2)…… 但是 (dan4shi4)……

This pattern can be regarded as literally corresponding to the English "although... nevertheless..."; however, while in English, the word "nevertheless" is often omitted, its counterpart Chinese word 但是 will usually be used.

Although it is the weekend, he is still working.

虽然是周末，但是他还是在工作。sui^{1}ran^{2} shi^{4} zhou^{1}mo^{4}, dan^{4}shi^{4} ta^{1} hai^{2}shi^{4} zai^{4} gong^{1}zuo^{4}.

Although I don't have much money, I'm happy.

虽然我没有很多钱，但是我很快乐。sui^{1}ran^{2} wo^{3} mei^{2} you^{3} hen^{3} duo^{1} qian^{2}, dan^{4}shi^{4} wo^{3} hen^{3} kuai^{4} le^{4}.

Although I can't speak Chinese well, I can understand when I read.

虽然我说不好汉语，但是我能读懂中文。sui^{1}ran^{2} wo^{3} shuo^{1} bu^{4} hao^{3} han^{4}yu^{3}, dan^{4}shi^{4} wo^{3} neng^{2} du^{2} dong^{3} zhong^{1}wen^{2}.

In spite of the rain, the sports meet is going ahead.

虽然下雨，但是运动会还是在进行。sui^{1}ran^{2} xia^{4}yu^{3}, dan^{4}shi^{4} yun^{4}dong^{4}hui^{4} hai^{2}shi^{4} zai^{4} jin^{4}xing^{2}.

In fact, there is another word to replace the word 虽然 without changing the meaning. This is:

尽管 jin^{4}guan^{3}

Although I don't have much money, I'm happy.

尽管我没有很多钱，但是我很快乐。jin^{4}guan^{3} wo^{3} mei^{2} you^{3} hen^{3} duo^{1} qian^{2}, dan^{4}shi^{4} wo^{3} hen^{3} kuai^{4} le^{4}.

In spite of the rain, the sports meet is going ahead.

尽管下雨，但是运动会还是在进行。jin^{4}guan^{3} xia^{4}yu^{3}, dan^{4}shi^{4} yun^{4}dong^{4}hui^{4} hai^{2}shi^{4} zai^{4} jin^{4}xing^{2}.

Or, to mark the continuous tense—

Although it is raining, the sports meet is carrying on.

尽管下着雨，但是运动会还是在进行。jin^{4}guan^{3} xia^{4} zhe yu^{3}, dan^{4}shi^{4} yun^{4}dong^{4}hui^{4} hai^{2}shi^{4} zai^{4} jin^{4}xing^{2}.

Although the meeting was still going on, he left.

尽管会议还在进行着，他就离开了。jin^{4}guan^{3} hui^{4}yi^{4} hai^{2} zai^{4} jin^{4}xing^{2} zhe, ta^{1} jiu^{4} li^{2}kai^{1} le.

16. Because... 因为 (yin^{1}wei^{4})……所以 (suo^{3}yi^{3})……

Because I'm ill, I ask for leave.

因为我生病，所以请假。yin^{1}wei^{4} wo^{3} sheng^{1} bing^{4}, suo^{3}yi^{3} qing^{3} jia^{4}.

Because there is a traffic jam on my route, I'm late for class.

因为路上堵车，所以我上课迟到了。yin^{1}wei^{4} lu^{4} shang^{4} du^{3} che^{1}, suo^{3}yi^{3} wo^{3} shang^{4} ke^{4} chi^{2} dao^{4} le.

Because the weather is bad, the sports meet is called off.

因为天气不好，所以运动会取消了。yin1wei4 tian1qi4 bu4 hao3, suo3yi3 yun4dong4hui4 qu3 xiao1 le.

He is taking a rest at home because he is not in good physical condition.

他因为身体不好，所以在家休息。ta1 yin1wei4 shen1ti3 bu4 hao3, suo3yi3 zai4 jia1 xiu1xi.

Here we should know that there is an alternative expression for 因为, which is—

由于 you2yu2

Because I'm ill, I ask for leave.

由于我生病，所以请假。you2yu2 wo3 sheng1bing4, suo3yi3 qing3jia4.

Because there is a traffic jam on my route, I'm late for class.

由于路上堵车，所以我上课迟到了。you2yu2 lu4shang4 du3che1, suo3yi3 wo3 shang4ke4 chi2dao4 le.

He is taking a rest at home because he is not in good physical condition.

他由于身体不好，所以在家休息。ta1 you2yu2 shen1ti3 bu4 hao3, suo3yi3 zai4 jia1 xiu1xi.

In fact, there are some cases when 因为 and 由于 are shortened to a one-syllable word, 因, especially in formal speech or serious writing. Here are some examples:

I ask for leave because I'm ill.

我因病请假。wo3 yin1 bing4 qing3jia4.

The meeting is, or will be, postponed for some reason.

会议因故推迟。hui4yi4 yin1 gu4 tui1 chi2.

He has not come because he is engaged.

他因事没来。ta1 yin1 shi4 mei2 lai2.

The sports meet is suspended because of the rain.

运动会因雨暂停。yun4dong4hui4 yin1yu3 zan4 ting2.

All right! As we see, this collocation is very important. However, you don't always have to use this pattern in its full form. You can also drop the first part without changing the meaning. For example:

There was a traffic jam on the way, and so I was late.

路上堵车，所以我迟到了。lu4shang4 du3che1, suo3yi3 wo3 chi2dao4 le.

You may also need to know another word to be used as an alternative to 所以, which is literally corresponding to "because of this". This is:

因此 yin1ci3

He has something important on, and for that reason asks for leave.

他有重要的事情，因此请假。ta1 you3 zhong4yao4 de shi4qing, yin1ci3 qing3jia4.

As we see, the word 因 has the same function as that of the English "because" or "because of". However, we should also know that it can be a noun meaning "the cause" or "the reason".

Cause and effect
因果 yin1guo3
Cause-and-effect relation
因果关系 yin1guo3 guan1xi4
You must know the cause-and-effect relation between them.
你必须知道它们之间的因果关系。ni3 bi4xu1 zhi1dao4 ta1men zhi1jian1 de yin1guo3 guanxi4.

To use two-syllable words for both 因 and 果, you can say—

Cause or reason
原因 yuan2yin1
Effect or result
结果 jie2guo3
For this reason, I decided to learn Chinese.
由于这个原因，我决定学习中文。you2 yu2 zhe4 ge4 yuan2yin1, wo3 jue2ding4 xue2xi2 zhong1wen2.
I read this book, and as a result learned Mandarin Chinese very fast.
我读了这本书，结果很快学会了普通话。wo3 du2 le zhe4 ben3 shu1, jie2guo3 hen3 kuai4 xue2 hui4 le pu3tong1hua4.

17. Rather than... 与其 (yu3qi2)... 不如 (bu4ru2)...; 宁可 (ning4ke3)... 也 (ye3)...

Rather than going to the library, it would be better to go on the internet.
与其去图书馆，不如上网。yu3qi2 qu4 tu2shu1guan3, bu4ru2 shang4wang3.
Rather than being idle with nothing to do, it's better to read for a while.
与其闲着, 不如看看书。yu3qi2 xian2zhe, bu4ru2 kan4kan4 shu1.
Rather than translating, it is better to write yourself.
与其翻译，不如自己写。yu3qi2 fan1yi4, bu4ru2 zi4ji3 xie3.
I'd rather follow you than going after him.
我宁可跟你，也不跟他。wo3 ning4ke3 gen1 ni3, ye3 bu4 gen1 ta1.
He'd rather spend more money to buy it.
他宁可多花钱也要买。ta1 ning4ke3 duo1 hua1 qian2 ye3 yao4 mai3.
I'd rather eat nothing than that.
我宁可什么都不吃也不吃那个。wo3 ning4ke3 shen2me dou1 bu4 chi1 ye3 bu4 chi1 na4ge4.
They'd rather die than yield or surrender. 他们宁死不屈。Ta1men ning4 si3 bu4 qu1.